# THE TIES
# THAT BIND

# THE TIES THAT BIND

## African American and Hispanic American/Latino/a Theology in Dialogue

*Edited by*

ANTHONY B. PINN
*and*
BENJAMIN VALENTIN

CONTINUUM

*New York* • *London*

2001
The Continuum International Publishing Group Inc
370 Lexington Avenue, New York, NY 10017

The Continuum International Publishing Group Ltd
The Tower Building, 11 York Road, London SE1 7NX

Printed in the United States of America

Library of Congress Cataloging-in-Publication Data
The ties that bind : African American and Hispanic American/Latino/a theology in
dialogue / edited by Anthony B. Pinn and Benjamin Valentin.
    p. cm.
Includes bibliographical references and index.
ISBN 0-8264-1326-9
    1. Black theology. 2. Hispanic American theology. I. Pinn, Anthony B. II. Valentin,
Benjamin.

BT82.7 .T54 2001
230'.089'68073—dc21                                                    00-065723

*For*
*William Hargrave*
*in*
*memoriam*
*and the Ancestors*

ANTHONY B. PINN

---

*For*
*Rev. Angel M. Valentin and Luz Belen Valentin*

BENJAMIN VALENTIN

# Contents

PART V

*On Pain and Suffering:*
*Theology and the Problem of Evil*

PART VI

*Building Bridges: Reflections on Context,*
*Identity, and Communities of Struggle*

# Acknowledgments

This project took shape over the course of several years and in spite of numerous unexpected "difficulties." As the editors of this volume, we take responsibility for the "rough spots," but we would like to share the value of this project with a variety of people. Although we cannot possibly mention everyone by name, we would like to thank our parents—Rev. Anne H. Pinn, Rev. Angel M. Valentin, and Luz Belen Valentin. We would also like to thank our siblings for their support and encouragement—Joyce Pinn, Raymond Pinn, Linda Bryant, Elieser Valentin, and Bethsaida Valentin. Anthony's work on this project would have been impossible without the support, encouragement, and kindness of his wife, Cheryl Johnson. Thank you always.

Within our academic community, we would like to thank Catherine Keller, Otto Maduro, Gordon Kaufman, Ada María Isasi-Díaz, Calvin Roetzel, James Laine, Paula Cooey, Jeanne Kilde, Charles Long, J. Deotis Roberts, Justo González, Zaida Maldonado Perez, Daisy Machado, William R. Jones, Joanne Rodriguez, Heather White, James H. Cone, and Peter Paris for guidance and support over so many years. There are academic organizations that should also be acknowledged and thanked for community and nourishment. Thank you to the Hispanic Theological Initiative and the Society for the Study of Black Religion. We must also thank the two institutions that provided support and "space" in which to discuss and shape these ideas. The editors thank the faculty, staff, students, and administrators of Macalester College and Andover Newton Theological School. The support of faculty and energizing enthusiasm of students made completion of this project that much easier. Anthony would like to extend a special thank you to the staff of the Macalester College library for patience and much needed assistance. He offers a special thank you to David Yesilevskiy who helped him scan documents with

11

good humor. His patience with someone who is computer-challenged is much appreciated.

Benjamin would also like to thank all the members of La Iglesia de Dios/The Church of God (1800 Third Avenue in New York City) for their love and multifarious support. Anthony would like to thank his humanist friends and supporters, including but not limited to Koren Arisian, the First Unitarian Society of Minneapolis, and the Humanist Institute of New York City.

In New York, Minneapolis, and beyond, the editors would like to thank the following persons for their encouragement, friendship, intellectual, emotional, moral, and editorial support: Ramon Rentas, Robby Seals, Richard Ammons, Ahmed Samatar, Peter Rachleff, James Stewart, Robert Pazmiño, Efrain Agosto, Harold Recinos, Alvin Padilla, Ismael Garcia, Fernando Segovia, Luis Rivera-Pagan, Rose and Danette Costas, Samuel Cruz, Hugo Magallanes, Victor Algarin, Daniel Rivera, David Traverzo, Omar Soto, Henry Sierra, the Marchany family—especially Melissa, Ana, Yadira, and Tonya—Wilfredo and Edith Vargas, the Hernandez and Lopez family—Jorge, Eddie "Polako," Karaly "Jennifita," and Lourdes, David and Milagros Vargas, Roslyn Friedman, Christopher Tirres, Michelle Gonzalez, Rudy Busto, Loida Martell-Otero, Manuel Jesus Mejido, Mereides Delgado, Gaston Espinoza, Francisco Lozada, Jr., Gilberto Medina, Hjamil Martinez Vazquez, and Noraida Diaz.

Finally, the editors would like to thank their editor Frank Oveis for his confidence in this project. And, we must offer a strong and loud thank you to the folks who contributed essays to this project.

# Introduction

One of the hallmarks of constructive theology is its emphasis on the historical character of all theological formations. This consideration has paved the way for the understanding that all theologies are influenced by background conditions as they are shaped by historical, sociocultural, and socioeconomic locations constructed through a limited range of experiences and exigencies. In the latter half of the twentieth century we have seen the development of liberationist and progressive theologies, as forms of constructive discourse, around the world that couple this historicist sensibility to an explicitly ameliorative and emancipatory impulse. Generally put, these have acknowledged that theology is best understood as a "secondary moment" of reflection: "life comes first, theology comes only thereafter, striving to understand and serve life."[1]

As this last description makes clear, liberation and progressive theologies attempt both to understand life and to enhance it. This responsiveness and yearning clearly characterizes the development of African American and U.S. Hispanic/Latino/a theology in the United States. The unfolding of these two theological traditions is based upon strivings to understand and serve existentially defined needs, particularly by placing attention on the manner in which African Americans and Hispanics/Latinos/as suffer injustices that are traceable to political economy and culture. In response to these "multiple jeopardies" and their debilitating effects, African American and Hispanic/Latino/a theologians, using the medium of theology, provide enhancing personal and collective images that promote sociopolitical adjustments for the well-being of members of their ethnic group as well as the greater U.S. society.

Although they have emerged side by side, and although there are tendencies evident within both of these theological analogues that advance a dialogical understanding of theology, the development and analysis of theologies within these two ethnic groups has occurred independently of each other. That is to say, African American and Hispanic/Latino/a theologians and religious scholars have rarely inquired into the possibility and even necessity of cross-cultural communication with respect to these two communities. To be sure, some attempts have been made from the vantage point of African American theology to scrutinize the similar uncertainties and "common journeys" shared by African Americans and so-called "Third World" constituencies—Africans, Asians, and Latin Americans.[2] Yet, this disposition has not extended to include conversation with Hispanic/Latino/a theologians, intellectuals, and activists who live and struggle alongside African Americans *within* the national context of the United States. Similarly, U.S. Hispanic/Latino/a theology has emphasized the importance of a dialogical and collaborative spirit—of *teologia en conjunto* (i.e., collaborative or joint theology).[3] Unfortunately, this emphasis has been limited thus far to "intradialogue" and "intracollaboration" among Hispanic/Latino/a theologians and has not yet made sufficient allowances for dialogue and collaboration with African American theologians, intellectuals, and activists. Thus, both theological traditions—African American and Hispanic/Latino/a— have failed to explore the possibility and desirability of a cross-cultural dialogue of people of color within the United States. Such work seems a natural development in light of what these two communities implicitly and explicitly share with respect to historical, racial, cultural, social, and religious geographies.[4]

Although not often acknowledged, the experiences and identities of these two groups are linked by a unique web of historical relations that began to develop even before the invention of the United States of America. This relatedness commenced at the end of the fifteenth century with the arrival of European explorers in the Americas, and is founded upon the subsequent Spanish/Portuguese/English conquest and colonization of most of Central and South America, Mexico, large segments of the Caribbean, as well as much of the territory that today constitutes the United States. A full discussion of the "making" of the Americas is beyond the scope of this introduction. Nonetheless, we believe it is safe to generalize that what emerged over time was a violent and unequal encounter having at its core socioeconomic motivations that intensify over time. Involving at least four groups of people, this contact and conquest destroyed various populations while giving rise to new populations of peoples with unique ties to the Americas.[5]

The proximateness of these groups of people in the Americas occasioned the emergence of a new cultural and even racial context as the European, Native American, and African populations increasingly "intermingled." Evidence of this "blending" of peoples abounds. Present day African American, Latin American, and U.S. Latino/a populations have clearly been marked by this history. Most acknowledge that African American and Latino/a cultures and identities are the result of a "fusion" of Iberian, Ameri-Indian, African, and Euro/American cultures. In this way, the history and identity of African Americans and Hispanics/Latinos/as are inexorably linked. The material, decorative, and expressive cultures present in this part of the world are marked by this exchange. This historical and cultural linkage accounts in large part for the sharing of many similarities between members of these two U.S. social groups that can be evidenced at times in their racial composition, religion, food, music, art, and other social mores and idiosyncrasies. In keeping with the theological and religious context of this particular book, one need only look at the religious traditions forged in the "New World" to see the manner in which existential conditions and cultural sensibilities melted into each other resulting in life affirming traditions such as Vodou, Santería, Candomblé, and Conjure to name only a few. Tied to the rituals of these religious systems are doctrinal or theological elements that also marked the merging of at least three worlds—Europe, Africa, and the Americas.

Beyond this historical and cultural connection, African American and Hispanic/Latino/a life and identity are also linked by a parallel history of struggle against multiple forms of jeopardies that have variously threatened and in many cases circumscribed the well-being of members of each of these ethnic groups in the United States. African Americans, for instance, have had to contend both with the lasting material and cultural inequities engendered by the long history of slavery, as well as the denial of equal citizenship rights and overall treatment due to the persistence of racism. In regards to U.S. Latinos/as, it is often taken for granted that the fragile American experiment in democracy also began with the plight of some of the early Hispanic peoples who inhabited this land. Hispanic/U.S. history was, after all, marked very early on with the violent North American conquest of Mexicans, Hispanic mestizos, and their lands. Moreover, Latinos/as continue to endure questions regarding their legitimacy both as citizens and as persons since they are often viewed as a problem people and as "perpetual aliens" in our nation regardless of their citizenship status or years of residence, and despite the fact that Hispanic history in North America actually predates the history of the United States. In this sense, Malcolm X's comments regarding African American origins also apply to Hispanic American origins: "we didn't land on Plymouth Rock, Plymouth Rock landed on us."

It is also true that both the African American and Hispanic/Latino/a populations living in the United States have had to contend with the reality of disproportionate poverty and unemployment levels; of limited or poor educational, income, housing, and health opportunities;

of the hurtful experiences of racist attitudes and negative stereotypes; and of the pervasive limitation of life choices and of hope itself. Thus, both of these groups share a parallel history of struggle in the United States. And, for both communities there is a sense in which this struggle is marked by a sense of "double consciousness." The words of historian of religion Charles Long ring true: "Blacks, the colored races, caught up into this net of the imaginary and symbolic consciousness of the West, rendered mute through the words of military, economic, and intellectual power, assimilated as if by osmosis structures of this consciousness of oppression. This is the source of the doubleness of consciousness made famous by W. E. B. DuBois. . . . This doubleness of consciousness, this existence in half-lights and within the quasi fields of human infection, is the context for the communities of color, the opaque ones of the modern world."[6]

We do not want to give the impression, however, that these two communities are only linked by what has been done to them. Rather, African Americans and Hispanic Americans/Latinos/as share a history of subversive activities and formations that promoted life and health in spite of oppressive forces. The cultural structures of both communities speak to this preservation and celebration of life.

In light of this common historical and cultural heritage, and this similar chronicle of struggle and affirmation of life, it is indeed surprising that African American and Latino/a intellectuals in general and theologians in particular have not made more of an effort to explore the possibility and desirability of interchange and collaboration between them. This inadvertency is even more bewildering given the need that presently exists for such cross-cultural communication and cooperation in light of continuing discrimination. Current indices demonstrate that the employment, economic, educational, and health standing of most African Americans and Latino/as has actually gotten worse in recent times. African American and Hispanic/Latino/a individuals and families are more likely to be unemployed and living below the poverty line than members of any other U.S. ethnic group. They are also less likely to have a college degree or even a high school diploma than members of other U.S. ethnic groups. At the same time, the African American and Latino/a population continues to increase dramatically. Recent statistics suggest that the U.S. African American population is roughly 33.1 million or 12.7 percent of the total U.S. population, while the Hispanic/Latino/a population in the United States is 31.7 million or 11.7 percent of the total population and counting. What will it mean for both communities to live in a country that is increasingly becoming "brown" yet still controlled by white Americans?

The increase in material inequality and population for these two ethnic groups comes at a time when "affirmative action programs are under heavy assault, and broad public sympathy for those minority individuals"[7] who have suffered the most from varied forms of subordination, disadvantage, and exclusion has waned. Indeed, although some have said that these are good times for America, these are trying and vulnerable times for African Americans and Latinos/as. In a time of increased economic anxiety and xenophobia such as ours, people can become more susceptible to simplistic and divisive ideologies that distract attention from the complex sources of their problems.[8] Members of historically disadvantaged groups such as African Americans and Latinos/as in particular can mistakenly come to see each other as competitors for dwindling opportunities rather than as potential political allies.

It is vital that African American and Latino/a thinkers of all kinds, and indeed critical theorists of justice in general, look to collaborate in searching for those causes and sources that may help us to "bridge the racial divide" and to harmonize the utopian energies of our distinct social groups. This task indubitably calls for verbal exchange between our distinct and currently fragmented constituencies.

Toward this end, *The Ties That Bind* brings the complex theological discourses of these two communities—African Americans and Hispanics/Latinos/as—together for the purpose of mutually-enhancing dialogue. This is an exercise meant to promote better understanding through a discussion of similarities and differences with respect to a few theological issues. To achieve this, two scholars, one from each of the two communities, were asked to write an essay on a particular topic. The two scholars addressing a particular issue were then asked to exchange essays and write a response in which similarities and differences in approach and content are discussed.

The book contains six major parts reflecting a concern with a guiding set of questions: (1) what is the thought structure of these two theological traditions and how has it developed historically and thematically in the United States?; (2) how can the overarching methodology of African American and Hispanic/Latino/a theology be interpreted?; (3) what are the sources employed by theologians and religious scholars in these two theological traditions?; (4) what are the historical linkages, similarities, differences, and possibilities for substantive dialogue between these two U.S. theological traditions; and (5) what are the sociopolitical implications of these traditions when presented in solidarity?

With this framework in place, Part I—"Theology in 'Black' and 'Brown': History, Issues, and Interpretation"—contains essays by Anthony Pinn and Benjamin Valentin. Both treatises explore the germinal thought found within African American and Hispanic/Latino/a theology, bringing to light the historical development, articulated concerns, and core themes of these respective theological traditions.

They also provide a critical and constructive glimpse of the inadvertencies and the challenges that each of these distinctive theological voices must speak to in the United States. Part II—"Theology and Its Reflexive Sources: Scripture, Tradition, Experience, and Imagination"—contains essays by Victor Anderson and Justo L. González examining the ways in which African American and Hispanic/Latino/a theologies have weaved together the use of scripture, religious traditions, notions of contextualized individual and collective experience, and imagination. Following the essays and responses written by Anderson and Gonzalez, Part III—"Theologizing with What's Popular: Theology and Popular Culture"—presents essays by Dwight N. Hopkins and Harold J. Recinos exploring the manner in which the popular, particularly popular religion, is employed in African American and Latino/a theology.

The work of women within the theological discourses marking these communities cannot be ignored. To do so is to miss a major component of the experiences and history of African Americans and Hispanics/Latinos/as. With this in mind, Part IV —"Women's Experience and Theology: Reflections on Womanist and *Mujerista* Theology"—proffers two articles that survey Womanist theology and *mujerista* theology. In these essays, Chandra Taylor Smith and Ada María Isasi-Díaz shed light on the development, themes, concerns, and distinctiveness of Womanist and *mujerista* theology. Following this, in Part V—"On Pain and Suffering: Theology and the Problem of Evil"—Dianne Stewart and Nancy Pineda-Madrid, provide interpretations of the way in which African American people in general and Latinas in particular have dealt with experiences of undeserved suffering, unmerited pain, and unjustified subjugation in their quest for subjectivity.

The volume's final part—"Building Bridges: Reflections on Context, Identity, and Communities of Struggle"—contains essays by Lee H. Butler, Jr. and Luis Pedraja. These writings generally explore possible points of constructive contact between religious bodies associated with African American and Hispanic/Latino/a communities in the United States. Following these essays, the book closes with concluding remarks and observations made by the volume's editors and a bibliography of selected works related to African American and Hispanic/Latino/a theology and the religious life of both communities.

Acknowledging both the previous lack of substantive dialogue between African American and Latino/a theologians, and the present need for coalition among disadvantaged groups, the contributors to this volume have come together to initiate a cross-cultural conversation. The conviction of each one of the authors in the following pages is that theology can and should become a discourse that serves to develop overarching meaning systems that encourage and sustain holistic imagination, notions of self and communal integrity, social activism and solidarity. Although the articles enclosed convey varied perspectives and distinct approaches to their assigned themes, the guiding aim connecting each one of the contributing authors is this: to think through and even to recast our respective theological traditions in the hopes of discovering, for the task of solidarity building communication, *The Ties That Bind* African American and Hispanic/Latino/a theology.

# PART I

## Theology in "Black" and "Brown": History, Issues, and Interpretation

# 1

# Black Theology in Historical Perspective: Articulating the Quest for Subjectivity

## Anthony B. Pinn

I AM CONTINUOUSLY DRAWN TO historian of religion Charles Long's recounting of a "creation myth" pertaining to the arrival of enslaved Africans to the Americas. He writes:

> The oppressed must deal with both the fictive truth of their status as expressed by the oppressors, that is, their second creation, and the discovery of their own autonomy and truth—their first creation. The locus for this structure is the mythic consciousness which dehistoricizes the relationship for the sake of creating a new form of humanity—master-slave dialectic.[1]

For Long, this complex reformulation is often expressed in terms of religious creativity by which the angst of dislocation is played out. That is to say, this movement from "second creation" to "first creation" is articulated through religious experience pointing to a fuller sense of human-ness, a fuller modulation of subjectivity or identity.[2] With this in mind, it is reasonable to argue that the various forms of African American religion (or religious experience) are, below doctrine and ritual, marked by a similar concern with the development of subjectivity or identity. In other words, they all, at a fundamental level, participate in a move against the essentialization or objectification of African Americans.[3]

Black theology of liberation—both informal and formal—is concerned with the articulation of this vision of and struggle for subjectivity. It is a primary mode of expression by which the struggle for subjectivity or meaning (i.e., religion) is stylistically recounted and

23

celebrated. In the remainder of this essay I will concern myself with tracing this theological discourse as a record of the quest for subjectivity, but with respect to an ever evolving sense of subjectivity beginning with race and moving into issues of gender, class, and sexual orientation.

## I. Subjectivity and Race: The Emergence of Black Theology of Liberation

The Civil Rights and black power movements (1955–1968) provide the impetus and paradigm shift that sparked the development of black theology. Having recently re-embraced a commitment to the public welfare of African American communities, black churches were developing a strong sense of a historic liberative agenda within the framework of the Civil Rights activities in the South.[4] Yet, there were those outside the church who questioned its motivations and capabilities for the securing of "secular" needs. The black power movement, for example, proposed a commitment to struggle inspired by Malcolm X *not* Martin L. King, Jr. For advocates of social transformation even through violent means, the quest for subjectivity—discussed in terms of full participation in a reorganized society—took precedent over the scripture, doctrine, and religious ritual that marked the Civil Rights movement.

In response, some within church circles denounced the black power movement as grounded in dangerous ideology and inflammatory rhetoric running contrary to more popular calls for tolerance and "brotherhood." Others sought ways to reconcile the Christian principles of the Civil Rights movement with the Malcolm X inspired demands of the black power movement. Early evidence of this wrestling is found in the platform adopted by the National Committee of Negro Churchmen (NCNC). In a full-page ad in the *New York Times* (July 31, 1966), the NCNC addressed four groups: national leaders, white churchmen, black citizens, and mass media. In each case an appeal was made for a rethinking of power dynamics that bred pain and suffering within African American communities. The riots and other events of the 1960s were presented as a minor threat to national security, the major threat being a failure of the nation to live in accordance with God's demand for justice and righteousness. A move into the full expression of God's will could not be achieved through rhetorical commitments to love (i.e., acceptance of the status quo) and appeals to U.S. individualism over against community (i.e., a healthy self-concept in the context of group dynamics—humanity). The oppressed must secure power in order to fully participate in the important processes of the nation.

This statement sparked a great deal of conversation—both pro and con—and was followed by other declarations, including the extremely controversial "Black Manifesto" prepared in the context of the national Black Economic Development Conference (Detroit— April 26, 1969) and read by James Forman at Riverside Church (NYC). This document critiqued the historically documented oppressive behavior of Europeans, and called African Americans to recognize themselves as connected to Africa. Furthermore, it called for black control over black economic development as a way of ending exploitation by "racist white America," a country that raped "our minds, our bodies, our labor" for centuries. In order to construct economic opportunity and self-sufficiency for African Americans, the manifesto called white Christians and Jews to provide financial resources because these groups aided in (and benefited from) the exploitation of people of color across the globe.[5]

Fueled by recent events including the assassination of Martin L. King, Jr., the "Black Manifesto" could not be ignored, particularly by concerned black clergy who were wrestling with the relevance of the Christian gospel in a context of modern racism. A statement issued by the Board of Directors of the National Committee of Black Churchmen (formerly the NCNC) responded to the "Black Manifesto" and to the growing unrest in major urban areas with an embrace of black power in light of the teachings of Jesus Christ (i.e., a "Christian conscience"). NCBC agreed with the charges against the Church as a contributor to oppression and recognized that it benefited from the enslaving of Africans. Beyond recognizing the white Church's guilt, NCBC maintained the appropriateness of financial compensation from religious organizations *and* private foundations for centuries of free labor provided by enslaved Africans.[6] This positive response to a critique of white racism was followed by a 1969 statement on black theology as the articulation of the Gospel's call to liberation within the context of the United States. More precisely defined:

> The word "Black" in the phrase was defined by the life and teachings of Malcolm X—culturally and politically embodied in the Black Power Movement. The term "theology" was influenced by the life and teachings of Martin Luther King, Jr.—religiously and politically embodied in the Black Church and the Civil Rights Movement. The word liberation was derived from the past and contemporary struggles for political freedom and the biblical story of the Exodus, as defined by the Black religious experience in the United States.[7]

Many figures participated in the early formation of black theology of liberation. However, as an academic discipline of inquiry, black theology emerges in the writings of James H. Cone. In his intellectual autobiography, Cone argues that, as a Christian committed to the freeing of African Americans from U.S. oppression, he was locked in a struggle to bring the Christian gospel in line with the radical social critique offered by Malcolm X. His was an effort to recover the liberative nature of the Christian gospel—the revolutionary actions of Christ—covered by centuries of Christian complacency. To do so required great attention to overlooked theological resources—African American history, African American cultural production, African American experience—as well as Scripture and the Christian Tradition. These resources brought African Americans into the center of theological discourse, particularly when viewed using a hermeneutic of suspicion that surfaced the duplicity of European renderings of history and faith. It was an assertion of the black church's relevance in the struggle for a liberated existence. This methodology marked a radical break from traditional forms of theological thinking in that it gave preference to lived experience and particularity as opposed to the more common universalizing of the particular experience of Europeans.[8]

In his first book, *Black Theology and Black Power* (1969), Cone argued for the legitimacy of black power because it relates to Christ's call for the liberation of the oppressed. Cone's argument was premised on a commitment to Christ as a radical, *black* Messiah who, in keeping with the will of God, disrupted status quo institutions and mind sets. Black theology took seriously the words found in the Gospel according to Luke, arguing that this proclamation was the core of Jesus's ministry:

> The Spirit of the Lord is upon Me,
> Because He has anointed Me to preach the gospel to the poor.
> He has sent Me to heal the brokenhearted,
> To preach deliverance to the captives
> And recovery of sight to the blind,
> To set at liberty those who are oppressed,
> To preach the acceptable year of the Lord.[9]

Cone's goal was to "identify liberation as the heart of the Christian gospel and blackness as the primary mode of God's presence." This volume was quickly followed by *A Black Theology of Liberation* (1970), the first systematic presentation of black theology.[10] In this text, Cone continues a refining of the epistemological and eschatological links between the plight of African Americans and God's commitments as expressed in scripture. Perhaps the most challenging component of this text was Cone's assertion that God is *ontologically* black. That is to say, God is so strongly identified with the oppressed—best understood in the United States with respect to African Americans—that God's very being is defined by this relationship. By extension, commitment to God's will as expressed in the Christian faith requires the "faithful" to maintain this same strong connection to the oppressed. Hence, true Christians in the context of the United States are also *ontologically* black.

In response to critiques by Cecil Cone and Gayraud Wilmore, subsequent work by Cone entailed the further development of this basic agenda through a more substantive presentation of the religious dimensions of African American cultural production. He also gave attention to the need for an increased ecumenical dimension to black theology. Although his theological agenda evolved as the nature of life in African American communities altered with time, Cone remained primarily concerned with racism as the major assault against African American subjectivity. For him, oppression in the United States is primarily marked by the damning effects of race as a social construction. Therefore, at this stage, black theology of liberation articulated black Christianity's vision of subjectivity as a push against racial objectification.[11]

Cone was not alone in this work; figures such as J. Deotis Roberts, Major Jones, Preston Williams, Henry Mitchell, Gayraud Wilmore, and William R. Jones also articulated a vision of black theology. Roberts, for example, provided philosophical underpinning for black theology and offered, in addition, a corrective to Cone's emphasis on liberation over reconciliation. For Roberts, the will of God at work in the world required a simultaneous commitment to liberating African Americans and reconciling them with white Americans. That is to say, according to Roberts, one could not move in a linear manner from liberation to reconciliation because they are mutually dependent. The emphasis remained on race, but in a way that emphasized mutuality and dialogical developments. The latter was further emphasized by Roberts in texts dealing with a comparative analysis of black theology and other forms of liberation theology such as South African liberation theology. Although Cone provided a critique of black churches, it was Gayraud Wilmore who provided the most nuanced challenge to black church public activities when, in *Black Religion and Black Radicalism*, he discussed the deradicalization of black churches in the early twentieth century, marked by the Great Migration of African Americans into Northern cities and the death of progressive leaders such as Bishop Henry McNeal Turner of the African Methodist Episcopal Church.[12]

## II. Subjectivity and Black Theology: Part Two

### (a) Subjectivity, Race and Class

Whereas the work of Roberts, Wilmore, and others pushed black theology to refine its method and agenda, it remained a theological discourse concerned with subjectivity in terms of race and racism. Cornel West, however, made an effort to extend the discussion beyond race to include the category of class. He argued that black theology as prescribed by Cone and others talked in terms of social transformation without providing a blue print for this new social structure. Furthermore, he argued that African Americans, based on Marxist analysis, suffered in the United States not only because they are black but also because of the dynamics of the class structure of society. West called black theology to an embrace of prophetic Christianity and its concern with a much fuller response to social injustice based upon a mature social critique and vision for a transformed world. In this way, West called black theology to become "public" discourse in new ways. Others, in recent years, have talked about black theology as a public discourse but they have done so without the same complex attention to and understanding of communication theory and social theory that informs West's discussion of this idea. This is not to say that all black theologians must "borrow" from Habermas, Foucault, and others. But, there is a sense in which West's conversation with these theoreticians has been beneficial within a discipline—black theology—which is often dismissive of theoretical issues. Too many have falsely argued that the urgency of black struggle does not provide the "leisure" necessary for the entertainment of abstract, theoretical considerations.[13]

West maintained the importance of dialogue concerning race, but argued that this must be combined with a critique of classism as a more meaningful engagement of "historical consciousness" with "present-day political struggles."[14] This historical consciousness is important to him because of a prevailing forgetfulness within American culture. For West, black theology in particular and liberation theology in general are liberative in part because of their ability to sting the conscience of the nation without the loss of a powerful quality of relationship with respect to both ultimate and mundane concerns connected to the conditions under which people live.[15] That is to say, black theology seeks to recognize and nurture the struggle for a textured subjectivity—integrity of existence that cannot be expressed within a limited conversation concerning race. The web-like structure of oppression as "will to power" and the structurally embedded ways in which it preserves itself must be tackled.

### (b) Subjectivity and Race: The Second Wave

Themes developed by pioneers in black theology were picked up by what is typically referred to as the "second generation" of black theologians.[16] However, in the work of this "second generation," there is a more complex understanding of race in that it is put in the context of other challenges to full humanity. For example, Josiah Young, trained by James Cone, argues for an increased sensitivity to and dialogue with Pan-African thought. As a result, Young pushes for a Pan-African theology that embraces a complex sense of cultural nationalism—through figures such as Alexander Crummell—based on epistemological and spiritual links to Africa. Dwight Hopkins has also expressed an interest in unpacking the religio-theological links between Africa and African Americans. He, like Will Coleman and George Cummings, has challenged the canon of theological resources presented by Roberts, Cone, and others by revisiting slave narratives as a primary mode of envisioning the liberative nature of black (Christian) religion.[17] An interesting twist to Hopkins's work includes his interest in conversing with African American literature, particularly the writings of Toni Morrison. He sees the utilization of such sources as an important step in the development of a constructive (and more systematic) black theology. The methodological "refinement" suggested by the work of Hopkins is also an explicit concern held by James Evans who has worked toward a systematic black theology.[18]

Theologians within this group are beginning to explore the religious imagery and doctrine prevalent in overtly Christian rap (e.g., DCTalk and Gospel Ganstas) and Islamic rap (e.g., Five Percent Nation lyrics by groups such as Poor Righteous Teachers, and Nation of Islam rhetoric in the lyrics of groups such as Public Enemy). One of the more prolific figures with respect to the theological exploration of African American musical production—from the Spirituals to rap music—is Jon Michael Spencer. In numerous publications, Spencer outlines a methodological approach—theomusicology—to musical production that takes seriously both the music *and* lyrics.[19] The exploration of this material not only nuances theological understandings of cultural production; it also serves to implicitly acknowledge the thematic links between early forms of musical production such as work songs and the blues and more recent developments in hip hop. However, this theological investigation of popular culture (particularly rap music) has meant an embrace of its liberative potential and a hard critique of its more problematic dimensions revolving around the often offensive depictions of masculinity and manhood.

Garth Kasimu Baker-Fletcher has raised interesting questions concerning the nature of subjectivity as presented within African American religiosity. He argues, drawing on recent literature related to the "Men's Movement," that African American liberation must entail a reevaluation of current notions of masculinity. That is to say, the further development of the African American community coupled with a reformulation of larger social relationships must contain a reformulation of the acceptable ways in which African American men relate to themselves and to African American women. Baker-Fletcher's work attempts to remove the residue of misogynistic attitudes and behavior for which many of the social protest efforts during the 1960s and 1970s (and elements of popular culture during this period and the present) are known. Some of his work entails creative conversation with African American women, the prime example of which is the co-authored book with his wife, theologian Karen Baker-Fletcher, in which his version of black theological discourse (Xodus Thought) is brought into dialogue with Womanist theology. This is an effort to place into a larger context of mutuality, based on more than the black male body, what is typically a male- and race-driven conversation. This type of work is still rare.[20]

### III. Subjectivity and Race/Gender: Womanist Theology

Race driven depictions of theology's role in the articulation of a quest for subjectivity were effectively challenged by black women who tired of having their experiences excluded from theological dialogue. In this way, black women forced a rethinking of subjectivity based on the manner in which they are essentialized or objectified through race *and* gender. An early articulation of this reformulation of libera-tion theology within African American communities was developed by Jacquelyn Grant who argued that the black church (and black theology by extension) is guilty of crimes similar to those with which the white church and larger society have been charged. That is to say, black churches and their theologians have universalized the experi-ences of black men, thus are guilty of oppressing black women. She argues that a proper theology of liberation for the African American community must consider, as a major resource and methodological concern, the experiences and history of African American women. Until this is done, and churches change their sexist policies, black churches remain far from Christian in orientation and black theolo-gians continue to serve as the "mouthpiece" of an oppressive organi-zation. This position was also embraced by thinkers such as Theressa Hoover.[21]

Although Grant, Hoover, and similar late twentieth century think-ers engaged in academic work are credited with the development of liberation theology for African American women, readers should also be mindful of the writings of figures such as Maria Stewart and Anna J. Cooper (during the 1800s) in that they argued for the inclusion of African American women in the full life of the black community (secular and religious) as well as the larger society. With respect to the twentieth century, readers should also note the groundbreaking work of Pauli Murray who, as the first black woman ordained an Episcopal priest, engaged and critiqued black (male) theology and feminist the-ology in a way that highlighted the unique position and potential of black women. These developments, from Maria Stewart to Jacquelyn Grant, are essential for an understanding of the second stage of black theology—the quest for subjectivity in terms of both race and gender. Nevertheless, theology done by black women is more fully defined during the mid-1980s with a hermeneutical and paradigmatic shift initiated by attention to Alice Walker.[22]

Both Katie Cannon and Delores Williams during this period, in 1985 and 1987 respectively, made use of Walker's category of womanism as the defining orientation and hermeneutical approach for theology done by black women.[23] It is in the work of these two that this shift in theology is first called Womanist theology, a distinct form of black liberation theology (subjectivity as freedom from race and gender oppression). Drawing on Walker, Cannon and Williams argued that a Womanist theology is concerned with the experiences and history of African American women as a defining element of religious activity and reflection within African American communities. To exclude or deny this is to participate in the oppression of God's people. Womanist theology, based on this concern, provides a new theological language that, if successful, allows black women to speak for themselves.

Using slave narratives, diary accounts, and other written records left by black women as well as a rethinking of Scripture, these theologians developed an understanding of God's will as intimately bound to the welfare of both men and women. Therefore, churches and religious thinkers must mirror this commitment to and recognition of women to be in line with the teachings and ministry of Christ. Such a perspective has been further developed in the writings of Womanist theologians such as Cheryl Kirk-Duggan, Traci West, M. Shawn Copeland, and Diana Hayes, as well as Womanists in other disciplines such as Cheryl Townsend Gilkes.[24] This work is meant to buttress the voice of women in the doing of theology and in the life of the church by giving due attention to "less conventional" and "more intimate and private aspects of Black life" that speak to the "real-lived texture of Black life and the oral-aural cultural values implicitly passed on and received from one generation to the next."[25]

An interesting conversation took place in the late 1980s that served as an essential moment of internal criticism for Womanist thought. In a piece published in the *Journal of Feminist Studies in Religion*, Cheryl Sanders, a theologian at Howard University and a Pentecostal minister, raised questions concerning the compatibility of Alice Walker's definition of Womanism and the central doctrines and commitments of the black Christian tradition. Her questioning revolved in large part around sexual orientation in that Walker's definition is open to same-sex relationships as an important expression of both sexual and non-sexual women's affirmation of self. Sanders argued that sexual orientation as embraced by Walker's definition ran contrary to basic teachings of the black Christian churches, and the uncritical appropriation of this definition might prove logically inconsistent with the beliefs of their audience.[26]

Womanist theologians took up this challenge and, I believe, their response sparked an important development in Womanist theology in particular and in liberation theology in black communities in general. It is after this roundtable discussion that one begins to see some attention given to the homophobia and heterosexism present in black churches (and black scholarship). Womanist theologians such as Renee Hill and more recently Kelly Brown Douglas have given more than superficial attention to this problem. Hill argues that a proper understanding of the ministry of Christ must entail a rejection of *all* oppressive tendencies including homophobia and heterosexism. Although others, including Emilie Townes, have voiced a rejection of these two forms of evil, it is in the work of Douglas that one sees this systematically worked through. Douglas urges black churches to address issues of sexuality within the context of the Gospel's message of liberation and transformation.

Womanist theologians have led the charge with respect to this issue, while the work of black (male) theologians will make passing reference to the evil of homophobia without systematic and constructive alternatives proposed. A few possible exceptions are Cornel West's sense of prophetic Christianity, the critique of the black church offered by Michael Dyson, and some writings done by Elias Farajaje-Jones. With respect to future work on homophobia and heterosexism, more attention to the politics of pleasure as played out in African American religion and a focus on the theological significance of the black body might prove theologically helpful. Yet, again, Womanist thinkers have taken the lead and their work is vital in that it marks another evolutionary moment in black liberation theology through a recognition of subjectivity as extending beyond race and gender to include sexual orientation.[27]

Besides this shift in conversation, another important transformation in black theology was initiated by Delores Williams's analysis of surrogacy as it is played out in the life of African American women. She argues that black women have historically served as surrogates on a variety of levels and that traditional depictions of the Christ event provide the theological rationale for this. Williams, as a counter, argues that a preoccupation with the suffering and death of Christ is a misread of the Gospel's significance. She, in place of this misreading, proposes a rethinking of Christology in which attention is placed on the ministry of Christ and little made of the passion.

What Williams's work makes possible is a sense of redemption that does not require suffering—the old "no cross no crown" paradigm.

Theology, accordingly, is purged of its preoccupation with Christ's surrogacy act on the cross as "sacred" and, in figurative and felt ways, appropriate for the Christ-like to mimic. According to Williams, this depiction of Christ (and God) has little potential for any type of meaningful inclusion of black women in salvation history. Rather, it reenforces their role in surrogate situations.[28] As part of this theological shift, Williams argues that the Christ event points to humans being shown an example of relationship, an example they attempt to destroy through the cross. Therefore, participation in God's plan for redeemed existence does not require death, rather it requires a commitment to healthy relationships. God does not require or condone black women's surrogacy. Hence, the cross must be remembered as evidence of the evil humans are capable of; it must not become a reified, theological symbol of required blood sacrifice.

This rethinking of the cross has also been explored by JoAnne Terrell. Linked to this, Jacquelyn Grant and others have raised questions concerning the importance of Jesus' gender, arguing that what is of most importance is the ministry of Christ. Grant suggests that we give priority to the manner in which Jesus Christ proposed a certain quality of relationship between God and humanity, and between humans. And this development of "family" should take theological precedence over Jesus' maleness. With respect to relationship, but outside this rethinking of the Christ event in light of women's experience, Karen Baker-Fletcher has argued that Christians have a responsibility to rethink humanity's relationship to the earth. Drawing on Alice Walker, Baker-Fletcher argues for a sense of interconnectedness with the earth, a mutuality that places humans within nature and makes its survival our survival.[29]

## IV. Complex Subjectivity: Additional Theological Riffs

Although black theology has evolved through a re-envisioning of subjectivity in light of an increasing number of essentializing practices within the larger society and within the African American community itself, Victor Anderson argues that there remains a troubling preoccupation with ontological blackness. He argues that black theology (and to some extent Womanist theology) has concerned itself with the ramifications of blackness in ways that force African Americans to identify with a rather narrow depiction of what it means to be black. Anderson argues that black theology must rethink itself in ways that move beyond ontological and essentialized notions of African American identity by allowing both individual fulfillment and inclusion in the African American community.[30] He suggests a further rethinking of the subjectivity which serves as the basis of black religion and black theology by arguing for the development of self-consciousness and self-identity within the context of community.

The appreciation for diversity and understandings of community as complex extends beyond the categories outlined by Anderson. Readers will note that most of what is currently discussed with respect to black theology—of all varieties—addresses the black Protestant experience. Theologians, however, like Diana Hayes, Bryan Massingale, Jamie Phelps, and Shawn Copeland have called for an understanding of African American religion that extends to the Roman Catholic faith embraced by more than two million African Americans. In light of this, black Catholic theologians have argued for the importance of Catholic ritual and teachings for the development of liberation theology within the African American communities. In addition to black Catholics theologically thinking through their faith stance, their writings also serve to form a more complex sense of black religiosity and the nature of spiritual struggle in African American communities.[31]

To recap, the work done by first and second generation African American (male) theologians as well as that done by Womanist theologians points to the growing complexity of subjectivity, even with respect to the modes of religious expression in African American communities (particularly with respect to Catholic and Protestant interaction). Current work does not go far enough.

### V. Black Theology Beyond 2000:
### Commentary on a Revised Agenda

What remains a rather under-explored component of black theology is the language used to explore religious experience. That is to say, most of what has been described above is couched in a rather apologetic appeal to the Christian faith as the central mode of religious identification within African American communities. Black theologians are correct to argue for the black church's historical presence and numerical significance; yet the church is just one way of articulating this quest for subjectivity. The challenge remains, I believe, an adequate response to the critique brought forward by Charles Long some years ago. Long argued that the religious experience of enslaved Africans and their descendants cannot be adequately understood using the Christian faith as the paradigm. It is more complex and more fundamental than the Africanization of Europeanized Christian faiths. In addition, Long suggests that theology—a European discipline about power and discourse about power—may not be the most useful mode of exploration if black theology does not make its first order of business a move away from traditional power discourse to an exploration of the soft substance of religious experience, the inner life of oppressed people. For him, the best approach to the religious experience of African Americans is hermeneutical in nature.[32]

It will take some time to adequately respond to Long, but I believe a good starting point is a critical assessment of the religio-theological language used to describe the religious experience of African Americans.[33] An assessment of this language and grammar may even point to the need for a more comparative approach to black liberation (and Womanist) theology. However, an *interest* in comparative work can only bear fruit if it is matched by a sustained conversation with those in other disciplines such as ritual studies, archaeology, anthropology, history of religions, and the visual arts.[34]

The language and methodologies offered by these various disciplines should push African American liberation theologians to better "handle" theological information in ways that do not force a christianization of "non-Christian" or "extrachurch" resources. Furthermore, these disciplines may help black theology make an important shift with respect to the utilization of non-written materials in which African American religious experience is grounded. For example, anthropologist Mary Douglas has done work on body symbolism that points to the multi-leveled signficance of the body, and this has meaning for an understanding of the body as a ritual device, marker of religious developments, and source of theological questions. In the long run, theological exploration of black bodies, beyond current levels, might provide black (and Womanist) theologies with an even richer understanding of what subjectivity means.[35] It is my hope that these methodological and resource shifts will also help clarify the "public" nature of black theology.

Finally, black theology must aggressively pursue dialogue with Latino/a theologians in the context of the United States. Conversation started years ago with Latin American thinkers, yet conversation with those who literally live "around the corner" has been much slower in developing. Continuing oppression in the United States, combined with the "browning" of the nation, necessitates such interaction.

# Response

## by Benjamin Valentin

In my years of reading both Hispanic/Latino/a and African American theology, I had gradually become intrigued with the need and possibility for dialogue between theologians of these two theological traditions. My conviction is that there is ample historical and sociopolitical reason for the cultivation of such a cross-cultural theological exchange. In reading Anthony Pinn's thoughts on the historical development of black theology it became apparent to me that there is also much theological ground for substantive dialogue between African American and Latino/a theologians. Indeed, there are various topics, concerns, and points of parallel distinction that could provide the basis for such an exchange. One could, for instance, point to a roughly concurrent historical and/or generational course of development, and the sharing of a similar founding impetus, between African American and Hispanic/Latino/a theology. Besides these two resemblances, it also seems to me that these theological traditions also share a similar methodological emphasis on the inclusion of popular sources in theological reflection and various overlapping thematic challenges. I believe that these parallel distinctions and concerns can both spark and facilitate further comparative analysis among African American and Latino/a theologians.

One of the points of commonality between African American and Hispanic/Latino/a theology that especially stood out for me when I read Pinn's essay alongside of mine is the great attention that both of these theological traditions place on the use of the "popular" in theology. That is to say, both of these theologies fundamentally seek to incorporate into theological construction the particular history, experience, and cultural production of the communities from which they emerge. In black theology this emphasis has paved the way for the use of slave narratives, diary accounts, and other written records left by black women and men, African American literature, and musical production—from the spirituals to contemporary rap music—as theological resources. In Hispanic theology this impulse has led to a strong emphasis on the interpretation of Latino/a *mestizaje* (i.e., cultural hybridity), the study of popular religion, and the inclusion both of Latino/a literary production and "lo cotidiano"—the everyday experience of Latinos and Latinas. In both cases the result has been the placement of African American and Hispanic/Latino/a experience and identity at the center of theological reflection. This methodological emphasis on the use of "the popular" (*lo que es nuestro*/what is uniquely ours), in the doing of theology is appreciable in African American and Latino/a theology and could provide an interesting basis for future comparative analysis.

It also seems to me that both of these theological traditions share some comparable challenges that could be jointly explored by theologians and religious scholars in these two groups. In his review of themes and works in black theology, Pinn sheds light on four internal critiques and challenges that still remain under-explored in that theology. He specifically mentions the following calls to question: (1) Cornel West's early summons for black theology to incorporate a fuller response to injustice by way of a mature social analysis, and to become public discourse in new ways; (2) Victor Anderson's warning that black theology has generally preoccupied itself with an ontological blackness that actually impels African Americans to identify with a narrow depiction of what it means to be black; (3) Charles Long's admonition that black theology and the study of black religion adequately consider non-Christian and extra-church African American religious experience. Pinn also notes the need for black theology to pursue dialogue with Latino/a theologians in the context of the United States. Interestingly, these critical notations closely compare with the issues I highlighted for closer attention in Latino/a theology: (1) U. S. Hispanic theology's tendency to restrict theological reflection and discourse to the internal concerns and the language of the institutional churches; (2) the need for theologies that can adequately engage, respond to, and influence the broader public life and discourse of the United States; (3) Hispanic theology's tendency thus far to focus predominantly on discussions of cultural justice, and not sufficiently on the multifaceted matrices that impinge upon the realization of a broader emancipatory political project and energy; and (4) the need for the development and promotion of socially binding theological discourse that can connect the sociopolitical and economic struggles of our Latino/a communities to the similar struggles of other marginalized groups in the United States. Given the comparability of these under-explored challenges, I believe that it would be fruitful for African American and Latino/a theologians to explore the possibilities of a revised agenda together.

# 2

## Strangers No More: An Introduction to, and an Interpretation of, U.S. Hispanic/Latino/a Theology

BENJAMIN VALENTIN

IN THE UNITED STATES, feminist and African American theologies have received much deserved notice for their original contributions to the task of theological construction. However, it is necessary to note that right alongside these liberation theologies, though with less publicity until now, Latino and Latina theologians have been developing a distinctive form of liberation theology written from the perspective of their lives in the United States. Although influenced in certain respects by the mode of liberation theology that emerged in Latin America, and also by feminist and African American liberationist theologies in the United States, these theologians have created an inimitable theological expression that has sought to analyze the existential conditions of U.S. Hispanic American life and to promote new strategies of personal meaning and sociopolitical adjustments, through the employment and reshaping of Christian and popular Latino/a religious symbols, for the well-being of Latinos/as and the greater U.S. society. Their voices deserve attention and appreciation in mainstream theological study, for they offer much reflective novelty and creativity, and also because they provide insight into the confounding realities of life in the United States and the varieties of religious experience found within it.

This essay intends to provide an introduction to the germinal thought found within U.S. Hispanic/Latino/a theology.[1] My study is made up of three parts: the first offers a brief account of Latino/a theology's historical background; the second elaborates the themes and reflective categories that have most engaged the attention of Latino/a theologians; and the third provides a personal assessment of

U.S. Hispanic/Latino/a theology that takes into account its great achievements and the challenges that it faces as we enter the twenty-first century in the United States.

## I. A Historical Tracing of U.S. Hispanic/Latino/a Theology

Hispanic/Latino/a theologians in the United States have been writing creative and systematic book-length theological reflections on the U.S. experience since 1975.[2] Although in a sense Latino/a theology is a rather recent theological tradition that may seem to be a novel elaboration to many in the mainstream of U.S. theology, I will suggest that actually it is already possible, and indeed useful, to speak of three stages in the development of U.S. Hispanic/Latino/a theology: (1) a *formative and prearticulated stage* marked by certain broad social events and circumstances that particularly shaped the thought, reflective categories, and activities of Latino/a theologians; (2) an *initial stage of articulation* that extends from 1975 to 1990; and (3) a *boom and maturation phase* that begins in 1991 and continues on to the present.[3] A brief examination and explanation of these historical stages of development is in order here.

### (a) The Formative Stage

Although the articulated stage of U.S. Hispanic/Latino/a theology begins in earnest in 1975, with Virgilio Elizondo's first book-length theological monograph on Latino/a life in the United States, it is necessary to note that its development as a theological tradition proceeds from a number of broader social and cultural factors that antecede this date. Broadly put, Latino/a theology has been rooted in and conditioned by the overall Hispanic experience within the United States.[4]

Although the thematic structure of Latino/a theology has clearly been impelled by the overall U.S. Hispanic/Latino/a experience, from its earliest beginnings during the Spanish colonial period to the contemporary moment, it has especially been shaped by more recent events and outcomes that have generally influenced Latino consciousness since the Second World War, most prominent among them the evolution of a fragile, yet appreciable, panethnic social identity. Indeed, the predilection toward a pan-Latino/a or Hispanic designation and posture, and the overall enchantment with matters of cultural recognition and identity in Latino/a theology, bears witness to the influence that the broader search for a positive and collective Latino/a ethnic identity has had on that theology. The staging moment of U.S. Hispanic/Latino/a theology is, therefore, particularly rooted in the emergence of a critical pan-Latino/a social consciousness among Latinos/as, one that arises principally as a result of, and in response to, a set of social developments that transpired between the decades of the 1940s and the 1960s.

Five social developments had special impact on Latino/a identity during this period. First, the U.S. Latino/a population grew rapidly, both because of the proliferation of those long-established Latino/a communities that had been living in U.S. territories even before the establishment of the United States as a nation, and because of an increase in migration and immigration, particularly from Mexico, Puerto Rico, and Cuba. Second, many Latinos migrated into U.S. urban settings, drawn by the demand for cheap labor in city factories; this gave rise to greater Latino/a visibility in some of the big U.S. cities. Third, Latinos/as became more aware of a growing U.S. xenophobia that often targeted them because of their increasing visibility. Fourth, there developed among Latino/a communities a heightened sense of the existence of long-standing forms of structural racism and pervasive discriminatory patterns in public life, which relegated disproportionate numbers of Latinos/as to indeterminate underclass status. Fifth and finally, there emerged in Latino/a communities a greater understanding of the economic and political delimitations that they faced in the United States.[5] These factors led to a heightened recognition of the need for a protean struggle to ameliorate dismal conditions that disproportionately affected them and other disadvantaged groups of people. This acknowledgment, in turn, engendered a new, more critical, identity among U.S. Latinos and Latinas.

This unfolding distinctive Latino/a consciousness noticeably fermented during the late 1960s, giving rise to a flurry of secularist, then religious, theological, and ecclesiastical movements for change. Various secular Chicano- and Puerto Rican-led advocacy organizations, such as La Raza Unida Party, the Young Lords, Brown Berets, Crusade for Justice, the Puerto Rican Socialist Party and Student Union, MECHA, MALDEF, CISPES, and CRECEN among others, arose during the 1960s to struggle for the overall self-determination of U.S. Latinos/as. Challenged by the secular Hispanic sociopolitical movements that emerged in the 1960s, the Latino/a churches, first through lay movements, then through national ecclesiastical leadership organizations, found it necessary to become involved in the spirit of social transformation that permeated the Civil Rights era. A progressive element in the church, motivated by these events, proceeded to apply the insights of the burgeoning liberation theology movement to the social situation in the United States in order to advocate for social, political, economic, and legislative change. The internal call within the church for ecclesiastical change, coupled with the strident external challenge of secular movements calling the church to authentic social witness, led to a flurry of lay and religious organizations whose goal it was to contribute to the betterment of the Latino/a condition in the United

States. Although conservative reactions from within the church and the secular realm often attempted to placate the liberationist stance of these movements, progressive visionaries always found a way to galvanize the prophetic elements of the Latino/a churches with those in the socio-secular realm in order to stir up the energies of Latino/a activism in the United States.

Lastly, the staging moment of U.S. Hispanic/Latino/a theology is also rooted in the initial dialogues between Latin American liberation theologians and the first generation of U.S. Hispanic/Latino/a theologians. Virgilio Elizondo was the first to initiate such an exchange, starting with his participation at the Medellin Conference in Colombia. Through the Mexican-American Cultural Center, which he founded, Elizondo continued to encourage dialogue between Latin-American and U.S. Hispanic/Latino/a religious leaders. To be sure, U.S. Hispanic/Latino/a theology was informed not only by these dialogues with Latin American theologies but also by the concerns and insights of U.S. African American and feminist theologies. The insights gained from these encounters with other liberation theologies, however, were not simply cut and pasted into the theological reflections of U.S. Latinos/as. Rather, they were employed as orienting thought forms and were then reshaped according to the particularities of Latino/a life in the United States.

### (b) Initial Stage of Articulation (1975 to 1990)

The initial stage of U.S. Hispanic/Latino/a theological articulation begins in 1975 and extends, I will suggest, until 1990. During this stage, the contributions of five theologians, Virgilio Elizondo, Orlando Costas, Justo González, Ada María Isasi-Díaz, and Yolanda Tarango, and the evolution of two autochthonous organizations for the support of Latino/a theological study, loom especially important. The seminal and formative contributions of these pioneering theologians and theological organizations deserve particular mention.[6]

### Virgilio Elizondo

As Allan Figueroa Deck rightly notes, "the history of contemporary U.S. Hispanic theology must begin with the work of Virgil Elizondo."[7] Elizondo, who continues to serve as the rector of the San Fernando Cathedral in San Antonio, is the first contemporary Latino/a thinker to explicitly articulate a U.S. Hispanic/Latino/a theology. He has been active as a religious leader since the early 1960s. From the beginning, his writings have demonstrated a creative synthesis by weaving together a concern for Hispanic culture in general; a celebratory analysis of Mexican American culture in particular; and

a Christian faith. This creative, yet critical, theological dialectic was
already on display in a 1968 treatise that Elizondo entitled "Educación religiosa para el Mexico-Norte Americano."[8] In this early writing, Elizondo can be found taking exception to the Catholic
Church's disregard for the particularities of Mexican American culture in its religious observances among Mexican Americans. Following a criticism of this ecclesiastical failure, Elizondo called for the
inclusion of Hispanic cultural elements in the Catholic religious
practices within Mexican American communities. He followed this
up, in his 1975 text entitled *Christianity and Culture*, with a full-
length theological study and expression of the consciousness that
emanates from the culture and religiosity of the Mexican American
people. In this work one can already detect Elizondo's first attempts
to translate the lived *mestizaje* (i.e., cultural hybridity) that characterizes the Mexican American as well as the overall Latino/a heritage
and experience.

Elizondo's most renowned work, however, appeared in 1983 with
the publication of *Galilean Journey*.[9] The importance of this work for
the present constitution of Hispanic/Latino/a theology cannot be
overstressed, for it was in this book that Elizondo first introduced an
elaborate theological interpretation of the concept of *mestizaje*—the
multiformed fusion of European-Iberian, Amerindian, African, and
U.S. American race and culture that constitutes the historical and
cultural reality of Mexican Americans and the majority of U.S. Hispanics. Drawing an analogy between Jesus' sociocultural identity as a
hybrid—a Jew of Galilean descent—and the present experience of "in-
betweenness" that is prevalent among Mexican Americans and Chi-
canos, due to their multivalent racial, cultural, and historical
hybridity, Elizondo's *Galilean Journey* proffers a Christology that encourages Mexican Americans, Latinos/as, and by extension all persons
of hybrid heritage, to affirm their unique *mescolanza/hybridity* in spite
of the rejection they may experience because of it in the United
States. Mestizo/a identity, as Elizondo conceives it in this work and in
his later *The Future is Mestizo*,[10] admits for much more than just pain
and dislocation: It is also a liminal space filled with potentiality, and
a prospective site of grace. Overall, this work provided a methodological model for later U.S. Hispanic/Latino/a theology: a Christian theological interpretation that emanates from the space of the self, of
identity, and begins with a contextualized historical and cultural reading of the Hispanic experience.

Elizondo was also one of the first theologians to argue convincingly
that a truly contextual theology had to take the popular religious
expressions and symbols of its people seriously.[11] The subsequent
trend within U.S. Hispanic/Latino/a theology of considering popular
religious expression, and other forms of autochthonous Latino/a cul-

tural production and memory, as legitimate sources for theological reflection owes much to Elizondo's initial insights in this area. In sum, Elizondo's creative scholarly work, and his work as an activist, have served as catalysts for subsequent U.S. Hispanic/Latino/a theological scholarship. Moreover, his involvement in the Mexican-American Cultural Center, which he founded, and his exemplary fusion of reflection and social practice, popular cultural expressions and Christian theology, and pastoral concerns and scholarship, continues to provide theologians with a model for authentic organic intellectual activity.[12]

### Orlando Costas

Protestant theologian Orlando Costas, a contemporary of Elizondo, also contributed to the initial articulated stage of U.S. Hispanic/Latino/a theology and to the vision of later theologians. Three central emphases can be found in Costas's theological works: (1) the need for theology to engage its present context reflectively and practically through social action for transformation; (2) the liberative potential that exists in a theology constructed from the underside of history; and (3) a call for an ecclesiastical model of evangelization that accents an integral and holistic liberative agenda, one that does not only call attention to spiritual enlightenment but more fully to the whole of life in all of its provinces.[13] David Traverzo, a more recent U.S. Hispanic/Latino/a theologian who has interpreted and expounded on Costas's legacy, describes Costas's theological system as "a Latino radical evangelical approach" that interweaves "the components of a biblical faith with a socially relevant and liberating thrust." In this way, Traverzo continues, Costas interprets Christian mission as "a transforming enterprise with a holistic framework that requires a contextual engagement from the vantage point of the dispossessed."[14]

As one of the original articulators of a contemporary U.S. Hispanic/Latino/a theology, Costas left behind a mature theological model for a liberative praxis that refreshingly accentuates contextuality, a view from below, and the subversive, yet empowering value of holistic reflection. Costas's work serves to continuously remind theologians that authentic transformation of the self, community, and nation always depends on a depth liberation that affects our whole being existentially, personally, culturally, and politically. Moreover, Costas's theological legacy continues to remind us that a theological system is true and viable only to the extent that it contributes to salutary, concrete, and justice-engendering results in our personal lives, families, communities, and societies. Rightfully, many contemporary U.S. Hispanic/Latino/a theologians, especially those of Protestant orientation, continue to remember and to build on Costas's legacy today.

## Justo González

As with Elizondo's involvement, the manifold contributions of Justo González cannot be over-emphasized. Although his first truly explicit articulation of a U.S. Hispanic/Latino/a theology appears in 1990, with the publishing of his masterful and influential book entitled *Mañana*, a treatise that offers one of the few full-fledged systematic treatments of the traditional Christian categories of doctrinal thought to be found within the annals of Hispanic theology, González's earlier contributions as a writer, organizer, activist, and theological mentor played a major role in the development of U.S. Hispanic/Latino/a theological thought. González's three-volume work on Christian history, for instance, published in 1970 under the title *History of Christian Thought*,[15] has long been a favorite of Latino/a seminarians and has in fact been commonly used in many seminaries as a central text in the study of church history. All of González's published works, even before his later systematic and more explicit Hispanic theological treatises, display a clear liberationist stance and methodology. Since he completed his doctoral studies in Church history at Yale Divinity School in 1961, González has not ceased writing and editing books. Overall, he has written over fifty books and three hundred articles which have been translated into several languages. Besides his many early works on the history of Christian thought and church history, González has more recently authored various other books on theology from a Hispanic perspective that have contributed greatly to the creativity and overall development of contemporary U.S. Hispanic/Latino/a theology. Among these are *Out of Every Tribe and Nation*; *Voces*; and *Santa Biblia*.[16]

González's contributions, however, go far beyond the publication of books. He has also founded many educational enterprises that have provided the means for scholars and church practitioners to focus on the theology of U.S. Hispanic Americans. He was, for instance, one of the founders and the editor of the professional journal *Apuntes*, a theological journal founded in 1980 and dedicated to the exploration and elaboration of a U.S. Hispanic/Latino/a theology. Until the 1992 appearance of the *Journal of Hispanic/Latino Theology*, this was the only U.S. Hispanic/Latino/a theological journal in the country. He has also been involved in the establishment or organization of other theological educational programs, such as the *Hispanic Summer Institute*, *AETH* (Association for Hispanic Theological Education), and funding programs for U.S. Hispanic American students in religion and theology, such as the *Hispanic Theological Initiative*, all of which have been designed to assist in the exploration of Latino/a religious expression within the United States.[17] Through his work as author, organizer, teacher and mentor, Justo González has bridged academic and pastoral concerns and has greatly contributed to the shaping of contemporary U.S. Hispanic/Latino/a theology. In countless ways, present Latino/a theologians and religious scholars, and indeed the movement of U.S. Hispanic/Latino/a theology itself, remain in debt to the original and multifaceted contributions of Justo González and to his overall mentorship.

### Ada María Isasi-Díaz and Yolanda Tarango

Ada María Isasi-Díaz and Yolanda Tarango advanced Latino/a theological thought immensely through their joint publishing of *Hispanic Women: Prophetic Voice in The Church*, in 1988.[18] This work represents the first book-length articulation of a distinctively U.S. Latina theology of liberation. Part of the uniqueness of this book lies in its integration of interview-like colloquials with lay Hispanic women in the theological reflective process, and the incorporation of Spanish chapter summaries in the text. The work also laid the foundation for one particular expression of Latina theology.

Ada María Isasi-Díaz, the most published Latina theologian to date, expounded on the premises set forth in the above treatise, developing, in the process, a distinctive form of Latina theological discourse which she labeled "*mujerista* theology." Its first public appearance can be traced back to a 1989 article that Ada María Isasi-Díaz published in *The Christian Century*, under the title of "Mujeristas: A Name of Our Own."[19] Noting how the naming process can be an act of self-determination, and how the volitional act of self-naming can lend orientation and distinctness to Latina theological articulation, she made use of the Hispanic term most commonly employed in Latino/a love and protest songs to refer to women (i.e., *mujer*) to designate her proposed Latina theology of liberation. Ada María Isasi-Díaz defines a *mujerista* as "a Latina who makes a preferential option for herself and her Hispanic sisters, understanding that our struggle for liberation has to take into consideration how racism/ethnic prejudice, economic oppression, and sexism work together and reinforce each other."[20] Following this definition, *mujerista* theology becomes a liberative process, "reflective action that has as its goal the liberation of Hispanic women."[21] In this connection, *mujerista* theology attempts to accomplish two enormously important tasks: first, to enable Hispanic women to understand the many oppressive structures that strongly influence their lives; and second, to help Hispanic women define a preferred future.[22]

To be sure, there are other Latinas who have contributed to the evolution of a distinctively U.S. Hispanic women's theology, and not all of these are *mujerista* theologians who make use of this term. Marina Herrera, the first U.S. Hispanic woman to earn a doctorate in theology, and Maria de la Cruz Aymes, for instance, also promoted a Hispanic women's theology in the United States through their early written articles and church-social activism. More recently María Pilar Aquino, who prefers to call her theological endeavor a Latina feminist liberation theology, Gloria Ines Loya, Rosa María Icaza, Jeanette Rodríguez-Holguin, Ana María Pineda, Lara Medina, and Daisy Machado, who has the distinction of being the first Protestant Hispanic woman to earn a doctorate in theology, have added their distinctive voices, among others, to Latino/a theology. The activity and literary production of these Latinas bears witness to the boom and maturation phase of U.S. Hispanic/Latino/a theology, which will next be discussed. Nevertheless, solely on the basis of their having published the first book length monograph on Hispanic theology from a Latina perspective, not to mention their other honorable and important strivings to provide Latina theology with its deserved visibility, Ada María Isasi-Díaz and Yolanda Tarango's place in the historical development of Latino/a theology deserves special acknowledgment. Latino/a theology as a whole is indebted to their activism and to their writings.

Finally, it must be acknowledged that the development of Latino/a theology during this initial stage of articulation has been greatly served by *Apuntes*, the first journal devoted to the study of Latino/a theology and religiosity, ACHTUS (The Association of Catholic Hispanic Theologians in the United States), and the Hispanic Summer Program, which was initiated by the Fund for Theological Education. These three establishments provided space for conversation and theological reflection among theologians and religious scholars on issues of Latino/a religiosity in the United States.

### (c) The Boom and Maturation Phase

Since 1991, U.S. Hispanic/Latino/a theology has burgeoned, displaying an impressive array of creative theological innovations. This creativity is especially grounded in, and clearly disclosed in, five developments: (1) the elaboration of *mujerista* theology as a unique expression of a Latina liberation theology; (2) the 1991 founding of the Association for Hispanic Theological Education (AETH), which was designed to study and better the state of theological education among U.S. Latino/a communities; (3) the emergence, in 1992, of a second theological journal (the *Journal of Hispanic/Latino Theology)*; (4) the initiation, in 1996, of the *Hispanic Theological Initiative*, designed to encourage networking among Latino/a theological and religious scholars, mentorships between Latino/a scholars and theological students, and scholarship programs for theological students; and (5) the rigorous growth in theological publications, including the appearance of seven anthologies, prior to this present volume, devoted to the elaboration of a U.S. Hispanic/Latino/a theology, three historical overviews of the U.S. Hispanic American churches, and a four volume study devoted to the study of Latino/a religion by PARAL.[23]

Besides these anthologies, many other individually authored books have appeared since 1991. These texts bear witness to the emergence of what could be called a second wave in the articulation of Latino/a theological thought, authored by thinkers who are slowly but surely ceasing to be strangers within the U.S. theological academy, such as María Pilar Aquino, Arturo Bañuelas, Orlando Espín, Roberto Goizueta Jr., Roberto Pazmiño, Harold Recinos, Jeanette Rodríguez-Holguin, Fernando Segovia, Eldin Villafañe, and other emerging Latino/a theological voices.[24] Along with the pioneers, most of whom are still with us and still contributing to the shape of U.S. Latino/a theology, these more recent articulators have helped to expand theological reflection in and on the United States. As Fernando Segovia rightly notes, this recent growth in theological production "represents but one facet of a much larger literary and academic boom in U.S. Hispanic American circles."[25] Spurred on by the recent interest in the long-ignored reality of Latinos/as in the United States, perhaps due to the heightened awareness of the Latino/a population increase, and the growth in the numbers of Latino/a scholars, U.S. Hispanic/Latino/a theology has recently taken enormous strides both in the proliferation and richness of its distinctive expression.

## II. A Summary of The Themes of U.S. Hispanic/Latino/a Theology

In view of the constant experience of racial and cultural discrimination and the consistent attacks on positive self-identity that Latinos/as have long endured, U.S. Hispanic/Latino/a theologians have placed great emphasis on issues related to cultural memory and self-cultural identity. The reasoning behind the emergence of this emphasis, and the privileging of the categories of culture and identity, in Latino/a theology is easily grasped when we examine the general history of Latinos/as in this nation. To put it bluntly and briefly, from the very beginning we Latinos/as have had to struggle consistently and zealously to keep alive our distinctive historical and cultural experiences in the United States, all the while also claiming our membership as legitimate citizens and active agents in this nation. The assimilationist dogma that frequently creeps into our national discourse has often, either overtly or more subtly, requested that Latinos/as erase their past in order to then become "authentic" U.S. Americans. These historical realities and dynamics have led Latino/a theologians, and Latino/a scholars in general, to the conclusion that identity and culture are salient topics which deserve their consideration.

This focus is perhaps most clearly manifest in the recurring use of, and significance attributed to, the concepts of *mestizaje* and *popular religion* in the writings of most Hispanic/Latino/a theologians. Even the most cursory reading of the emerging tradition of U.S. Hispanic/Latino/a theology would show that these two motifs hold special significance for Latino/a theologians. These two themes, along with the concept of *Teologia en Conjunto* (theology done in joint collaboration and in community), can be seen as core topics in Latino/a theology.

### (a) Affirming Our Mestizaje and Mulatez

Latino/a cultures and identities are always in some way the result of a syncretic, eccentric, and disjointed fusion of Iberian, Amerindian, African, and Euro-American culture. The most commonly used term in literature to speak of this ambiguity and multilayered hybridity at the heart of Latino/a cultural history and identity is *mestizaje*. The term *mestizaje* generally refers to "the process of biological and cultural mixing that occurs after the violent and unequal encounter between cultures."[26] In the case of Latinos/as, this hybridity involves the fusion and influence of all of the aforementioned cultural heritages at different historical moments. Latino/a identity and culture is actually, therefore, the result of a confluence of contexts and cultural heritages that at the very least includes Iberian, Amerindian, and African influences, and certainly the influence of Euro-Anglo cultural traditions and life experiences in the United States. Undoubtedly, this hybrid past and present is responsible for much of the uniqueness of Latino/a identities. It is evident in our corporeal features, customs, foods, music, dances, celebrations, religiosity, sensibilities, and overall consciousness. Indeed, we Latinos/as have managed in every way to develop new cultures and identities that juggle, blur, and blend the historic and cultural genealogies that make up our heritage into a meaningful existence. Latinos/as in the United States have lent living credence to Homi Bhaba's assertion that hybridity could in fact give rise to "something different, something new and unrecognizable, a new area of negotiation of meaning and representation."[27] It is important to bear in mind, however, that affirmation of the lived transcultural experience of Latino/a *mestizaje* has involved relentless inner and outer struggle, and has always in fact required a strong resolution to transcend menacing existential, political, cultural, and even geographic borders in order to survive sanely and wholly in the United States.

The process of translating this lived Latino/a *mestizaje* into written discourse can actually be traced back to the early twentieth century writings of the Latin American intellectual Jose Vasconcelos.[28] In more recent years, however, it has crossed the U.S. border and found a home in the writings of such Chicano-Latino/a scholars as Daniel Cooper Alarcon, Guillermo Gomez-Peña, Cherríe Moraga, and especially Gloria Anzaldua, writers who have given *mestizo/a* discourse a newfound recognition and a refined theoretical status.[29] Yet, even before hybridity discourse and the concept of *mestizaje* was to become popular in U.S. cultural scholarship during the late 1980s, a Mexican-American theologian by the name of Virgilio Elizondo had already been working on the interpretation of U.S. Latino/a *mestizaje*. It is proper to say, therefore, that Virgilio Elizondo is a pioneer of the more recent discourse on Latino/a *mestizaje* among Latino/a scholars. Without a doubt he was the first theologian to employ the concept of *mestizaje* as a theological starting point from which to interpret the historical experience of U.S. Hispanics. Following his influential lead most Hispanic/Latino/a theologians have come to view *mestizaje* as an important and fertile locus for theological reflection.

In whatever manner the term *mestizaje* is employed, the main thrust behind this concept's usage in Latino/a theology is a concern with the proper remembrance, defense, and celebration of cultural identity and difference. Hence, the notion of *mestizaje* (i.e., Latino/a racial and cultural hybridity) is employed within Latino/a theology as an explanatory category that synchronously depicts the cultural and even racial hybridity that characterizes Latino/a identities; highlights who we are as Latinos/as; helps point to what is different and new about Latino/a identity in the United States; and provides fertile ground so that new positive formations and celebrations of Latino/a cultural identity may take hold in the United States in spite of the depreciating pressures often exerted by the dominant Euro-Anglo culture. Finally, *mestizaje* is also utilized as a heuristic device that can help promote the acceptance and even affirmation of difference, and as an imaginative source for overall human unity across the boundaries of difference.

### (b) Popular Religion

The concern with cultural affirmation and identity in Latino/a theology is not only revealed in the prominent role granted to the theorization of *mestizaje*, but also in the status accorded to the study of U.S. Hispanic popular religion, particularly popular forms of Catholicism and Protestant Christianity. The concept of popular religion most generally connotes those sets of religious beliefs and practices that are either distinct from or, rather, not *fully* the product of religious specialists or of an elaborate "official" ecclesiastical organizational framework. This wide-embracing term, "popular religion," "points to the ways in which individuals take religious belief, interpret it in practical terms, and put it to work to do something that will give order and meaning to their lives"[30] independently of the consent of theologians, priests, religious professionals, or ecclesiastical offices.

The Latino/a fascination with popular religion is rooted in the perception that it embodies an ongoing, albeit clandestine, form of Latino/a self-definition and communal resistance against assimilatory pressures in the United States. To put it plainly, Latino/a theologians suspect that the study of Hispanic popular religious expression may provide an aperture to one of the central ways that Latinos/as have attempted, through a religious medium, both to maintain their marginalized cultural traditions and to take their identity back in the United States. Hence, theologians have defended popular religious expression as both a legitimate site of faith and authentic religious form that mediates the divine, and as fount of salutary remembrance, defense, and celebration of Latino/a cultural identity and difference.

### (c) Teologia en Conjunto—Theology in Community and Collaboration

U.S. Hispanic/Latino/a theology is also highly characterized by a collaborative spirit, a motivating impulse that has even been given name in Latino/a theology and received prominence as a theme in itself: *teologia en conjunto* (i.e., collaborative or joint theology). This sensibility materializes in the form of two different but interrelated emphases. First, Latino/a theologians stress that theology should be done in dialogue with one's community of faith. The ultimate hope in such an exchange is that the theologian be influenced by the specificity of his or her community and that, in turn, the community be enriched in some way by the theologian's participation. As Luis Pedraja puts it, Latino/a theologians generally believe that "doing theology as dialogue avoids the Enlightenment's model of doing theology as an abstract observer."[31] In brief, these theologians strive to become "organic intellectuals" who work in and on behalf of the religious communities they may be a part of. The second emphasis that materializes within this overall collaborative sensibility is that of doing theology in cooperation with other Latino/a theologians as a communal exercise.

This overall collaborative and dialogical spirit is exemplified in a number of ways. One of the earliest examples of this communal and collaborative approach was Ada María Isasi-Díaz and Yolanda Tarango's 1988 book, *Hispanic Women: Prophetic Voice in the Church*. In this book Latino/a theology was described as a "communal process," and the method employed to give body to this notion was the use of ethnographic accounts, which elucidated the experiences of lay Hispanic Catholic women, as central components of the authors' life-based theological interpretations.[32] Another example of the emphasis on collaborative and communal engagement can be found in Justo González's call for, and description of, Hispanic theology as a *Fuenteovejuna theology*: a communal reflective enterprise that envisions all as one.[33] This overall spirit can also be seen at work in Roberto Goizueta's descriptions of a theology of *accompaniment*,[34] as well as in the many convocations organized by Latino/a theologians to discuss their work together and in the proclivity toward the production of theological anthologies that allow for inner collaboration.

## III. A Personal Assessment of Hispanic/Latino/a Theology: Conclusions

U.S. Hispanic/Latino/a theology has definitely come a long way in a rather short time. Coming into published existence between 1975 and 1990, with the writings of a precious few theologians, it has rapidly achieved a high level of articulation and has distinguished itself as one of the most creative emerging theologies in the world. I agree with M. Shawn Copeland's intimation that "the most conspicuous achievement of U.S. Hispanic/Latino/a theology is its own liberation."[35] In other words, this theology established a distinctive identity over and against subordination to Latin American liberation theologies, even as it continued a supportive bi-directional dialogue with these theologies. But, in addition to this achievement, U.S. Hispanic/Latino/a theology has also been at the forefront of such influential theological innovations as: the creative employment of autochthonous cultural productions and cultural memory in theological reflection; the theorization of the concepts of *mestizaje*—cultural hybridity—and popular religion; the elaboration of a distinctive women's theology of liberation; the advancement of historical Jesus study through the presentation of his *mestizo* and border sociocultural identity as a Galilean; the development of an ecclesiology that emanates from the context of the *barrio* (the inner city); a reading of the Bible from the eyes of Hispanics/Latinos/as; the promotion of postcolonial studies within biblical hermeneutics; the development of a distinctive Christian ethics based on Latino/a notions of *dignidad*; and many other innovative developments.[36] All of these developments demonstrate, as Fernando Segovia notes, that not only has U.S. Hispanic/Latino/a theology emerged with a boom: it has also "gone on to develop deep foundations and to mature and flourish as well."[37] Although, as a participating insider, I am proud of Latino/a theology's rapid maturation, I suggest that there are certain challenges, directions, and issues that deserve closer attention. I will close this essay with some general observations and comments in support of the further maturation of U.S. Hispanic/Latino/a theology.

First, I believe that U.S. Hispanic/Latino/a theologies have often tended to restrict theological discourse to the internal concerns and the language of the institutional churches. To put it bluntly, this theology often operates under the misguided assumption that theology is solely and entirely a reflective endeavor of the church and for the church. As such, I have observed that much of our theological reflection defers to the language and concerns of the church and becomes, in the end, a mere analysis and interpretation of the faith of those already existing within the theological circle of a particular institutionalized church. My personal concerns with this *ecclesiocentrism* are that first, it does not serve to motivate Latino/a theologians to reflect upon the full spectrum of Latino/a religious experiences, theological orientations, and what may be called "extra-church" realities and sources. Second, it can also serve to divert our attention away from the larger sociocultural matrices that make up theology's reflective context. Third, by restricting theological reflection to the language and internal concerns of the church we may unknowingly limit the potential orienting capacity of our theologies within the greater national public context. Increasingly, I see a need for theologies that can adequately engage, respond to, and influence the broader public discourse of the United States in the realm of civil society. Yet this can only be accomplished if our theologies reflect on more than just the life of the church. Although we need theologies that reflect on the existence and condition of the church, we also need theologies that at least strive to interpret the broader contours of U.S. public life and seek to stimulate discussions that may have widespread public interest beyond the confines of local churches and seminaries.[38]

Second, I believe that Latino/a theology has tended to limit itself to discussions of culture, identity, and subjectivity, and has, therefore, given too little attention to the critical scrutiny of the multifaceted matrices that impinge upon the realization of a broader emancipatory political project and energy. To be sure, this stress on identity and culture arises from a legitimate concern with the survival of Hispanic/ Latino/a people as a people in the United States. Nevertheless, I suggest that a theology that aims to promote social justice cannot be limited to discussions of culture, identity, subjectivity, and difference.

The predilection toward, and the emphasis on, matters of local cultural identity and difference in our theologies has unintentionally served to engender certain debilitating oversights. First, our enchantment with a general discursive paradigm of culture and identity recognition has served to displace other pertinent issues and axes of social stratification from the reflection chart. One unfortunate outcome, for instance, has been the deflection of class issues and social politics from a central point in our theologies. Yet, we should bear in mind that the axes of identity and culture are always in fact embedded in a larger web of shifting social, political, and economic relations that must be equally kept in mind when theorizing on matters of identity, culture, or difference. Hence, these matters must be understood in relation to broader societal constituents, stratifications, and crises that transcend the space of the self and the local, and yet, nevertheless, influence everyday personal and local realities.

So also the proclivity toward the theorizing of culture, identity, and cultural difference has apparently diverted our attention away from the longing for and need in society for connectivity, affiliation, coalitional energies, and the development of progressive alliances of struggle. Aimed primarily at valorizing local cultural specificity and the reclamation of positive self and group identity, our discourses have not reflected enough on the possible harmonizing of diverse emancipatory interests in society and the importance of cross-ethnic alliances of struggle. Yet, the task of alliance building and the need for coalitional energies is particularly pressing today, due to the increase of social antagonism, the fracturing of emancipatory social movements, the deterioration of a spirit of solidarity, and the increasing chasm between the haves and have-nots in our society. We must also bear in mind that the utopic dream of coalition and connection is especially pertinent for those historically subordinated persons and groups in society that by themselves lack the power to single handedly transform present institutional structures. The prospect for progressive institutional transformation in our society ultimately hinges on our abilities to facilitate and sustain holistic social arrangements that can engender political coalitions across racial, cultural, gender, class, and religious lines. Toward this goal I believe that we need to attend to the cultivation of a broad public perspective in our theologies, one that critically reflects on the social whole and addresses issues of economic inequity and power as well as matters of social relations and social politics. And, as I see it, this undertaking should allow for the development and promotion of a socially binding theological discourse that can connect the sociopolitical and economic struggles of our Latino/a communities to the similar struggles of other marginalized groups and the progressive sensibilities of other constituencies in the United States. In brief, we need to couple our issues of cultural politics to an adequately comprehensive social theory and political project invested with broad-based egalitarian commitments.[39] By attending to these priorities, and by diversifying and amplifying our mode of address to include both new themes of interest and pertinence as well as recent innovative disciplines and theories, I believe that we can continue to improve on our distinctive Latino/a theological voice and quite possibly even further the likelihood of our becoming *strangers no more* to the broader U.S. public realm.

# Response

## by Anthony B. Pinn

The late twentieth century within the context of the United States marked a rupture in socioeconomic, political, and cultural paradigms that affected communities across perceived lines of demarcation. After reflecting on the development of African American liberation theology and reading Valentin's thoughts on the historical development of Hispanic/Latino/a theology, the similarities and differences with respect to the religious-theological consequences of this period in U.S. history are in better focus for me. In the remaining pages of this response to Valentin's paper, I would like to quickly note a few of these commonalities and points of distinction with an eye toward future solidarity and collaboration.

These two forms of liberation theology share an understanding of what are several essential theological resources. In reading Valentin's essay it became clear that both make use of the community's history, experience, and cultural production as vital theological material. In addition, both draw from the Christian tradition and argue for a social gospel in which God, through Christ, expresses a commitment to social transformation on behalf of the oppressed. This is coupled with an appreciation for the contribution of the social sciences to the unpacking of religious history and theological meaning. What is also noteworthy is the manner in which theological developments take place within the context of community. Put another way, both Hispanic/Latino/a and African American theologians understand the importance of working in light of and in response to the needs of a "real" community of concern. To use popular terminology, there is a quest within both communities to develop and nurture organic intellectuals. Theology is not done by an individual in isolation; rather, it is a joint venture. In this sense theology is a "second" act, a hermeneutic process by which religious-based praxis is articulated and discussed. Connected to theology as a second act is an understanding of truth's experiential nature. Hispanic/Latino/a theology as presented by Valentin would agree with James Cone: truth is experienced and experience is truth. The existential realities of the people must never be compromised or ignored.

African American theology, in its various forms, plays off a rather unique church history. That is to say, whether African American theologians embrace the church as spiritual "home" or not, it is impossible to ignore the shadow it cast over the development of African American communities. Independent African American denominations (e.g., African Methodist Episcopal Church, the African Methodist Episcopal Zion Church, the National Baptist Convention, and the Church of God in Christ) have at times provided praxis sparked by their commitment to the social gospel and social transformation. It seems, from Valentin's presentation, that Hispanic/Latino/a theology is not as obviously grounded in the formation of independent Hispanic/Latino/a denominations forged in response to overt racial discrimination. In addition, whereas most African American Christians are Protestant, most Hispanic/Latino/a Christians are Catholic.

By extension, the attempt to dehumanize Africans during the slave trade combined with the church structures developed by enslaved Africans and their descendants have resulted in a certain focus within African American theology. That is to say, survival of enslaved Africans and the liberation of their descendants entailed a commitment to self-consciousness and subjectivity as the basic concerns of African American religious thought and activity. And most African American theologians have maintained these two concerns as central to the doing of liberation theology. This practice is not restricted to church-based or church-sympathetic theologians; it is also present in the work and agenda of humanist theologians such as myself. This seems present in Hispanic/Latino/a theology as well. Yet, Valentin, while noting the preoccupation of Hispanic/Latino/a theology with cultural memory and self-identity, suggests a need to move beyond these elements to foster a public discourse that addresses a large range of issues affecting quality of life and life options within Hispanic/Latino/a communities. On the other hand, African American theologians tend to see this quest for subjectivity as interrelated to all other issues. For example, political involvement must be premised on full humanity.

Tied to this sense of full humanity as the religious-political thrust of these two communities is an unfortunate history of discrimination. That is to say, as Valentin notes in his essay and I discuss in my essay, both theological traditions and the religious institutions they speak to and from have been guilty of sexism. Male theologians within both communities have traditionally overlooked the history and voices of women, and in this way they have compromised the liberative potential of liberation theology. In both cases, it is not until the emergence of Womanist theology in African American circles and Hispanic women's theology (e.g., *mujerista* theology and feminist Hispanic theology) that sexism receives a full and strong critique. In both cases, women argue that theological vision connected to the Gospel must entail a reproach of sexist practices both inside and outside the church. This theological and academic critique of sexism within African American thought is present as of the late 1970s and, within Hispanic/Latino/a thought, it is present as of the 1980s.

Another tragic similarity within both theological communities is the relatively scarce critique of homophobia and heterosexism. Although late in its development, one notices an increasingly "seasoned" understanding of the ways in which oppression is web-like in nature as well as the ways in which the oppressed easily become oppressors.

Although there is a significant difference with respect to religious history, Valentin's essay notes a common concern by some Hispanic/Latino/a theologians with the Christian-bias within their community's theology. This has also been expressed by several African American theologians. In both cases, theologians are calling for greater attention to "popular" religion as a theological resource, one that is intimately linked to a unique understanding of "ultimate orientation" and "ultimate concern." What is profoundly interesting here is the strong connection between various forms of popular religion within these two communities. For example, as George Brandon and Mary Curry have noted, both African Americans and Hispanic/Latino/a communities have a historical link to African-based traditions such as *santería*. In this way, the experience of contact and conquest as well as what Valentin refers to as *mestizaje* and what some within African American theology refer to as *creolization*, resulted in shared religious visions grounded in African, European, and indigenous world views.

By recognizing and drawing on the "cultural hybridity" of both communities, fruitful theological attention can be given to the "popular" forms of religiosity present in both. Our recognition of this religious link between these two communities is a late twentieth century occurrence, linked to the immigration of Cuban and Puerto Ricans to the United States in the 1950s. However, these traditions are of theological significance to both communities. As Valentin notes, a proper understanding of religious identity requires an exploration of all forms of religious expression within a given community. It should be noted that the religious exchange between these two communities through popular religion has not always been smooth. Referring again to the work of Mary Curry, there has often been friction over the proper language for ritual within traditions such as *santería*. Arguing for Spanish as the language of ritual-based gatherings has often isolated African American practitioners. This debate over language is further complicated by the use of Yoruba and accompanying issues of religious purity.

It is important to mention the linguistic distinctions between the theological ventures of these two communities within the context of more "mainline" and "mainstream" religious formations. African American theologians, as a form of cultural recovery, might talk in terms of linguistic Africanisms within African American culture but these holdovers are not strong enough to use as a definer of cultural identity. However, Hispanic/Latino/a theologians often present their work in Spanish as a way of emphasizing a certain set of cultural meanings and assertions. In this way, the use of Spanish marks cultural nuance and texture.

Finally, there are similarities between these two communities and theological traditions that hold the promise of substantive exchange. Yet, are there misrepresentations and misunderstandings, "feuds" resulting in us living in proximity but without in-depth conversations? The answer is not provided in the essays written on theological history. Nonetheless, the essays do provide clues. Let me suggest one: Perceptions of one community by the other are too heavily premised on socioeconomic and political competition fostered by a society larger than either community. But perhaps theology, with its concern for materiality, provides a space in which to recognize this deception and speak truth against it.

# PART II

## Theology and Its Reflexive Sources: Scripture, Tradition, Experience, and Imagination

# 3

## Scripture, Tradition, Experience, and Imagination: A Redefinition

### Justo L. González

THE TITLE OF THE SUBJECT assigned to Dr. Anderson and myself was suggested by the editors, and provides an excellent opportunity to reflect on the nature of theology as well as on the self-understanding of the people doing theology. Significantly, it closely parallels the so-called "Wesleyan quadrilateral" of Scripture, tradition, experience, and reason—although Wesley himself never referred to such a "quadrilateral," which in fact is a North American attempt to systematize the sources of Wesley's theology. Also very significantly, on the fourth point the editors have substituted "imagination" for "reason." To this point I shall return later, as I examine each of these four in sequence.

**Scripture.**    As is the case with the vast majority of Christians, Latino/a Christians also declare that Scripture and its authority are crucial for the theologian's task. We insist, however, that our own experience and perspective provide insights and/or interpretations of the text that are important contributions, not only to our own theology and liberation, but also to the church at large.

In his introductory article on the matter, written for *The New Interpreter's Bible*, Fernando Segovia lists four Hispanic approaches to the Biblical text, to which he adds his own.[1]

The first such method is exemplified in the work of Virgilio Elizondo, particularly in his now classical book, *Galilean Journey: The Mexican-American Promise*.[2] Elizondo selects, as Segovia declares, a "canon within the canon," which consists of Jesus of Nazareth as he is presented in the Synoptic Gospels. (Segovia points out that the Gospel of John is hardly mentioned. One could add that the same is true, even to a greater degree, of the Epistles of Paul and the latter part of the canon of the New Testament.) Jesus of Nazareth, the man from Galilee, thus becomes the paradigm through which not only the Bible, but also the current situation, are to be read.

Elizondo finds the Galilee paradigm particularly helpful, because the Galilean stood at the margins of both Jewish and Gentile society—neither a full Jew nor a Gentile, and yet somehow both. This is similar to the situation of *mestizaje* which is the experience of Mexican Americans—neither fully accepted as an American nor fully accepted as a Mexican, and yet both at the same time. Therefore, the *mestizo* Jesus provides a paradigm for the liberation and the liberating task of the *mestizo* Mexican American. And the movement from Galilee to Jerusalem which is central to the Synoptic story points to the need to confront the centers of power, and to expose their active participation and complicity in the oppression of the marginalized.

The second approach that Segovia describes is exemplified by Ada María Isasi-Díaz.[3] He calls this approach "a canon within the canon from the outside." What he means by this is that, while Elizondo bases his approach on a particular part of the biblical narrative, Isasi-Díaz considers the praxis of liberation the central hermeneutical tool, and even the basis on which to select a canon. Segovia's conclusion is that for Isasi-Díaz

> Whatever traditions contribute to and advance the liberation of Hispanic women are accepted as revelatory and salvific; whatever traditions detract from and impede such liberation are to be considered neither normative nor authoritative. In the end, therefore, the Bible remains subordinate to the praxis of Hispanic women.[4]

In fairness, however, one must add that the reason why Isasi-Díaz follows this procedure is her concern that in the received tradition of Hispanic women—both Catholic and Protestant—the process of colonization and oppression has been such that it

> has resulted in a variety of Christianity that uses the Bible in a very limited way, emphasizing the traditions and commandments of the church more than the scriptural basis of Christianity.
>
> It is not surprising, therefore, that in the lives of Hispanic women the Bible does not play a prominent role. They do not read the Bible and know only popularized versions of biblical stories—versions Hispanic women create to make a point but that often distort or imaginatively interpret the original versions. Their Christianity is informed by Christian tradition and practice rather than by the Bible . . . Biblical revelation and truth are not negated, but they are not given much attention, simply because they are not part of the daily experience of Hispanic Women.[5]

The third approach to Scripture which Segovia analyzes is what he calls "the Bible as straightforward liberation," exemplified in the work of Harold Recinos and his *barrio* theology. In this approach, the entire Bible is read as a history of liberation, in which "prophetic" theology seeks to liberate the people from the bonds of oppression justified by "royal" theology. In this approach, the Bible is the history of an oppressed people with whom God sides.[6]

Fourthly, Segovia turns to my own approach, which he calls "the Bible as non-innocent liberation." In this interpretation, he focuses on my notion of a "non-innocent reading of history," and summarizes what this means for our reading of the Bible:

> The Bible argues for a salvation that is deeply social and historical, not just otherworldly. . . . On the other hand, however, the message of liberation is also said to be highly ironic. Since the biblical protagonists of the OT and NT all carry (including Jesus himself) closets full of skeletons and by no means represent embodiments of high ideals, purity and perfection, the real heroes of the Bible are rather history itself, which keeps moving despite such unlikely channels and repeated, even radical, failures, and the God of history, who chooses such people for the divine plan.[7]

Finally, Segovia offers his own approach, not so much as an alternative to the others, but rather as an addition or correction to them. This he calls the "strategy of intercultural criticism." In arguing for this strategy, Segovia correctly reminds us that the text is always "other," and that it reflects, expresses, and is intended to shape a culture which is radically different from our own. This means, in the first place, that the text should never be approached as if it were readily accessible, as if it had no otherness. The text must be respected, just as we demand to be respected within a culture in which we are often the "other." It also means, however, that those of us who have learned to live as "others," as people for whom interculturality is a way of daily life, have much to contribute to the reading of the text. Thirdly, it means that in such interpretation we also have to take account and to be in conversation with the "others" who are also reading—or who in the past have read—the text.

Having surveyed these various approaches, and the books and articles in which these and other authors discuss and employ the Bible, it is clear that, although all of these authors have a deep commitment to ecumenism, some of the old divides between Catholic and Protestant still stand. The first two authors, as well as Segovia, are Roman Catholic; the other two are Protestant. Significantly, apart from Segovia, who is a biblical scholar, the work of the Protestant writers refers more often to Scripture than does that of the Catholic ones—and also to a wider segment of the canon of Scripture. The statement quoted above, to the effect that Hispanic women do not read the

Bible, would baffle thousands of Protestant Latinas who do read the Bible regularly and assiduously—even if not always with a liberating hermeneutics. This shows that, although we are trying to construct an ecumenical Hispanic theology, we are still heirs of a deeply divided tradition, and that we still have much to learn from each other.

Having said this, however, it is important to underscore the general agreement among Latino/a theologians that a proper reading of the Bible must be liberating—that it must throw light on our current situation, help us understand it, and support us in the struggle for justice and liberation. This coincides with the traditional reading of Scripture in African American religion, where God is the Liberator of Israel from the bondage of slavery.

Given our different circumstances, however, we may emphasize, besides the Exodus event, which is crucial for all of us, certain other themes that may be of particular interest to Latinos/as. One of these is the exile. A large number of Hispanics in the U.S. are literally exiles—some for political reasons, some for economic reasons, some for a mixture of reasons, but all exiles nevertheless. Even those who are not exiles, whose ancestors have lived in the United States for generations—or whose ancestors were engulfed by the United States in its process of expansion—are often treated as aliens, as people whose homeland is elsewhere. Thus, even though not literally exiles, many such Hispanics find the paradigm of exile particularly helpful.

Then there is the issue of language and culture, and how they are used to marginalize people. The Galilean paradigm of Elizondo is a way to bring this out in the Bible. Galileans are marginalized because they do not speak like Judeans, and because they have contacts with outside cultures which the Judeans lack. That is often the experience of Hispanics in the United States. For us, it is important that at Pentecost the Spirit does not make it possible for all to understand the language of the speakers, but rather to hear "each in their native tongue."[8] For us, the bicultural experience of Paul/Saul, and his upbringing as a Jew and a Pharisee, and also as a citizen of Rome and a citizen of Tarsus, is crucial to understanding the nature of his mission as well as ours.[9]

**Tradition.**    Protestant Hispanics have been taught that tradition is not important for their understanding of Christianity, and therefore for their own self-understanding. In general, what was at stake in the process of converting from Catholicism to Protestantism—at least as the converts and their evangelizers understood it—was a rejection of "tradition" in favor of the Bible. This is deeply rooted in Latino/a Protestantism, and in its more virulent forms becomes an attack on the "idols" of Catholic tradition in the name of pure scriptural Christianity..

What we have not often understood is that the "tradition" against which most of the Protestant Reformers wrote and preached was not the "tradition" that we were invited to abandon. They opposed a "tradition" which was almost identified with the magisterium of the church, and which was therefore greatly controlled and even manipulated by the hierarchy. If they rejected some of the "traditions" of the people, this was not because they were against their ancestral cultures and practices, but rather because such traditions had become a tool for alienation and domination on the part of those who controlled them.

The traditions we as Protestants were required to abandon were sometimes employed by the hierarchy, and even used for exploitation. When I was growing up, to be given a "proper" burial in the cemetery of Havana, which was owned by the Roman Catholic Church, cost a small fortune; those whose families did not pay were eventually exhumed, and their bones cast on a mountain of bones. This, however, was not the case with most traditions. Indeed, most of the religious traditions with which my grandparents grew up had developed at a time when there were few priests, if any, and these essentially lay practices developed as a way to keep the faith alive and to transmit it to later generations. In that process, they became closely entwined with the culture of the people. Novenas, rosarios, velorios, días de santos, procesiones, and so on, were not under the control of priests—mostly foreigners, in any case—but of the people. They were part of the culture passed from generation to generation—mostly by the "abuelitas" whose task this was.

Therefore, when Protestantism came into the Latin world bringing its blanket rejection of "tradition," converts were being required to abandon, not only the decrees of Trent or of Vatican I—of which most had never heard—but also and foremost the traditions learned on their grandmothers' laps. In other words, they were invited and required to reject much of their culture and of its defining traditions. There were places where Nativity scenes were rejected as "pagan," and Christmas trees and Santa Claus substituted for them. People who grew up with memories of their grandmothers dressed in mourning for their grandfathers could not dress in mourning when their grandmothers or mothers died. People who were named after one of the saints of Christian tradition were precluded from celebrating that saint's day.

Elsewhere, I have described this process as that of being left "hanging on an empty cross." One of the supposedly significant differences between Catholic and Protestant Hispanics is that the former have a crucifix and the latter an empty cross. This has been justified on the basis that ours is a risen Lord, and therefore the cross must be empty. But in fact it was a criticism and condemnation of the manner in which Latino/a culture traditionally deals with death and suffering, and the imposition of what was an alien way to deal with such matters. While acknowledging the value of the empty cross, I remind us:

> But there is also a negative side to the empty cross. We hang on an
> empty cross in the sense that we hang from it, that it is we who have
> been and are being crucified on it—if not individually, at least in our
> culture, tradition, and identity. The danger of an empty cross is that it
> will not remain empty for long. In the crucifix, Jesus hangs in our stead.
> In the empty cross, there is always the danger that it will be our people,
> our culture and tradition, that will hang in Jesus' stead![10]

In brief, what I have been arguing to this point is that the supposed
primacy of scripture over tradition in Protestantism has been used to
substitute other traditions for ours—traditions that are not necessarily
more biblical than our ancestral ones.

The case of Roman Catholicism presents its own complexities
when it comes to tradition. What do we mean by "tradition"? Do we
mean the magisterial tradition of the hierarchical church, expressed
at Trent and at the two Vatican councils? Do we mean the religious
practices of the people, as expressed and passed on by the abuelitas?
In this respect, in spite of their sharp differences, the three councils
just mentioned stand on one side of the divide, and the religion of
the people on the other side. Trent was a reforming council in its own
way. It sought to regulate the life of the faithful in the manner the
hierarchy thought best, both in matters of theology and in matters of
practice and worship. Vatican I, with its declaration on papal infalli-
bility, was the high point of the process whereby the hierarchy, with
its claim to being the custodian of tradition, claimed ever increasing
authority in the church. Vatican II was also a reforming council. Its
reforms moved in two directions. On the one hand, it sought to purify
the church from many of the practices that had slowly crept into the
lives of the faithful, and which the more "enlightened" theologians
and prelates considered superstitious. On the other, it sought to connect the faith more closely with the various cultures and situations in
which the church existed in different parts of the world. The impact
of the first of these elements was felt most strongly among Latino/a
Catholics in the early years after Vatican II. This was a time of conflict
between a reformist clergy and a body of the faithful who insisted on
keeping their customs and traditions. It was only later that the second
prong of the Vatican II reforms led to greater recognition of the traditional religious practices of each culture. As a result, what was at
first called "popular religiosity," and later "popular religion," has
gained wider recognition within the church, and particularly among
Hispanic theologians. Needless to say, this leads to conflict with what
to some seem to be the established norms of the tradition.

One of these Hispanic theologians, Gary Riebe-Estrella, comments
that "as this collision between Latino/a religiosity and United States
mainstream Catholic pastoral agents takes place in parishes today, it

is often centered on the place of the eucharist."[11] He adds that, while the eucharist has been the center of church life in the United States and in much of the Northern Hemisphere, "the Catholic experience of most Latin Americans over the past five hundred years is of a Catholicism whose ritual life does not revolve around a celebration called eucharist."[12] In conclusion,

> Pastoral ministers in the United States, concerned that there be a Mass on the feast so that the central importance of Christ—the divine become human—is highlighted, have failed to understand that the central beliefs of the Catholic faith can be imaged in quite different ways in different cultural worlds and that the prayer forms that express these beliefs can be equally diverse.[13]

Along the same lines, Orlando O. Espín reminds us that "just as important as the written texts of Tradition (or, in fact, more important) is the *living witness and faith* of the Christian people. However, they do not seem to be taken as seriously by those who study Tradition."[14]

In other words, what constitutes tradition must be defined in such a way that it does not favor a particular group or culture over others—or, to state the matter negatively, that "tradition" must not be understood in such a way that it denies the validity of the faith as expressed by a different people and culture.

**Experience.**    This leads directly to the question of "experience." When North American theologians speak of "experience," most often what they mean is one's personal religious experience, one's encounter with God, one's sense of calling and mission. Yet this is a very narrow understanding of experience. Gary Riebe-Estrella, in an essay on the nature of the church for Hispanics,[15] draws on cultural anthropology in order to distinguish between "sociocentric organic" and "egocentric contractual" cultures.[16] What this means is that Latino/a societies by and large are such that individuals find their meaning through their place in a complicated network of relations, and that those relations are considered prior to the individual. By contrast, in egocentric contractual societies the individual finds meaning by defining his or her own strengths and weaknesses vis-à-vis others in the group, and then joins the group—or forms a group—in what amounts to a contractual arrangement on the basis of those strengths and weaknesses. Thus, while in an egocentric contractual society maturity is a process of individuation, in sociocentric organic societies maturity is a process of socialization.

It is important to remember that such clear-cut distinctions between cultures are often exaggerated and romanticized. In most cases they are not determined exclusively by cultural traits, but also by economic orders, systems of production, means of communication, and so on. Therefore, to claim that certain traits in a given society at a particular time or place are typically "Hispanic" or "Anglo" is always risky, and must be understood as a generalization and over-simplification whose purpose is to help the "other" understand something about ourselves and our view of the world. Still, the distinction that Riebe-Estrella proposes is helpful in clarifying the role of experience in Latino/a religion as many of us have lived it. When most North-Atlantic theologians—and certainly most North American theologians—speak of "experience," they are referring to the most private level of religious life. Of the four elements in the quadrilateral, scripture, tradition, reason, and experience, only experience stands within the realm of the intimate. The other three stand outside the individual and are objectively verifiable. Over against them, experience can only be verified by the one who claims it. It is for this reason that so many theologians have been so leery of the concept itself of "experience" as playing a role in religion and theology.

This is not necessarily what is meant by "experience" in the Latino/a context. While it is true that many Protestant Latinos/as and Latinas understand "experience" in this fashion, and even that some Catholics are being drawn into the same understanding, this is the result of cultural pressures from the surrounding egocentric contractual culture. In traditional Latino/a culture, experience is not the private apprehension of an individual who claims, for instance, to have seen God, or to have heard God commanding something. Experience is rather the accumulated wisdom of the community, something that has been lived and known by it even before any of its living members can remember. To claim, as the hymn says, that one knows that Jesus lives because He lives in one's heart is a typical statement of an egocentric culture, and one which would have very little meaning in a sociocentric setting. In the latter setting, it would be more appropriate to say that the assurance that Jesus lives comes from the experience of His presence in the life of the community—not in "my" heart, but in "our" heart, meaning the "heart" that has been developed through the generations of community life. If someone claims to have had an "experience" of God's presence, this is immediately placed and judged within the context of the community's experience of such presence—unless, as is the case with many Protestants, our participation in the dominant ethos, and the atomizing pressures of the technological age, have led us to accept an individualistic understanding of experience.

This in turn widens "experience" in a way that would be inadmissible for many who defend and propose the famous "Wesleyan quadrilateral." For most of them, "experience" in this context means "Christian experience"—meaning an experience of a "personal encounter" with Jesus and/or with God. For many Latino and Latina theologians, the "experience" to be brought to bear in the religious life is the wisdom that the community of faith has acquired through the ages—some of it even antedating its knowledge of the name of Christ. Such experience includes both "lo cotidiano" and "lo atávico."

"Lo cotidiano"—the everyday—is an emphasis developed first of all by feminist critical theory, mostly because in most societies women are put in charge of "lo cotidiano"—cooking, cleaning, nurturing—while men claim for themselves the extraordinary, "lo histórico." Indeed, we have even allowed ourselves to be convinced by the obviously false claim on the part of (mostly male) biblical scholars, that Yahweh is a god of history, while the Baals are gods of nature—a claim that implies that Yahweh is particularly interested in the affairs of men, in "lo histórico," and not in "lo cotidiano," which we have imposed on women as the main object of their work and concern.

With reference to the importance of "lo cotidiano" as a source for theology, María Pilar Aquino states that:

> The methodological importance of daily life is grounded on its being the privileged locus for an intercultural theology, since the cultures and religious experiences of our communities converge in it. Theologically, daily life has salvific value because the people themselves, in *lo cotidiano* of their existence, let us experience the salvific presence of God here and now in their daily struggles for humanization, for a better quality of life, and for greater social justice.[17]

The "cotidiano"—the everyday—provides a people with that experience we call "wisdom," for it is the tried out ordering and understanding of life that has proven to work through the collective experience of the community.

Over generations, however, "lo cotidiano" becomes so ingrained in a people, that it becomes part of its subconscious self-definition. The wisdom acquired through the centuries, even when suppressed, remains for generations, and emerges again as soon as circumstances allow. This is what I call "lo atávico."

"Lo atávico" refers to the cumulative experience of countless generations past, which though repeatedly suppressed surfaces as soon as it is permitted to do so. The European invasion of the Western Hemisphere suppressed much of the cultures that had flourished here for centuries. When Africans were brought as slaves, their traditions were also suppressed. When Protestant missionaries arrived, while they disagreed with their Roman Catholic predecessors on most things, they agreed that such suppression was a good thing, for these ancient American and African cultures were idolatrous and perhaps even inspired by demons. To their condemnation of all that was African and

American in origin, these Protestant missionaries added a similar condemnation of all much that was Spanish and Portuguese culture and tradition.

Though suppressed, these things insist on coming to the surface. The story of the Virgin of Guadalupe, for instance, shows the atavistic longevity of ancient religions, now clothed in a Marian mantle. Much of what goes on in a Hispanic Pentecostal service can be connected with similar practices in ancient African rites. Some of the music that becomes most popular in both Catholic and Protestant religious celebrations shows signs of ancient rootage. All of this is part of what we mean when we speak of "experience" as a source for theology.

This may seem heretical and syncretistic. Yet, it is not much different from what the early church did in claiming Greek philosophy as part of its inheritance. They did this by means of the doctrine of the logos, which claimed that any truth that the Greek philosophers knew had been given to them by the same logos who is the true light that enlightens every one, and who was made flesh in Jesus Christ (Jn. 1:9, 14). By means of this doctrine of the logos, the church of the early centuries was able to appropriate all that seemed good in Greek philosophy and culture, and thus to develop an understanding and a practice of the faith that took into account much of the collective "experience" of the Greco-Roman world. Yet, when missionaries—both Catholic and Protestant—came to these lands, they apparently decided that the logos had never been here. What existed here was nothing but idolatry, false wisdom inspired by demons, darkness that had to be enlightened. When Africans were brought over as slaves, they too were considered to be absolutely lacking in logos. They too were in demonic darkness, and had to be enlightened by their white masters.

I do not mean to imply that the Gospel need not have been preached and taught in these lands or to its African population. What I mean is that the Gospel that was taught was truncated. It was a Gospel about a god who had been left without witnesses in America and in Africa until the missionaries arrived. It was a Gospel about a logos who had never crossed the Atlantic or the Sahara. It was a Gospel about a partial god. It was therefore, in a very real sense, a pagan Gospel, for the essence of paganism is precisely the limited scope of each of its various gods. Those who preached such a Gospel had little real authority to accuse others—as they did—of syncretism or of heresy!

The doctrine of the logos implies that experience, as I have defined it here, is much more than what a society has learned through trial and error. It is not purely human. It is the result of the activity of the divine logos. Therefore, in a very real sense, it is a form of revelation.

**Reason/imagination.** As I pointed out at the beginning of this essay, the title that was given to me is generally parallel to the so-called Wesleyan quadrilateral, except that instead of "reason" it speaks of "imagination." It is important to consider this difference, both in its values and in its dangers.

First of all, the dangers. To say that Hispanic—or African American—theology is grounded on imagination rather than reason is to surrender the claim of rationality to the dominant theologies of the white North Atlantic. A standard claim on the part of many of those theologies, whereby they discount much of what we have to say, is that our theology is "emotional" or "intuitive" rather than "rational." On that basis, whatever we have to say is often reduced to the quaint, the inspirational, or at best a footnote to "real" theology. In order to refute such an attitude, we must insist that, while it is true that "imagination" is crucial for our theology, that makes it no less rational.

Then, the values. To speak of "imagination" rather than merely of "reason" points to the need to widen the self-understanding of theology. Theology is indeed a rational enterprise; but not to the detriment of imagination, commitment, and aesthetics. If any doubt that these can be brought together, let them read the compelling, cogently argued and beautifully executed book by Alejandro García-Rivera, *The Community of the Beautiful*.[18]

Perhaps what we need is not so much to choose between reason and imagination, as to redefine reason in such a way that it includes imagination. If it is true, as many are telling us, that modernity is coming to a close, it is also true that the understanding of "reason" fostered by modernity is also coming increasingly under attack. Modernity taught that reason was objective, universal, timeless. Whatever was proven by "reason" could stand the scrutiny of any rational being, at any time and in any place. Such claims were based on the mathematical sciences, whose method modernity expanded into a universally valid understanding of reason. Indeed, this is the essence of the Cartesian method: to reduce all thought and all truth to propositions such as those in a geometric theorem.

In the "reason" of modernity, the universe is a closed system of causes and effects. This understanding of "reason" became compelling—and in many quarters still is—due to the phenomenal success of the physical sciences and their application in technology—the same technology that became the main weapon in the hands of the colonial enterprise.

Such an understanding of reason, however, is not self-evident, nor is it invulnerable to challenge. Ever since the time of Kant we have known that reason, rather than simply understanding and reflecting the world, also sets its own limits on the world, and molds it in such a way as to make it understandable. Thus, for instance, causality is a "law of nature" simply because we cannot understand the world without it, and not necessarily because the world follows that law. Then, with the work of Freud and Marx, as well as with their many successors, it has also become evident that "reason" never exists in isolation of the mind that thinks, and that the mind never thinks in isolation of the stomach and the "heart"—in other words, that reason, no matter how objective it claims to be, always reflects the physical and emotional contexts within which it operates.[19]

Since I have mentioned the example of causality, the same example may serve to illustrate how the decline of modernity opens the way for an understanding of reason that includes imagination. In modernity, we have been taught to think in a single direction, from past, to present, to future. To "understand" something is to understand its past, and how that past has caused the present. In another writing, I have both explained and commented on this view:

> What has made this view particularly prevalent in modern society is the success of the physical sciences. In the physical sciences, to "understand" something is to be able to explain its causes. And, when we today speak of "cause," we mean what the ancients called "efficient cause." The efficient cause of a billiard ball's moving into a pocket is that another ball hit it. And the efficient cause of that other ball's movement was that the cue hit it. And the efficient cause of the cue . . . and so on, and on, always backwards, into the past, to find the cause of things.
>
> But that is not the only way to look at reality. In fact, throughout much of history most of humankind has believed that things are ultimately caused not so much by other events as by a purpose; not so much by their beginning as by their end. This is what medieval philosophers called the "final cause," or the "teleological cause." Things happen, not merely because something happened before, but also and above all because they are being called from a future toward which they are moving. Thus, when medieval philosophers said that God was the ultimate "cause" of the universe, they meant not only that in the beginning God made all things and set them in motion, as a first efficient cause, but also that God calls all things from the future, as their ultimate teleological cause.[20]

Such an understanding of the universe, and of history and its causes, implies that there is an important place for imagination in reason. Modern "reason," which limits history to a closed system of efficient causes, would imply that any hope for a future order that is in truth different from the present, is in fact irrational. Thus "reason" is brought to bear as a weapon in favor of the status quo, and against any dream of drastic change. Over against that understanding of "reason," what many Hispanic theologians, and what both the Latino/a and the African American church have always experienced, is an understanding of reason in which imagination plays an important role, in which a radically new future is conceivable, in which revolution is possible, in which God's Kingdom may still come!

# Response

## by Victor Anderson

Dr. González's essay, "Scripture, Tradition, Experience, and Imagination: A Redefinition," opens conversation among Hispanic and African American theologians on a number of important themes that have been shaped by our social and cultural histories as minority groups in the North American context. A significant place to start the conversation is by reflecting on theological method. At least, this is how I understand the suggested topic that the editors assigned to Professor González and myself. I also read Dr. González's essay as an essay in theological method. I think that it is fair to say that contemporary African American theologians, especially black liberation theologians, have paid little attention to theological method since the development of the black liberation hermeneutics of the 1970s. The critical corrections that Womanist theology provided black theology was a matter of expanding and enlarging the interest of the theologians beyond race and class consciousness to include the social and religious interests of black women in constructive black theology.

As I have said in my essay, the recent turn of African American theologians to the slave narratives represents a resurgent interest in refining and substantiating a fundamental theme in black liberation theology. A central postulate of black liberation theology is that the primary sources of black theology are derived from theological reflection of black folk culture and the social experience of black people in the Americas. A corollary postulate is that, as a discipline, academic theology is at its core "constructive." In the next few paragraphs, I want to develop these two points and relate them to certain concerns I share with Dr. González.

The first postulate, that the primary sources of black theological reflection are black folk culture and social experience, is prima facie non-problematic. On this point, I have no disagreement with other African American theologians on the centrality of taking seriously the sociocultural history of African American people as a point of departure for African American theology. The postulate simply grants a certain priority to experience as a fundamental component of theological discourse. Of course, this primacy is not peculiar to minority theological discourse. As González himself indicates in his essay, taking experience as a condition of theological reflection has been a basic supposition in much of Western theology, but especially in the Protestant tradition. This does not mean that experience has played no important role in the Catholic tradition. Rather, its place was rather marginalized to spiritual formation and ecstatic or mystical piety.

In Catholic and Protestant theologies, experience also played a role as a criterion for testing the "reasonableness" of theological claims. Therefore, it is not so much taking experience as a basic resource of theological reflection that is problematic. Rather, it is the primacy that is granted to experience in North American minority theologies that signals a departure from the conditions of justification in Western theology. That is, while experience was recognized as a criterion for testing the reasonableness of theological claims in Western theology, it was regarded with suspicion as being non-analytically successful for confirming the apriority of theological claims. Experience was viewed narrowly to depict the particularity, historicity, and narrative structure of human activities. For many African American theologians who have abandoned any quest for a religious a priori on which to test the adequacy of theological claims, privileging the historical, existential character of life over rational analytic descriptions constitutes a fundamental disposition of African American theology.

I share this starting point with black liberation theologians and other minority theologians. However, I think that where I differ from many is on how black life and experience are construed or "taken hold of." That is, far too many African American theologians tend to treat black life and experience as if they were of a single thread. I suggest that such a preoccupation with defining black life and experience as a singularity is to make what is particular a totality. Such a totalizing strategy distorts more than it explains about the worlds of difference that constitutes black life and social experience. Moreover linguistic totalities such as Black Religion, Black Experience, and the Black Church are dangerously oriented toward bracketing from African American theological reflection the differences in experience, life, hopes, dreams, fortunes, and tragedies that structure the irreducible world of African Americans. Therefore, I have suggested that in this first postulate experience is fundamental to the development of African American theology. However, a serious discussion needs to be held on what are the best and more adequate ways to take hold of the opaque life-world of African American people in North America.

My worries about totalizing the social experience of African American people seem also a concern that González shares when he discusses Hispanic theology. He worries that some Hispanic theologians do not attend adequately to the worlds of difference that shape the theologies and spirituality of Hispanic peoples. He also senses the need for minority theologians to attend to the differing religious, social, and intellectual cultures that are shared by people with various languages, social experiences, and religious practices and sustained in Catholic, Protestant, Pentecostal, and folk religions throughout the Americas. I think that a continuing discussion on theological method has to take seriously better and worse ways of granting "Experience" in minority theology a place of primacy, for the answers are most ambiguous.

A corollary to the postulate that the experiences and the social world of African American people are granted a privileged status in African American theology is that such a theology is a constructive project. Professor González and the editors rightly see scripture, tradition, experience, and imagination as constituting reflexive matrices of theological reflection. I must admit that I share Professor González's concern about bracketing "reason" or "rational discourse" from these other intersecting sources of minority theology. The omission of critical reason as a reflexive source invites a negative claim that plays into long-held beliefs among theologians of the dominant culture that minority theologies are distinguishably non-rational.

I appreciate the criticism among minority theologians that seeks to displace reason as the basic criterion of theological adequacy, while they foreground the social, historical, and cultural forces at work in theological production. I also am aware of how much of Western theology is often depicted as rational, analytic, and cut off from the real interest of minority peoples (the non-rational others). However, I hesitate to see "imagination" as a substitute for critical rational thinking in minority theology. Minority theologians have to think critically through the claims we make not only about the ways our social experiences and lives are to be construed. We also have to think rigorously about whether the claims we make about ourselves, religion, doctrine, scripture, and tradition achieve cogency in understanding and justification, notwithstanding how tenuous the justifications might be.

The constructive task of minority theologians is not exempt from the burden of intellectual reasonableness and adequacy that is expected of critical scholarship. If African American and Hispanic theologies are to remain vital intellectual sources for furthering academic theology in American universities, seminaries, and colleges, then the constructive activity of our theologians requires the constant burden of intellectual rigor. What I am saying ought not to be understood as denigrating African American and Hispanic theological methods that make central the stories of our struggles, elicit the present miseries of our peoples, and find new ways of reading the Bible out of our social locations. Rather, my point is that, even among us minority theologians, not all the stories we tell about ourselves are equally valid and not all the ways we describe the lived situation of our peoples are equally adequate. Surely there are better and worse ways of reading the Bible, even if we share the same social location.

How we test the adequacy of our theological claims and constructive projects is a critical question in minority theology. Taking up this question may open both African American and Hispanic theologians to engage critically, revisit, and further our discourses on theological method. At stake in our theological methods are two mandates. The one is to further critical scholarship among minorities in the theological academy, and the other is to provide the best and most adequate interpretations of the social, cultural, and historical situations of those whose lives, stories, interests, and hopes we have made the starting point of our theological reflection.

Carrying out both mandates requires ongoing conversation among minority theologians on theological methods. The conversation certainly will accent our common intellectual and social interests. It will also foreground our worlds of difference constituted by our various experiences, social standings, ethnicity, languages, and religious communities which are always present at the conversation table.

# 4

# "We See Through a Glass Darkly": Black Narrative Theology and the Opacity of African American Religious Thought

VICTOR ANDERSON

To A GREAT EXTENT there has been little discussion or debate over theological method over the last thirty years in African American theology and religious thought. I think it is safe to say that the question of method has been subsumed under the problem of black sources for black liberation theology. Besides considerable glosses on James Cone's liberation hermeneutics, particularly by black feminist and Womanist theologians, the liberation hermeneutics has remained quite stable throughout subsequent stages of African American theology.[1] Cone rightly questioned the adequacy of traditional European and Western theological methods for interpreting black religious faith. His critical turn was to make way for research programs in black religion that take black sources themselves, whether black church history, literature, or popular culture as contributing to a fundamental canon for black theological and religious reflection. The impact of Cone's critique of the theological methods of the West extended to the very meaning of history, narrative, religious identity, and moral consciousness in black religion. Therefore, at the beginning of the black theology program, history and narrative problematically burdened African American constructive, moral, and philosophical theologies.

In this essay, my focus is on two paths toward answering the problem of theological method among contemporary African American theologians and religious thinkers. The primary attention is given to a research project proposed in a collection of essays entitled *Cut Loose*

78

*Your Stammering Tongue: Black Theology in the Slave Narratives* (1991; hereafter cited as *CLST*).[2] Sometimes this path is called the slave narrative theology program. My reading of this research program isolates two concerns, namely, the black liberation theologian's alienated consciousness and a hermeneutics of narrative return. In the first concern, I examine the slave narrative program in relation to the apparent alienation of the black theological academy from much of contemporary black cultural life. And in the second concern, I look at the ways that black theologians return to historical black materials for grounding their contemporary constructive theologies. In my critique of this path, I focus on several ambiguities in the slave narrative research program that I think test its persuasiveness.

In the last part of this essay, I propose an alternative path for dealing with black sources of religious insight. It is a path dependent on the phenomenological hermeneutics of Charles H. Long. This path accents the opacity of religious insight into the study of black religion. From my point of view, Long's talk of opaque theologies substantiates what I shall call the grotesquery of religious knowledge.

### Black Liberation Theology's Alienated Consciousness

During the late 1980s, a group of young African American scholars (particularly Dwight N. Hopkins, George Cummings, and Will Coleman) who were studying and teaching in the Berkeley, California, area met continually to discuss the future of black liberation theology in their black theology forum.[3] They exchanged papers and engaged in an exploration of slave narratives as a source for contemporary black liberation theology. Behind their explorations lay a set of problems that had plagued Cone's original formulation of method in black theology. The problems centered on the strained and often alienated relation of academic black theology to the black churches and black culture. Black church theologians questioned whether black theology could be a theology of the black churches if it disentangles itself from the creeds, confessions, and liturgical practices of the traditional churches. Others asked in what sense could black theology be black, if its theological method is derived from white, European theologians such as Karl Barth and Paul Tillich, and European philosophers such as Albert Camus and Jean Paul Sartre. Still others wondered how black theology could be relevant to a culture of black radicalism and revolution and remain theologically and morally Christian. This was the question of many who embraced the ideology of black power and associated Christianity with white oppression.[4]

Cone addressed some of these questions in many of his writings.[5] Yet, the historical problem of alienated consciousness lies in his call for a radical departure of black liberation theology from white theology and European religious sources. If black theology maintains the posture of radical departure from European Christianity, the black theologian has a difficult time showing how black theology is the theology of the black churches. And the black liberation theologian is likely to remain an alienated theologian. If the theologian gives up his or her radical claims to black exceptionalism, then the claims that he or she wants to make for the epistemic privilege of blackness in black theological reflection are likely to be undercut, losing their countercritical bite. As Cone attempted to overcome this dilemma, he emphasized the "commensurability of black sources" for the construction of black Christian liberation theology. He turned to the spirituals and the blues as cultural sources of black theology. Problems remained. On the one hand, the spirituals and blues proved difficult sources from which to disclose the normal, routine, religious beliefs of African American peoples and to render them regulative theological and moral judgments. To many, the spirituals appeared too otherworldly to be of much use for the purposes of black liberation theology and its claims for black radicalism, protest, and resistance.[6] On the other hand, much of the blues were regarded by the black churches as degenerative, secular, and misogynist expressions of black hopelessness.

Decades after beginning his research program, Cone would say that as he assessed the history of black liberation theology, if it failed to connect the academic black theologian and the churches, the failure belonged not only to black theologians but also to the black churches. He exclaimed that the black churches continue to be governed by the creeds and confession of white, European religious authorities and not by the indigenous sources of black life.[7] After several decades, it appears that black liberation theology and many black theologians remain alienated from the regular life and practices of the black churches and much of black culture. However, this alienation remains a major provocation behind the recent turn of some black theologians to slave narratives.

A primary source behind this alienation is the class differentiation of black theologians from others in the community. To be sure, we African American theologians are an elite class of educated intellectuals, often exhibiting bourgeois tendencies that alienate us from the underclass strata of life both in the black churches and black culture. And black liberation theologians, committed to liberation and radical politics, as regulative ideals of black Christianity, are often alienated from the churches for whom they desire to speak but whose piety is characteristically evangelical, reformist, and liberal in disposition, doctrine, and politics. Such churches are not likely to be moved by the revisionist agenda that define the constructive content of much of black liberation theology. Black theologians are also alienated by

class from the strata of black society, namely, the poor urban underclass, whose voices they want to evoke and whose desperation they
now raise as the new rallying call for the advancement of black liberation and the mobilization of the black theological academy.

The shift from race dependent discourse to class is generational. In
the early formulation of the black theology of liberation, the radical,
revolutionary interests of liberation centered on the oppressive structures of U.S. and South African legislative discrimination and poverty
justified by a history of racist public policy. Now, facing the twenty-
first century, black theologians are defending the cogency of their
liberation project and its justification by race in a climate of greater
class differentiation among blacks themselves than was experienced
in the 1960s and 1970s. From my point of view, it is quite clear that
race and racism galvanized black liberation theology in the late 1960s
and 1970s. It proved a powerful site for amalgamating the disperse
interests of African American theologians around a radical, revolutionary liberation rhetoric. It forged widespread agreement among
both theologians and church persons on the meaning of God—the
social, political, and economic liberator of the poor, Jesus—the one
who walks with the poor and disinherited in their situation, and the
church—the mediating spiritual and political institution of social justice.

However, on the dawn of the twenty-first century, it is not very
clear whether racial discourse can garner such agreement among the
theologians. What is clear is that the fragility of black liberation theology in the United States is being tested by a class differentiation
that is nonreducible to the racial categories of white over black.
Rather, class differentiation cuts across the various levels of the black
community itself, raising the question whether the black community
may not be facing "an incommensurability of values and interests"
among the various classes that now define the black community.
Black life in the United States is differentiated by the wealthy, entre-
preneurial, celebrity, and professional classes and the white collar-
and blue collar-working middle and lower classes. It is also differentiated by a desperate urban underclass constituted by the homeless, an
undereducated and underemployed class of black youths, and a rising
society of incarcerated black young males. The contemporary challenge to alienated black theologians is whether, from their internal
resources, they can speak univocally for the poor and underclass and
express the real interests of the black community today.

In great appreciation for the work of contemporary African American theologians, many of these concerns are being addressed. In his
systematic theology, for instance, James H. Evans proposes that the
academic theologian's alienation from the religious life of black people can be transcended. It can be transcended when "black theology

is rooted in the faith of the church and the faith of the church is given intellectual clarity and expression in black theology."[8] Evans answers the alienation problem in a hermeneutical return to a common black narrative. Here, it is claimed that a hermeneutical return to African chattel slavery discloses values, commitments, teachings, and a wisdom that sustained blacks under the unprecedented experience of chattel slavery. Evans also contends that this wisdom can be brought forward into the present to challenge a black culture that is now struggling with the push and pull of a secular, materialistic, hedonistic, narcissistic, and pessimistic culture.[9] For Evans, then, the return of black theologians to slave narrative sources is sparked by the need to reground contemporary black culture in a morally nurturing myth.

In books such as *CLST* and *Shoes That Fit Our Feet*,[10] Hopkins also proposes that the forms of alienation separating black liberation theologians from the black churches and much of black culture can be challenged effectively by a hermeneutical return to distinctive black sources as the basis for contemporary black theology. The hermeneutics of narrative return connects contemporary black life to a historical life of creative resistance and communal focus. Such a narrative can minimize what Hopkins sees as a rabid individualism plaguing black culture. He turns to the slave narratives, or more appropriately, the ex-slave narratives.

## Slave Narratives as a Source of Black Theology

The Slave Narrative Theology Project is a very ambitious program in black theology. Notwithstanding the many questions surrounding the collection of the slave narratives themselves,[11] there is a consensus among Hopkins, Cummings, Coleman, and Sanders that the wealth of folk materials contained in the slave narratives ought to have an authoritative function in the development of contemporary black theology. Their task, at least, is to make a case for their canonical standing. On this point, Cummings writes:

> This collection of essays shares a common view that the slave narratives are a legitimate source of the experiences of black oppressed people in the USA, as well as of the theological interpretations of their experiences of enslavement. Concomitantly, the slave narratives provide a means to return to the religious genius of the ancestors, who were forcibly taken from Africa and made to serve in the brutal crucible of chattel slavery. The narratives provide us with insight concerning the religious and cultural world-views that informed black slaves' theological interpretation of the experience and can be the basis upon which contemporary black theologians can incorporate the "thematic universe" of the black oppressed into their discourse.[12]

Hopkins concurs with Cummings, suggesting that the lessons slaves inferred from slave experience protected them cognitively from "fall[ing] prey to a white capitalist theological precept that glorifies individualism and private-property democracy." Hopkins then challenges contemporary black theologians "to promote individuality and communalism, not individualism and selfish motivations."[13]

Among the collaborators of the slave narrative program, the hermeneutics of narrative return signals a return of black theology to indigenous historical and narrative sources for religious insight and moral guidance. For them, the slave narratives evoke a great cloud of witnesses whose heroic legacy of survival, resistance, and hope mediates the fragility of African American life today and binds together our present generation so much in need of a heroic black faith. Each theologian regards the slave narratives as authentic historical representations of slave religion as it developed in the "invisible institution" of the antebellum South. According to Coleman, the invisible institution of slave religion was antecedent to the development of the independent African American churches.[14] From this premise, Coleman then critically sets slave religion in relation to the black churches in such a way that the former, the invisible institution, "was not so much an organization as it was an organic syncretism that enabled slaves to combine their Afrocentric religious beliefs with the Eurocentric ones of their masters. The consequence of this merger was their own unique form of African American Christianity."[15]

Hopkins, Cummings, Coleman, and Sanders hold that the ex-slave narratives authentically represent religious beliefs and moral practices constitutive of slave religion as it was practiced in the invisible institution. They also argue that the slave narratives exhibit a religious unity that is subject to theological formulation and moral inferences. Substantively, Hopkins has made the most of these possibilities in *Shoes That Fit Our Feet.* He argues:

> Enslaved Africans realized that God had created them originally with a free soul, heart, and mind. Yet white American Christians had re-created them in the demonic image of a distorted Christianity. Hence, for the slave, the purpose of humanity was to show fully the spark of God's created equality implanted deep within black breasts. To return to original creation, then, African American slaves pursued a resistance of politics and a culture of resistance.[16]

Hopkins' constructive task is to draw appropriate theological and moral inferences from the religious stories of African American slaves. He highlights Jesus—the mediator of God's agapic love, friend and mother, king and priest, provider of hope to the oppressed, and the one who directs the slave's path toward freedom and justice. This narra-

tive should challenge "the so-called secular black community repre-
sentatives to dig within and rely on the same African American
freedom impulse," says Hopkins.[17] While Hopkins accentuates God,
Humanity, and Jesus, Cummings maps the religious utterances of the
ex-slaves under the theology of the Spirit and Eschatology. Ironically,
however, for all their talk of Africanisms, both Cummings and Hopkins structure the slaves' religious utterances, bracketing the church,
under the traditional European loci of systematic theology: God, humanity, Jesus, spirit, and eschatology.

Coleman approaches the narratives with a hermeneutical concern
to elicit, by means of a linguistic-poetic method, the way the slaves
created their own black existence, religion, and reality through the
power of their interpretations, symbols, and metaphors. According to
him, "Slave narratives speak to us through symbols and metaphors
that redescribe the experiences of African American people under
slavery. . . . Historically, the oral tradition of African American slaves
placed a high value upon the power of speech. It was evocative,
driving internal mental, emotional, and spiritual experiences into the
exterior reality of the African American slave."[18] In other words,
through interpretation, the ex-slaves created an ontology of religious
significance by making a reality of what they subjectively experienced.

Among the collaborators, it is Sanders who explores the ethical
aspects of the ex-slaves' religious utterances. According to her, "the
ex-slave interviews provide day-to-day moral data that can be used to
analyze the ethical perspectives of the ex-slaves. Many of them testi-
fied of the experience of conversion, understood here as a conscious
moral change from wrong to right, involving reorientation of the self
from complacency or error to a state of right religious knowledge and
action."[19] Sanders applies an interpretative structure to the narratives,
which she believes elicits from them some description of the concrete
situation of the slaves, their loyalties, norms of moral reasoning, and
their religious beliefs concerning God, humanity, and human destiny.[20] Her essay is revealing because it shows the divergent ways that
ex-slaves remember their situation. Their attitudes range from nostal-
gia to abomination. But according to Sanders, all of their moral esti-
mations of slavery were based on the criterion of humane treatment.[21]
Their loyalties—either to their ex-masters, whites, or to others—were
grounded in their own judgments of who were "good Christians" or
exhibited Christian virtues.[22] And the norms of their moral reflection
were shaped by their sensing persons to be good Christians, Bible
believing, and obedient to God.[23]

Sanders also shows how theologically divergent the ex-slaves interpreted their recollection of emancipation. What they all had in common, she says, was the presumption that freedom was central to their

overall interpretation of religion. And the primary inference that Sanders draws from her analysis of the ex-slave narratives that she examines is that:

> The conversion experience did not transform them [the ex-slaves] into
> adherents of the slave ethic taught and upheld by their oppressors, even
> if it did make them "better" slaves by bringing an increased measure of
> moral integrity and conscientiousness into their lives and labors as
> slaves. If there is any social ethic at all among the ex-slave converts, it
> is indeed an ethic of liberation and not one of submission to the insti-
> tution of slavery or to the bondage of oppressive religious beliefs and
> ideas.[24]

In a recent book, *Empowerment Ethics for a Liberated People*, Sanders
reiterates the claims of her initial studies of ex-slave narratives.[25] However, her aim is to press more strongly than she does in *CLST* the ways
that the ex-slave narratives function as testimony to the present generation of black Christians. For these ex-slaves, it was "Christian Religion" that was central to their liberation ethics and played a
determinant role in forming the moral consciousness of African
American slaves of previous generations. The moral wisdom that she
attempts to bring forward into the present from these testimonies is
that "the religious testimony of the former slaves should be read as a
graphic illustration of the most critical hermeneutical challenge facing Bible-believing Christians, namely, the struggle to be faithful to
God's call to freedom and justice in the midst of a society that offers
attractive compromises with the evils of oppression."[26]

To be sure, Hopkins, Cummings, Coleman, and Sanders acknowledge that there exists an inherent diversity of approaches and organization of the materials constituting the slave narratives. Nevertheless,
each author also sees a thematic unity in the ex-slave's religious utterances. These utterances substantively express the definitive, exceptional, and liberation faith of African slaves in the United States.
According to Hopkins, the slaves maintained faith in a "God [who]
ruled with unquestioned omnipotence and realized release from total
captivity. And Jesus assumed an intimate and kingly relationship
with the poor black chattel."[27] Hopkins continues: "Slaves emphasized both the suffering humanity of Jesus as well as Jesus' warrior
ability to set the downtrodden free. Moreover, the slaves distinguished their humanity from the white slave master. For blacks,
God and Jesus called them to use all means possible to pursue reli-
giously a human status of equality."[28] A similar configuration of
themes are rehearsed by each theologian throughout their various
essays. Other themes include the slaves' rejection of sacred and secular spaces, otherworldliness, their affirmations of the intercession of

spirits and Spirit possession, and the privilege of community over individualism.

I think it is fair to say that for Hopkins and his colleagues, the slave narratives represent and express the African American cultural world that slave religion created. In slave culture, the slaves' "dogged and creative strength fashioned a new black collective self behind the closed doors in the slave quarters or deep in the woods late at night. Here slaves developed a culture of survival that included all the dimensions of a thriving but enchained community."[29] Slave religion gave rise and fulfillment to the new black consciousness in black religious history. It formed "a collective African American being, a new people in the hell of slavery, the most common bond among all who suffered as chattel was slave religion," says Hopkins.[30] For the members of this theological program, the slave narratives are unexplored and unmined sources for a distinctive, common spring from which the nurturing of black theology may depend for its vitality, substantive unity with the historic black faith, and moral wisdom. In the hermeneutics of narrative return, the alienation of black theology from traditional black Christian faith is overcome by a traditioning of slave religion and its moral consciousness. It is also overcome by admitting the slave narratives into an authoritative canon for constructive black theology.[31]

As a point of criticism, I do not want to get into seemingly interminable debates over Africanisms, retentions, and so on, in African American religion. For now, I am quite content to leave such debates to religious historians. However, as a philosophical and moral theologian, I am more interested in the kinds of inferences constructive theologians make from such arguments than I am in establishing the facticity of such things. Rather, I confine myself to what I see as a problem of equivocation operative throughout the slave narrative research program. Stating the problem, however, is not easy. I think that when these theologians examine the religious utterances of the ex-slaves, from which they correlate utterances typical of black liberation theology, the correlation is so strong that the ex-slaves' talk of freedom, human dignity, justice, and redemption is translated into liberation rhetoric of black radicalism, struggle, protest, survival, resistance, and hope. In other words, the evangelical–abolitionist theological categories in the ex-slave narratives are instances of continuous liberation motifs from slave religion to the present. Therefore, the ex-slaves' talk of freedom is equivocated with a liberation ideology. In which case, it is not so much black theology that is in need of justifying itself to the black churches, which are typically evangelical in faith, liberal in politics, and reformist in social action. Rather, the black churches have to assess their social and theological practices in light of a prior history of radicalism and subversion that characterized slave religion.

Not only does the slave narrative theology identify nineteenth century black evangelicalism with black liberation theology, it also appears to collapse slave religion into the ex-slave narratives. The collaborators argue that these slave narratives authentically represent slave religion. Well, it is true that the narratives represent the religious understanding of late nineteenth century and early twentieth century ex-slaves. But what these ex-slave narratives disclose theologically about slave religion (historically conceived) is debatable. This problem is linked to the equivocation of ex-slave evangelicalism and black liberation.

What the theologians are working with are the narratives of ex-slaves whose utterances display the spirituality and piety of Second Great Awakening evangelical conversionist theology, abolitionist editing, and the formation of institutional black churches in the post–Civil War period. The *CLST* collaborators' case for black theological and moral exceptionalism depends on whether the ex-slaves interviewed authentically recall the antebellum conditions of slave religion as it was practiced in the invisible institution, that is, in distinction from the postbellum redaction that abounds throughout the narratives. Therefore, the question is what has the historically specific evangelical theology among ex-slaves to tell us about the religious beliefs and worship practices of antebellum slave plantation communities. That, seventy-odd years removed from antebellum conditions, the ex-slaves maintained an authentic historical memory of antebellum slave religion is to my mind doubtful.

My criticism is that these theologians do not adequately take into account the historical thresholds that occurred from the earliest formations of the invisible institution of the plantations to the formal conversion of slaves by evangelicals and the abolitionist debates on the meaning of Christianity prior to and after the Civil War, but especially during reconstruction. These theologians see a direct correlation between black theology, slave religion on the large plantations in the antebellum era, and the formal organization of the ex-slaves into Protestant churches prior to and after emancipation. For them, such a correlation seems evident from the slave narratives. I have no doubt that the ex-slaves' evangelical beliefs are faithfully expressed in their narratives. However, the *CLST* writers assume what I do not, namely, that there is a direct correlation between their own commitments to black theology, the evangelical faith of the ex-slaves, and antebellum slave religion.

Hopkins says: "Blacks felt the powerful living presence of divinity in the midst of their daily burdens and concentrated in the Invisible Institution. These radical religious experiences colored their biblical interpretation; and thus, they produced a theology of liberation."[32] Although ex-slaves and black liberation theologians may favor the idea of freedom in their theological understanding, the equivocation of black evangelical religion with black theology distorts what freedom and religion mean in both historical contexts and traditions. My criticism seeks to discourage such cognitive reductions in black theology, if what remains is a distorted understanding of the differences in religious experience and theological thinking that provide black history and black religion with multiple trajectories in interpretations of and postures toward religious protest, spiritual development, theological positions, and political engagement.

I do not object to black theologians' interest in relating contemporary black religious thought historically to the religious beliefs, patterns of worship, and the moral consciousness developed by African slaves in the context of American slavery. I am just not very convinced that the identification of black theology with black evangelicalism in the ex-slave narratives and ex-slave narratives with slave religion will be very effective in these theologians' attempts to overcome the forms of alienation that characterize the black theological academy's relation to the black churches and black culture.

## The Opacity of Black Religious Knowledge

Like these African American theologians, I also think that the adequacy of African American religious thought ought to be tested in light of black religious experience and history. Therefore, I have no doubt that historical research into black cultural life is central for theological and religious reflection. However, I am persuaded by another path for appropriating black sources of religious insight. It is a deconstructive path that resists suspending the worlds of difference that African slaves and black Americans created for the sake of theological unity. Among African American religionists, Charles H. Long comes closest to the method I commend.

For Long, the significations of black religion constitute historical relationships between the signifier and the signified. However, he is always clear to admit that if the relationship between the signified and signifer is arbitrary, then the religious significations are open to changes, transformations, and reconstitution as the relationships are altered through their various exchanges of power. Long suggests that "the languages and experiences of signification can be seen for what they are and were, and one might also be able to see a new and counter-creative signification and expressive deployment of new meanings expressed in styles and rhythms of dissimulation."[33] In black religion, religious experience is the center of such changes, adaptations, adjustments, novelties, and differences.

While Long does not employ the aesthetic category of the grotesque to describe creative possibilities of black religious experience, in several places, he comes close to this language. Referring to the sense of terror that Pascal experienced in his contemplation of the "the eternal silence of infinite spaces" that marked his modern mathematical consciousness of nature, a consciousness that he himself contributed to, Long also suggests that he "struggled simultaneously with the fundamental problems of human creativity and human nature" (55). Both terror and wonder were present together in the experience. They are mixed and unresolved. Elsewhere, I described such an experience as the grotesque.[34] Here, creative possibilities and terrifying dread embrace in Pascal's meditations, as he faced "the creativity that has come into being through the new understanding of nature, [and] God as a structure of intimacy has disappeared and a new world latent with creative possibilities and terrifying dread appears" (55).

The grotesque signals the unresolved ambiguity of apparently opposing dispositions and affections entailed in Pascal's experience of the infinite. Before such a reality, any number of unresolved affective and cognitive responses might be elicited in the experience. On the affective level, appreciation and fear, love and loathing, and cries of ecstasy coupled with anguish are all possibilities. On the cognitive level, sometimes experience of the divine might be taken hold of in belief and bafflement or speech and silence. In his attempt to analyze the duplicity of these religious responses, Long appeals to the aesthetic category of irony.

For Long, such cognitive doublings as those between belief and bafflement or speech and silence are radically ironic (60). They are ironic in the sense that silence presupposes words, yet the power of silence—its manifestations—remains undisclosed. Long admits that the mere absence of words is not equivalent to silence. Rather, "silence forces us to realize that our words presuppose a reality which is prior to our naming and doing." It is not every instance of silence that captures Long's phenomenological gaze. Rather, it is archaic silence that Long seeks to expose in speech. In this case, speech is a testimony to the silence. For as the archaic condition and possibility of speech, the silence radically transcends the speech act. With this recognition, "We are given a philosophical orientation that sees all language as enveloped in silence. In other words, the interrelation of language and silence gives us a new understanding of the totality of the language and ranges of experience of the human being. The value of the new position is that it is possible to include within it that which goes by the name of rationality and that which is historical," says Long (61).

Both the possibilities of speech and action and thought and life are constitutive qualities of human existence. Each is an ontological structure, for each is co-present as a fundamental quality of the human being. The unity between speech and action, thought and life, and rationality and historical existence lies in the archaic silence that conditions their possibilities. It does not fundamentally lie in the historical understandings, languages, or cultural experiences of any one group or people. Therefore, while historical existence is taken for granted or the ordinary position for religious reflection, historical existence by virtue of its particularity is not a totality. It is not to be degraded, but it is also not to be equated with the infinite. As Long notes, "the religious being knows that humanity participates in a reality which is more than historical and cultural" (58). As I suggested elsewhere, the totalization of geography, history, and culture in the European self-estimation remains the great cognitive, moral, and religious fault of Western expansionist ideology. European genius disclosed itself in the garb and power of infinite speech and action, naming and transcending the "silent" other against which European culture named and defined itself. This double signification, between the signifier and the signified, enacts power relations that, from Long's perspective, create intrinsic ironies for both the signified and the signifier. Tracing the ironies requires attention to the ironies through the history of their effects.

The method of research is dialectical. One the one hand, historical consciousness of such effects entails black existence as having been signified by colonial powers that turned their racial significations into a symbol system of meanings that totalized both black and white self-consciousness. On the other hand, the totality that signified black existence also, at the same time, conditioned a history of recoiling effects. The recoiling responses by the signified are displayed in their own creative powers of word and symbols to constitute themselves both against the negations and within emancipatory effects of Western racial significations. Long sees this double signification entailed within W. E. B. Dubois's famous double consciousness thesis. He says:

> Blacks, the colored races, caught up into this net of the imaginary and symbolic consciousness of the West, rendered mute through the words of military, economic, and intellectual power, assimilated as if by osmosis structures of this consciousness of oppression. This is the source of doubleness of consciousness made famous by W.E.B. Dubois. But even in these symbolic structures there remained the inexhaustibility of the opaqueness of these symbols for those who constituted the "things" upon which the significations of the West deployed its meanings. This doubleness of consciousness, this existence in half-lights and within the quasi fields of human infection, is the context for the communities of color, the opaque ones of the modern world (190).

I find Long's talk of opacity a provocative metaphor for thinking about the double significations he sees in racial symbolism. I also think it equally effective in thinking about theological method. The metaphor should not be associated with any cognitive failure on the part of the theologian to understand race and religion. Therefore, the opacity of black religious thought is not connected to epistemic obscurity. Rather, in a more benign sense, the image is of a glass having become opaque as a result of being cast into a fire or of a stained glass window so intensely colored that light is blocked from fully illuminating what is inside. In both cases, the opaque quality of the darkened glass and stained glass window denies the quality of transparency to both objects. Opaqueness, therefore, becomes an identifying characteristic of both objects.

The metaphor strikes at the very root of modern epistemology. It balances scientific, philosophical, and theological goals of making transparent, clear, and distinct what in historical existence is the taken for granted, unexamined, and often distorted understanding of ordinary experience. To borrow Francis Bacon's language, sources of religious insight are "put to the rack" in order to force from them their truth value. The intellectual task is to expunge from the murky, opaque, non-translucent and ambiguous historical conditions of human life the concealed universal and necessary values. The truth lies underneath or behind the historical. However, the shady language of opacity runs counter to the languages of epistemic certainty, clarity, and transparency in both Western theological method and philosophical thinking. As an aesthetic metaphor, opacity installs a limiting factor on such intellectual preoccupations.

For many African American theologians and religionists, the principles of clarity, transparency, and distinction remain regulative intellectual ideal ends. However, in our attempts to understand and render black existence and black religion cognitively, morally, and spiritually transparent, which is a legitimate aspect of theological method, we also bump against the opaqueness of black life and black religious experience. Unfortunately, too many African American religious thinkers have not transcended the Western epistemic paradigm preoccupied with ocular clarity and transparency in theological method. The opacity of black religious life reminds us academic theologians of something that many ordinary believers know all to well, namely, that in matters of black faith and life, "we see through a glass darkly."

Black sources of religious insight are testimony to the opacity of black religious reflection. Whether one turns to autobiographies, spirituals, folktales, folk music, slave narratives, ex-slave narratives, and in our participation with black popular culture and religion, opacity balances our intentions to make transparent their meanings, values, purposes, and uses. Such a preoccupation with distilling from black sources their clear, distinct, universal, and exceptional counter cultural intentions and values puts at risk what brings the black academic theologian to black sources in the first place. What is put at risk are their particularlities, their historical creative testimonies to different worlds of black experience and creativity. Their ironies are suspended for clarity, their moral ambiguities for ethical transparency, their serendipity for the strategic, and their creative plurality for the simple, universal, and necessary. The risk is one of hermeneutical violence to the opaque ones whose very opaqueness leads us "crawling backward" into the religious and historical experiences that gave rise to worlds of religious difference that are the stuff of the study of black religion. Long says that such methodological attention to these worlds, their power and manifestations, will enable African American religious thinkers "to make common cause with folklorists, novelists, poets, and many other nontheological types" whose intellectual goals are to understand and interpret black historical existence and its political, moral, religious, and cultural meanings (196).

Engaging black sources in such a way as to take advantage of not only the familiar sources of religious insight, but also attending to the opacity of these sources is a regulative aspect of a deconstructive theology. The adequacy of African American theology, today, depends on its ability to take into itself the widest ranges of sources from black history and culture. Story telling, myth making, memory recovering, theologizing black culture, dancing, shouting in churches and fields, leaping on stage, engaging music that uplifts the spirit and that evokes black tragedies but also general human ones as well, making and watching films that depict the struggles of blacks toward freedom and those that depict the often ironic and comedic realities of black life are all potential creative sources of religious insight. Each is also a thing most opaque.

Black sources of religious insight are as wide as black culture is expansive and as open as black culture is expressive in its significations, creative possibilities, and their grotesqueries. Being open to the unresolved ambiguities of black religious life, its powers and manifestations, is basic for judging the adequacy of our theological judgments.[35] Therefore, if our hermeneutical task is to disclose both the light and the dark features of our religious lives, black theological hermeneutics warrants a balancing of ocular metaphors, that is, a balancing of the clear, transparent, and distinct, by the opaqueness of black religious life. Ritual and dance, drama and stories, sermons and singing, scriptures and doctrines, and black academic theology are all potential channels of religious insight. However, what is taken up and refracted through these channels is never without its unresolved ambiguities of light and dark, hope and tragedy, limits and openings to religious experience and insight.

My position is not a comfortable one to hold. Nevertheless, I think that it is an important balance to other paths in African American theology. If by attending to the opacity of black religious life and sources, openness to more religious knowledge not less, more criticism not less, more stories, poems, biographies, and narratives, more myths and even better ones emerge in the creative encounter with these sources, then the aesthetic path I have taken through the grotesque and the opaque will have been worthwhile. Such a commitment seeks to take hold of the widest ranges of black religious experiences and to interpret these experiences in the largest contexts of black historical existence and culture. Still, this hermeneutical activity is met everywhere with the grotesqueries of black existence and black religious life.

# Response

## by Justo González

As I seek to compare Dr. Anderson's essay with the manner in which Latinas and Latinos/as approach the "reflexive sources" of theology, the first and most important point of contrast appears in his very first sentence, where he declares that "there has been little discussion or debate over theological method over the last thirty years in African American theology and religious thought." In contrast to that, in Hispanic/Latino/a theology questions of method have been dominant. Indeed, in the late nineties the concern was expressed in the annual meeting of the Academy of Catholic Hispanic Theologians in the United States (ACHTUS), that we had centered our attention on issues of method to the detriment of issues of content.

These issues of method have developed mostly along two lines: hermeneutics—especially biblical and historical hermeneutics—and the question of sources—specifically the sources of popular religion and communal experience. Along the first line, a significant proportion of my own production has been devoted to this task. More recently, the issues of the postmodern critique of modernity, and of a post-colonial reading of the Bible and of history have come to the foreground, particularly in the work of Fernando Segovia and of his younger students Frank Lozada and Leticia Guardiola. Along the second, Orlando Espín and others have long been insisting on the place of popular religion as a source of theology, and Ada María Isasi-Díaz, María Pilar Aquino, and many others have shown the importance of the Latina communal experience as a source for theological reflection.

As I continue reading Dr. Anderson's essay, many parallelisms may be drawn between his concerns and those of many Latina and Latino theologians.

First and foremost, there is the issue of the possible alienation between theology and the believing community. The effects of class to which Anderson refers are also at work in the Hispanic theological community. It is difficult to live and make headway in the North American academic world, and not to leave behind the community from which one has sprung and received at least the initial impetus for the enterprise itself.

How does the Hispanic theological community respond to this? Obviously, with much ambiguity, ambivalence, and confession of sin. Still, there are some important concrete signs of a response.

Institutionally, one sign of such a response is the ethos that has governed the Hispanic Theological Initiative (HTI) from its inception. Its purpose has been, not only to increase the number of Latina and Latino scholars in the field of religion, but also to encourage a different form of being such a scholar—a form that is more communal, mutually supportive, in constant dialogue with the grassroots, and in the service of church and community.

Individually, another sign of such a response is the refusal on the part of many Latino/a scholars to reject what some call "the two c.v. syndrome," where scholarly essays and activities are listed on one c.v., and church activities on another. As a matter of principle, a number of Latino/a scholars have insisted on listing in their bibliographies both academic publications and others of a more popular nature, and even in mixing the two so as to make them undistinguishable to the reader of such bibliographies.

Theologically and methodologically, much of this response takes the shape of centering attention on popular religion as a genuine subject and source for theological reflection—in a way parallel to the use of slave narratives in the work of African American theologians. Hispanic theology has repeatedly insisted on the wisdom transmitted by the "abuelitas"—grandmothers—and has sought, not to refine that wisdom into sophisticated academic categories, but rather to transmit it as expressed, and to use it as a critique of traditional academic theology. Indeed, even among Latino/a theologians, there are some who fault their peers for not being sufficiently critical of popular religion, and thus limiting themselves to the description and exposition of such religion—often in a romanticized way that ignores its more subtly oppressive dimensions.

There are also in Latino/a theology discussions parallel to the issue raised by Anderson, of the genuine "blackness" of a theology whose method is derived from white, European theologians. This discussion, however, is for us a second step beyond the discussion of our own identity. Until recently—and then by a fiat of the U.S. Bureau of the Census—we were not a race. Then, even more recently, the Census has allowed us to define ourselves in many different ways. When needed for some political or economic purpose, we become "white" or "Hispanic white"; and, when another purpose requires a different set of categories, we become something else. In fact, as a people we carry within ourselves Amerindian, African, European, and even Asian genes. As individuals, most of us carry at least two of those set of genes, and many carry more than two.

For these reasons, the issue of identity is crucial in Hispanic/Latino/a theology. The names themselves, "Hispanic" and "Latino," and the need for the slash, show how difficult these issues are. They are prior issues to any "Hispanic/Latino/a" theology. And yet, they are unsolvable, for a people can never be defined without being dissected, immobilized, destroyed. As a result, we are constantly doing theology, politics, literature, and all the rest of our lives, in a "provisional" way, while we find out and decide who we are!

As Hispanics, we cannot find our identity solely on race, for our experience shows us that race itself is a political construct, with purposes of definition and control. To put it another way, even though we are told that racism is the result of the encounter of races, the truth is exactly the opposite. We suffered racism before we were a race. From our experience, the very notion of "race" is the result of racism, the result of the desire of one group to control or to eliminate another, and to justify such actions on the name of a supposedly objective difference called "race."

Nor can we seek a purely Hispanic/Latino/a theological method, as opposed to a white, European method, because historically, culturally, and even genetically white Europe is part of our very mixed ancestry. Much as we hate what our European ancestors did to our native ancestors, they too are our progenitors. This is true, not only in the genetic sense, but also in religious and cultural matters. Most of us speak the language of the conquerors, worship their God, and read their Bible. We may speak, worship, and read in a different manner; but we are still their heirs, and to deny them is to deny part of our very being.

It is for these reasons that the present volume is of such interest to us. We are interested in black theology because blackness is also part of our genetic and cultural inheritance and identity. If we are not in dialogue with it—just as if we are not in dialogue with European theology—we are stifling the dialogue that must take place within ourselves!

# PART III

*Theologizing with What's Popular: Theology and Popular Culture*

# 5

## Black Theology on God: The Divine in Black Popular Religion

### DWIGHT N. HOPKINS

THIS CHAPTER EXAMINES HOW black theology of liberation develops its view of God based on the popular religion of enslaved African Americans. Because of the significance of the Bible for black chattel, the Hebrew and Christian scriptures also play crucial roles in African American theological reflection. In a word, the everyday experiences of enslaved black folk plus the Bible are two dominant sources out of which popular conceptions of the divine emerge. For black theology, theological sources for God arise from, energize, and permeate the total way of life of black folk. Hence, for a black theology of liberation, culture is an integrated living tapestry in the world through which the divine manifests. In this sense, one does not discover a sharp sacred–secular dichotomy. If religion suggests a sacred, comprehensive, and integrated style of being for all reality and culture suggests the site of popular religious dimensions of black experiences, then black theology claims its God-talk and God-walk from the popular religion of the folk's total way of life.

By popular religion, I mean the sacred life experiences of nonelites—the poor, working class people, the marginalized, and the least in society. This is in contrast to the quantitative notion of popular religion. The quantitative sense connotes the numbers of believers who adhere to a specific religious sensibility. For instance, Christianity is the majority religion in the U.S.A. Claiming millions of adherents, it is a popular religion; the majority of the populace recognize it. However, popular religion, in my usage, concerns a sacred way of life believed in and practiced from below, from society's bottom. Moreover, this view of the popular as it pertains to religion entails life and death questions about the ultimate values and meanings for the poor in the U.S.A.

Black religious folk were made poor. Despite their backgrounds as legal experts, priests, doctors, academic scholars, warriors, parents, children, scientists, business persons, workers, statesmen, women, and so on, in their own West African countries, Africans were forced into the status of the lowest in the "New World" by European Christians and their slave trade. It is this involuntary movement downward into a subordinate social class which also determines the meaning of popular. When Africans forged themselves into a new phenomenon (i.e., black Americans) and created a new sacred way of life (i.e., black religion), they became the locus and the bearers of a popular religion.[1]

Specifically we can learn from enslaved African American realities and biblical insights to seek the development of a doctrinal statement on God. The divine is a spirit revealing and incarnating itself in the material. God, in constructive black theology, is the spirit of total liberation for us. The struggle for liberation and the practice of freedom unfold in the enfleshment of this theological doctrine. In this chapter, we discover that God is for us through divine acts, being, knowledge.

### The Acts of God—Ethics—What Does God Do

The primal hope-act of God is the exodus story. It signifies the paradigmatic expression of covenantal partnership of co-constitution of the oppressed self into a new liberated self. Divine intent works with marginalized humanity through liberation to exit out of physical restraints of Egyptian bondage (wherever it exists today) and into material free space undergirded by a spiritual belief in the power of Yahweh and the human community. The spirit of total liberation or holistic freedom of Yahweh is never in itself, but is always an empowering "ruach" (e.g., breath) for poor humanity. The finger of God is for us; and the divine spirit breathes on us for us.

That is, to encounter the identity of God's liberating spirit—the divine face of freedom, we look for what God is doing in the ongoing process of embedded transcendent ethics of holistic spiritual and material humanity. Divine ethics (e.g., the doing of God) do not escape us in an ephemeral invisibility or in a distant space acting on us absent from us. The work of God is actively present for us in the poor's attempts to construct themselves anew. God for us is always located socially with the poor communities on this earth. To believe otherwise is to deny and fracture the original covenant of the spirit's presence for broken humanity. God does wherever and whenever marginalized humanity cries out in the pain and pleasure of forging a new self. Divine activity is revealed in the voice of the voiceless fighting to make a way out of no way. There is the action of Yahweh.

The acts and ethics of God are also in direct response to society's monopolizers of power who project their fears upon the Other (in the

instance of black theology, the Other is the African American oppressed community in solidarity with other groups of struggle). Some-
what similar to the Israelites of old, black people today embody the
otherness of skewed social relations, skewed not in their favor. For
instance, the new king who came to power in Egypt stated:

> These Israelites are so numerous and strong that they are a threat to us.
> In case of war they might join our enemies in order to fight against us,
> and might escape from the country. We must find some Egyptians and
> put them as slave-drivers over them to crush their spirits with hard
> labor. (Exodus 1:9–11)

In today's society, race remains a negative indicator of black evil
and untrustworthiness. It results from a projection of fear and anger
against black folk. It serves, for those with resources to propagate such
a vision, as a thesaurus for criminality, slovenliness, sexuality, entertainment, and non-intellectual labor. The social location of racial
formation is either outstanding or standing out. The black self is
perceived to excel beyond the norm (therefore an outstanding exception) or is expected to fail (hence a palpable disaster which, in commonsense understanding, is the African American norm); either an
unbelievable Herculean success or a predicted collapse beneath the
pressures of life. Race matters still in American religion and culture as
demonic presence (with accompanying synonyms) and as truncated
two options of standing out or out standing. "They are a threat to
us."

The projected threat of a defined community marked by color pig-
mentation then operates at multi-levels. The monopolizers of power
in society define a mission to "crush their spirit with hard labor." The
oppression of African Americans (particularly the poor) is spiritual
and material. The latter oppression is to extract profit, either by a
disproportionate presence in the unemployed ranks or by a general
asymmetrical income and wealth scale detrimental to African American workers.

On the spiritual plane, the attempt is to crush the memory, vision,
and desire to struggle for liberation and to practice freedom. Consequently, too often this attempt anesthetizes marginalized African
American communities into a blurred perception of who has the
power to create a threat with them as the Other, and it implements a
systematic locking out of the majority of black humanity from the
earth resources created by God. In contrast and in response, God
works with the oppressed black community to co-constitute a new
liberated, spiritual, and material humanity. God is a spirit of freedom
for us.

The fundamental act of God (e.g., the doing and ethics of the
divinity of liberation for us) is earthly emancipation for those in

bondage, both spiritual and material; and this act operates in a co-constitution fashion. The poor and brokenhearted are co-agents with divine intent resulting in the fashioning of a new emancipated human self. In a word, God works with us through the act of freedom as we constitute ourselves from oppression to a full reality of the highest potential of a liberated humanity. God liberates us totally and holistically. The basis of a new self is found in the ethics of divine freeing on earth. As one former slave asserted in faith:

> Indeed I, with others, was often told by the minister how good God was in bringing us over to this country from dark and benighted Africa, and permitting us to listen to the sound of the gospel. To me, God also granted temporal freedom, which man without God's consent, had stolen away.[2]

Though sacred power pervades the spiritual dimension as well, the giving of full humanity—the spirit of liberation for us—is all the time manifest in the temporal realm. For the earth's dispossessed, "the sound of the gospel" is temporal freedom. We cannot encounter the language of the gospel, the work of Yahweh, without it being embedded or embodied in the tangible. The temporality of freedom might manifest in miniature acts of God or in obvious major divides in the breaking of restraints which enchain oppressed humanity. Regardless, God's ethics and doing come to us or are granted to us as a sign of divine grace. The gift of the spirit of total liberation is the manifest presence of a holy, omnipotent God whose constancy of being for us is eternal and whose glory appears in mercy, whose patience of working with and for us (despite our frail limitations) reflects the fullness of divine wisdom. The power of God to work on behalf of the oppressed never ceases.

God offers a liberating presence. We are not alone, for the covenantal engagement between Yahweh and the oppressed (both on the spiritual and material planes) arises out of the haunting testimony of the enslaved African American poor and the cries of the biblical witness. In the exodus drama, Yahweh proclaims to those in bondage:

> I have seen how cruelly my people are being treated in Egypt; I have heard them cry out to be rescued from their slave-drivers. I know all about their sufferings, and so I have come down to rescue them from the Egyptians and to bring them out of Egypt to a spacious land. (Ex. 3: 7–8)

The power of God to work for the oppressed is eternal. In the divine time of patience and knowing all about the plight of the poor, Yahweh's demonstrative glory comes as the harnessing of divine might for the "little ones" of this earth. For the marginalized believer, God's acts are real.

In this believing of those without access to resources to live their full humanity, we discover a faith to act on the covenantal promise of Yahweh. The doctrine of God is liberation for those who believe and act on this faith. It is faith in liberation from personal and collective demons and for the practice of freedom in a new God-centered self and life. For example, having departed from slavery, Etna Elizabeth Dauphus confessed the following to an interviewer:

> In setting forth her reasons for escaping she asserted that she was tired of slavery and an unbeliever in the doctrine that God made colored people simply to be slaves for white people; besides, she had a strong desire to "see her friends in Canada."[3]

Etna Dauphus exemplifies the co-constitution of the self (e.g., the divine and human agreement of transformation from the old to the new humanity). God provides the faith in liberation (as the divine intent for us) upon which the sufferer is freed with an emancipating belief to act (in response to and in accord with that which is offered by Yahweh) on the word or doctrine of the freedom spirit for us.

The divine gift of God, therefore, is both the active presence of the spirit for us (e.g., Yahweh acts on the hearing of the cries of the oppressed) and the granting of free agency as liberating commonsense to the oppressed. The doing of the spirit for us is manifest might of God and the gift to us to act freely with divine purpose. As one fugitive ex-slave penned in his autobiography: "In no situation, with no flowery disguises, can the revolting institution [of bondage] be made consistent with the free-agency of [humanity] which we all believe to be the Divine gift."[4] The intertwining of divine act, human faith, divine gift, and human agency is the empowering covenant for a God-human co-constitution of oppressed humanity.

Moreover, oftentimes Yahweh's act of liberation deploys others on behalf of the oppressed. Though the marginalized of society, fundamentally, work in response to and in concurrence with God's doing, the divine grace of acting for and with the oppressed manifests in signs not necessarily from the marginalized community. Indeed, there are times when the poor have to be shrewd enough to perceive divine doing in the camps of the non-oppressed. Divine ethics of liberation can be, at times, clouded by the agency chosen by God to implement divine intent.

For instance, former chattel Rev. W. B. Allen relates how he, during slavery, refused to pray for the southern whites who wanted slaves to beseech God for Confederate victory. In contrast, Rev. Allen continued to pray for the victory of the northern forces, not out of any love for the Yankees, but because God's plan demanded the enslaved African American to achieve emancipation. Therefore, in response to divine initiative, black folk had to pray for the fulfillment of God's liberation ethics. Rev. Allen commented in reference to his white plantation owners:

> I then told them that God was using the Yankees to scourge the slaveholders just as He had, centuries before, used heathens and outcasts to chastise His chosen people—the Children of Israel.[5]

In order to work with God, the oppressed must be open to and astute in reading the signs of the times which indicate God's doing. Consequently the marginalized have a vocational necessity to respond to and co-labor with God, even when the spirit of liberation for us appears in non-oppressed sectors of society. In other words, the constitution of the self (through a God and poor people's covenant) requires the majority of society (e.g., those at society's bottom) to employ a hermeneutics utilizing a liberative lens. Otherwise the gift of the spirit of liberation can be obscured by ruling sectors of any community claiming that they are acting for the least of the community. An interpretive liberative lens perceives the divinity of freedom employing whomever to aid the victims in the latter's movement for emancipation, even if the poor share no affection for the emancipation tools used by Yahweh.

Rev. Allen, in his popular usage of a radical interpretation from the poor's perspective, also stated: "Of course, I didn't have any love for any Yankees." It is in the dynamic of our act of prayer for emancipation responding to God's act of manipulating forces on the poor's behalf that we must carry out a consistent interpretive worldview in the reading of the signs of the times.

## The Being of God—Ontology—Who Is God

The spirit of total liberation for us expresses not only in God's acts but also in the being of God. God is an emancipating being for the oppressed of the earth and frees humanity spiritually and materially in an ongoing manner. This suggests the total and holistic being of the divinity as a constant dynamic, a process without beginning and without end. When Yahweh responded to the cries of the oppressed Israelites, Yahweh announced the ontology of God in the following proclamation:

> God said, "I am who I am. This is what you [Moses] must say to them: 'The one who is called I AM has sent me to you' . . . This is my name forever; this is what all future generations are to call me." (Ex. 3:14, 15)

The I AM God is a verb to be, one of the simplest yet most complex and versatile action verbs in human languages. Thus the I AM God is both present, in the sense that the divinity exists here and now, and future present, in the sense that the sacred one will always be I AM WHO I AM. Yahweh not only acts on behalf of and in conjunction with the oppressed and poor, but, moreover, God is a God whose being is I WILL BE WHO I WILL BE. I AM and I WILL BE signify a oneness and eternity in the spirit of liberation for us. God is for us and God will always be for us. For instance, while running away from slavery, Henry Bibb contemplated boarding a steamboat to a free state and immediately beseeched the being of God to embolden him in his emancipation journey from chattel states to northern territory:

> before I took passage, I kneeled down before the Great I Am, and prayed for his aid and protection, which He bountifully bestowed even beyond my expectation; for I felt myself to be unworthy. I then stept boldly on the deck.[6]

I AM is the spirit of interminable aiding, protecting, and rendering boldness. For the oppressed, in this moment, I AM becomes a comforting and defiant mood which transforms the human frail temperament of passivity and fear into one of empowered feelings for freedom. In this fearless disposition (e.g., the site of the spirit's self-depositing of the liberating attributes of the I AM), of the human person, one discovers a profound transference of I WILL BE WHO I WILL BE. God shares with and gives us a part of God's being of holistic freedom; what former slave Henry Bibb termed a bountiful bestowing beyond the human expectation. Precisely in the holy transfer point of divine being into the human being is where one confronts the co-constitution of the marginalized from the poor, obsequious insecure self into a comforted and dauntless new humanity.

The comforting of the Great I AM, moreover, comes to the being of the poor not in a general character but in a familiar way which allows the liberating spirit to more easily deposit its aiding, protecting, and bold self into the weak and broken hearted. Ex-chattel Kate Drumgoold offered a graphic portrayal of the familiar personality adopted by I AM.

> So God has been a father and a loving mother and all else to me, and sometimes there has been enough of trials in this life to make me almost forget that I had this strong arm to save me from these trials and temptations; but when I fly to Him I find all and in all in Him.[7]

I AM assumes both parental genders—mother and father—so that the fear of the weak and marginalized will open itself more quickly to familiar personalities and allow the entrance of divine liberating comfort. Therefore the divine being is not a patriarchal reality with the attendant trappings of subordination of women. On the contrary, to fully be the spirit of liberation for us, the very nature of God's being (e.g., the sacred ontology and who God is) is gender equality with full powers of emancipating comforting shared between mother and father, woman and man.

Any being masking as God but suffering from a designation as only male (without the equal sharing of spiritual and material power and a simultaneous naming as female) is a demonic personality whose intent, consciously or unconsciously, is not to bring freeing comfort to the oppressed. Instead such a demonic being can only render an oppressive hierarchical configuration among the earth's marginalized voices. For the very name of the spirit of liberation for us is gender inclusive and free of gender asymmetry. Therefore the transference of emancipatory comfort shared in the human spirit of fear and hesitation must image the mother-father ontology of the God I WILL BE WHO I WILL BE. The Great I AM's being is gender inclusive and holistic, not privileging any one gender, while ensuring the full liberation of all regardless of gender designation or racial color.

In addition, David Walker, a free black living in the northern section of the United States during the slavery period, links the sovereign rule of God with a reinterpreted ontological substance defining sovereignty as God being for the oppressed.

> God rules in the armies of heaven and among the inhabitants of the earth, having his ears continually open to the cries, tears and groans of his oppressed people and being a just and holy Being will at one day appear fully in behalf of the oppressed, and arrest the progress of the avaricious oppressors.[8]

God is a just and holy Being whose justice is the partiality to the groans of those who are heavy laden with unjust oppression. The justice of I AM becomes known or appears only in relation to the lack of justice expressed in the cries of the downtrodden and brokenhearted. Therefore in order for the divine being of liberation justice to become operative, the suffering of manifest cries from the marginalized must go up to God. The being of God is never in and of itself, but is always in a co-creative posture with the locked out ones of a society.

Closely related to justice is the holy dimension in the ontology of divine freedom. Holiness is sacred glory—a revelation of the brilliant power and presence of liberation offered by the divine to the poor in cooperation with their cries of pain and resistance. Like justice, holiness or glory shines forth similar to the sun. It brings new life to those in need but, at the same time, can burn the oppressive demonic and systemic configurations strangling those without resources to realize their full humanity. Holy glory of the Being I AM operates in a dual fashion. The isness of God appears as justice for the weak, but destroys and "arrests the progress of the avaricious oppressors."

### Knowledge of God—Epistemology—How Does God Reveal

Our knowledge of God (e.g., the spirit of total liberation for us) flows from the divine revelation which accompanies the acts and being of the divine freedom in cooperation with the efforts of self-affirmation by the oppressed. In a word, God not only acts on behalf of and with society's marginalized and presents a sacred being to be with those with suppressed voices, the spirit of total liberation is also for the poor in an epistemology of liberation.

In the beginning as witnessed in the narrative of Genesis, God created all the resources of the earth, heavens, water, animals, birds, plants, light, the entire universe, and women and men. The creation of all that is visible testifies to the macrorevelation of the spirit of liberation for us. For us, God gave the breath of life into the larger biological and material systems on earth. Originally, all of human-kind had access to the created, visible resources. The totality of creation, therefore, locates on a grand scale our knowledge of God's reality and intent of equal sharing of the earth's rich resources for all humankind. The poor only have to observe the manifestation of nature to remember the divine revealed purpose that all there is belongs to all of God's humanity. Whatever access to any part of creation is blocked by other human beings (who may have committed the sin of monopolization of any aspect of creation) should be a stark indicator of what belongs to all people. For the poor, this reminder indicates that their journey toward full spiritual and material humanity necessitates a struggle to regain equal ownership and distribution of God's gift to all.

While sharing his previous story of bondage in an anti-slavery meeting, escaped slave James Curry's beliefs and biblical interpretation corroborate this knowledge of God found in the liberation creation account.

> When my master's family were all gone away on the Sabbath, I used to go into the house and get down the great Bible, and lie down in the piazza, and read, taking care, however, to put it back before they returned. There I learned that it was contrary to the revealed will of God, that one man should hold another as a slave. I had always heard it talked among the slaves, that we ought not to be held as slaves; that our forefathers and mothers were stolen from Africa, where they were

free men and free women. But in the Bible I learned that "God hath made of one blood all nations of men to dwell on all the face of the earth."[9]

Divine revelation (e.g., the spirit of total liberation for us displayed epistemologically) becomes evident when the slave's biblical interpretation suggests Yahweh's creation comprising two parts. One manifestation allows us to know God's emancipatory nature through the definitive creative act in equality among all nations and human beings. For the oppressed, the Bible verifies the original intent of equality among and non-privileging of skin colors. Despite the evil of racial discrimination brought about by the acts of white skin privileges, the poor know of divine purpose for ultimate power sharing in social relations—symbolized in one blood among all people regardless of color.

The second dimension of creation of the spirit for us is God's allocation of the created earth for all humanity in the realm of geography and movement on a grand scale. The actual lands of the earth reveal knowledge about divine intent being the dispersal of all peoples freely throughout the globe. No one should suffer impediments in their movements, nor should anyone endure forced removal from a corner of God's earth. The stealing of others from one section of the earth and the monopolization of land and resources by a small elite contradict Yahweh's revelation. To know God, therefore, we can look to the visible testimony of the expansive globe—"to dwell on all the face of the earth." The epistemology of God embodying the liberating spirit for us is also a macroecology marked by spacial and mobility arrangements.

Not only do we know God through major issues of power, wealth, and macroresources, God also reveals the divine liberating spirit for us in everyday micro-, more focused social relations. This is not to say that the macroissue of political economy (i.e., what classes and races own and monopolize wealth in society) does not pertain to narrower, less global concerns. On the contrary, even on a microlevel, we find God's self-epiphany given to us as an offer for the poor and all who side with them to co-constitute the self with sacred intent and to achieve a full spiritual and material humanity. In this regard, micro-epistemological unveilings manifest, among other things, as God inspired cartography and love between individuals.

The biblical Song of Songs exhibits love as an everyday, microsocial relationship. In the Song of Songs, a sacred bond of spiritual and sexual relationship between a man and woman embodies the possibility of full humanity defined by holy love. Part of the spirit for us, therefore, is the recognition of the need for men and women to be free to love each other equally on diverse levels; and this is authenticated by the biblical witness. Though this Hebrew Scriptures' book has often been interpreted by Jews as an analogy for Yahweh's relation to a chosen people and by Christians as Christ's connection with the Church, nevertheless both concur that a sacred intimacy of being loved and giving love in freedom applies. For my purposes, the text also reveals knowledge of God's emancipatory love between men and women.

> The Man
> My love, you are as beautiful as Jerusalem. . . .
> Let the king have sixty queens, eighty concubines, young
> women without number!
> But I love only one, and she is as lovely as a dove. . . .
> I am trembling; you have made me as eager for love as a
> chariot driver is for battle. (6:4–12)

> The Woman
> Then let the wine flow straight to my lover . . .
> I belong to my lover, and he desires me.
> Come, darling, let's go out to the countryside and spend the night
> in the villages.
> We will get up early and look at the vines . . .
> There I will give you my love. . . .
> Darling, I have kept for you the old delights and the new. (7:9b-
> 13)

Part of being fully free and present with one's lover in a divinely sanctioned intent, thus locating a site of knowledge about God, is appreciating the natural beauty of the other. An epistemology of sacred freedom is an aesthetics of natural attraction on a microlevel. It is, moreover, an embracing of the physical body of one's lover in harmony with metaphors from nature, thereby underscoring a truly liberated intimate human union as a congruent non-dominating connection to the naturally created order. The trembling and eagerness for love and the giving of love also mark an awareness of sacred presence in the midst of a monogamous consummation. The giving of the self in a free equality of sharing, sanctioned in holy intimate love, testifies to one form of self-constitution of the self which displays to the self, the other, the community, and nature, the reality of how God reveals God's purpose of liberation.

After love between individuals, the second microrelation, cartography (e.g., mapping as an additional revelation of God for us on a microlevel) is expressed in an ex-slave spiritual. The partial lyrics speak to calling on the appearance and knowledge of divine presence to be a pilot in a barren space; hence the cartography and mapping dimension of sacred reality. The slave song testifies to the oppressed person's comprehension when the holy appears as pilot: "Guide me,

O thou great Jehovah, Pilgrim through this barren land." Here through song, oppressed humanity calls out from a restricted and deleterious space for aid from God for us. To know God, then, is commensurate with how the marginalized understand the sacred–human connection and constitution not only in macropictures inclusive of political economic resource configurations, but also in space (e.g., bareness), geography (e.g., land), and cartography (e.g., holy mapping).

In addition to micro- and macroconfigurations, racial cultural identity, moreover, serves as a third site for divine knowledge of God for the oppressed. The identity of the marginalized African American race and culture within an unequal society does not materialize at the expense of other races and cultures. Precisely because of the enforced de-centering of oppressed African American race and culture from stated and unstated normative claims in the U.S.A., God reveals God's self to affirm that which evil systems and persons suppress. Another ex-chattel attests to this epistemology of aesthetics and way of life (e.g., race and culture) in the following:

> The Lord, in His love for us and to us as a race, has ever found favor in His sight, for when we were in the land of bondage He heard the prayers of the faithful ones, and came to deliver them out of the Land of Egypt. For God loves those that are oppressed, and will save them when they cry unto Him, and when they put their trust in Him.[10]

Knowledge of sacred love for the oppressed race displays itself in the divine favor for the racial dimension of the oppressed; in a word, God embodies holy self within the color of the downtrodden. On this racial-cultural identity level, among others, Yahweh is for the liberation of the black race as the divine–human dynamic (of the faithful crying out and trusting and the divinity hearing and delivering) unfolds.

Similarly, a former slave's biblical interpretation depicts knowledge of who God is for oppressed humanity today. He says:

> Ethiopia shall yet stretch forth her hand and all nations shall bow unto her. I long to see the day that the Ethiopians shall all bow unto God as the One that we should all bow unto, for it is to Him that we all owe our homage and to be very grateful to Him for our deliverance as a race. If we should fail to give Him the honor due there would a curse come to us as a race, for we remember those of olden times were of the same descent of our people, and some of those that God honored most were of the Ethiopians, such as the Unica and Philop, and even Moses, the law-giver, was of the same seed.[11]

God expresses what God's actions and being are in the racial heritage of the biblical witness and its genealogy down to present African

American people. The Ethiopia paradigm locating divine intent, consequently, speaks to the awareness of God in black races and culture and to the need for all who would support marginalized black humanity to acknowledge divine intent (e.g., for "all nations [to] bow unto her"). Ethiopia, in the biblical story, embodies polyvalent purposes. On the one hand, it accents a special place for poor African Americans by affirming (e.g., "God honored most") their confidence in their black phenotypical selves and ebony way of being in the world. Ethiopia underscores acceptance of racial cultural identity. At the same time, and not in contradiction, God presents comprehension of the sacred self to all who would engage and embrace Ethiopia for their own relation to God. Ethiopia underscores a universal epistemology for all by all accepting African American racial cultural identity.

Knowledge of God comes through language, a final exemplar of sacred epistemological encounters. Language, especially proclamation of what God has done for the unlettered and the outcast, acts as one powerful medium for God's making God's self known. Usually it is in the oppressed's attempt to claim her or his voice amidst a context of demonic stifling circumstances that one discovers God's ordaining significance for the poor to speak with liberating power. One African American woman during slavery instructs our contemporary juxtaposition of talking and sacredness:

> I also held meetings in Virginia. The people there would not believe that a coloured woman could preach. And moreover, as she had no learning, they strove to imprison me because I spoke against slavery: and being brought up, they asked by what authority I spake? and if I had been ordained? I answered, not by the commission of men's hands: if the Lord had ordained me, I needed nothing better.[12]

Preaching, in this instance the prime example of language, comes from the commissioning of Yahweh's ordination of a poor black, unlettered woman who suffered both from the white Christian community and from backward theological perspectives in her own oppressed community. Moreover, the potency of the poor accepting divine holiness in language can even cause oppressors to be fearful and, consequently, threaten imprisonment of the oppressed voice asserting its God-given right to utter a word about the goodness of God. The fear of losing racial, gender, and formal educational privileges surfaces the demon within the victimizing group and forces them to restrict authority in sacred language matters to a human hierarchy with the bottom rung occupied by black women.

In this regard, by supporting the restructuring of hierarchy into equality by lifting up the bottom rung, recognition of black women's preaching or saying a sacred word aids the knowledge of God by perceiving divine revelation in the African American poor woman's voice. Furthermore, as another former black female slave indicates, the language reality of God's knowledge offered to the least in society, accompanies a divine-human co-constitution dynamic. "Chile, God's a talkin' man an' you gotta talk back to him."[13]

## Conclusion

This chapter investigated the notion of popular religion as a source for black theology's constructive work regarding God. The primary sources in the popular religiosity of African Americans, in this instance, are the Bible and enslaved black folk's sacred life experiences. Because black theology is a theological believing and doing from the stance of liberation, liberation has been the operative norm in the folk's popular religion.

Black theology is a broad rubric constituted by diverse disciplines, communities, and liberating practices. In this chapter, we examined what would be a systematic theological approach to the divine. Consequently, we explored constructive statements on God's action, being, and knowing—ethics, ontology, and epistemology. Black theology as liberation theology needs to continually rely on its own indigenous sources and how the folk have employed these sources as non-elites and as the bottom of U.S. society. By lifting up this banner, it joins its natural allies from the ranks of all people of color in the struggle for a full humanity for all who would side with the liberation journey of the least in society.

# Response

## by Harold J. Recinos

Popular religion is an important focus for theological research in both the Latino/a and African American communities. The symbols, discourses, and practices of popular religiosity are not decided by clergy and the institutional church, thus theologians who take popular religion seriously are given a unique opportunity to understand a complex field of cultural identity. In the black and Latino/a experience popular religion plays a vital role in orienting the relational and political views of determining subjects.

In the Latino/a and African American communities popular religion shapes cultural attitudes about politics, gender, family, political society, worship, preaching, the afterlife, God, the prophets, Jesus, and the Bible. Moreover, a very important social function is the role of popular religion in constructing responses to situations of powerlessness. The Latino/a and African American variety of popular religion discussed here argues that non-religious elites articulate, in the context of their marginalized existence, values and practices that oppose the domination of larger political and economic structures.

I will not attempt in what follows below to provide the reader with an exhaustive discussion of the similarities and differences present in Latino/a and African American popular religion; instead, I will first point to selected similar aspects of popular religiosity to demonstrate how this mode of faith is a defining characteristic of the Latino/a and African American religious experience. Second, I will name a number of dissimilarities between Latino/a and African American popular religion that suggests the need for further study.

In Latino/a and African American contexts one type of popular religion (examined in my essay and that of Dwight Hopkins) privileges the practices of liberation and gives rise to theologies related to the expectations and experiences of ordinary people. The symbols and collective understanding of marginalized Latinos/as and African Americans center theological identity on the God who exists in suffering. The liberative form of Latino/a and African American popular religion says the daily life of the poor who struggle against life-denying systems is not a matter of indifference to God. Latino/a and

African American popular religion share the belief too that God always promises a future of freedom and equality.

The God who exists in suffering is central to the action orientation of Latino/a and African American popular religion. The popular religious identity that conveys the social ideas of those who bear the burden of the presently regenerating necrophilic economic, political, and cultural system adapts people to their own condition of oppression by mobilizing political action. Hopkins uses in his constructive theology slave narratives to show how popular religious social ideas mobilize action; I enlist the testimony of Salvadorans to show how the social order is imaged and challenged. Latino/a and African American popular religion are concerned to address the massive and intolerable levels of suffering in the world caused by poverty, institutionalized violence, and the systems of power that kill God daily by way of crucifying racist practices. In this sense, God is "the spirit of total liberation" (Hopkins), or "the liberator God who proffers life" (Recinos). In other words, the experience of powerlessness rooted in slavery, poverty, and exclusion is culturally reconstituted by Latino/a and African American popular belief in God into a distinctive social force.

Latino/a and African American popular religiosity reflects the social power present within a historically shaped collective understanding of God. If we look at the differences between these popular religious experiences, new possibilities for dialogue will be fostered that are mutually enriching and mutually critical. Although the religion of the oppressed shares an identity of opposition to that oppression, the imagined oppressor wears different masks across cultural communities.

Hopkins reflects that the fundamental sources of black theology's concept of God is the popular religion that codified the everyday experience of enslaved black humanity and their reading of the Bible. From these sources, Christianity can learn to read the scriptures from an alternative understanding and seek to make new doctrinal statements about God. Popular religion and the Bible are vitalizing sources for Latino/a theology as well; however, the social ideas and political action shaped by Latino/a popular religious identity mostly focuses on Jesus of Nazareth and political discipleship rather than on making new doctrinal statements about God.

Latino/a popular religious experience is different from African American popular religion in terms of how the foundational experience of slavery shapes the oppositional identity of the oppressed in their everyday experience. Latino/a popular religion understood in the context of conquest and capitalist development draws on the narratives of enslaved Native American, Africans, and the mostly *mestizo* (mixed-race people) poor to articulate a constructive Latino/a theology that exposes the epistemological limitations of dominant cultures in North Atlantic capitalist society. Latino/a popular religion has steadily shaped a liberation theology that took in the social experience of racial, ethnic, and linguistic pluralism in the Americas; thus, liberation theology imagines the experience of God in terms of making strangers companions in the struggle for justice. If Latino/a and African American popular religion are united by the deep scars left in the people by oppression and suffering, they are apart in their prevailing ideas of solidarity with the non-oppressed sector of society. In Latino/a popular religion, the non-oppressed or privileged sector of society is composed of allied economic classes who come in many colors and cultures; thus, drawing on our own sources to construct theology tells us the non-oppressed sector of society is more than the white dominant system.

# 6

## *Popular Religion, Political Identity, and Life-Story Testimony in an Hispanic Community*

### Harold J. Recinos

I AIM TO EXPLORE the role of Salvadoran refugee popular religion in terms of its use of the public symbols of Christianity and those termed "social martyrs" to create meaning that actuates resistance to powerlessness and to construe self-identity as a response to a world of political repression. This essay will focus on the relationship between religious beliefs and ritual shaped by liberation theology discourse and Salvadoran self-identity and behavior centered on efforts to alter abuses of power.

For me popular refers to a defining characteristic of a social class which has a common identity, based, among other things, upon a situation of inequality. The social class in this case is the Salvadoran refugee poor of the Mount Pleasant locality of Washington, D.C. The common identity factor is Salvadorans' shared undocumented status. Thus, I focus on Salvadoran refugee popular religion as the belief and practices of a social class engaged in reinterpreting the meaning of Christianity from their own perspective as shaped and amended in the context of struggle and commitment to social change.

In my understanding popular religion in the Salvadoran community serves the interest of radical politics with symbolic processes that support the insertion of the poor as change agents into political settings. This variety of Hispanic popular religion is part of a "poetics of power" in which religious institutions and symbols are resources for political action. Moreover, the cultural practices evidenced in Salvadoran popular religion are best viewed in relation to issues of class, capitalism, and power.[1]

My research sites were two developing Salvadoran base Christian communities located in the Mount Pleasant area of Washington, D.C.

I was also a participant observer of popular religious ritual events and conducted numerous informal conversations in various settings in preparation for a period of collecting testimony with Salvadoran refugee men and women. Salvadoran refugee men and women in my study were either: (1) placed on death lists, (2) fleeing out of a well-founded fear of persecution, and/or (3) came to the States out of economic motives.

## The Politics of Popular Religion

Popular religion as a belief system culturally responds to and influences political and economic power in the Latino/a world. Popular religious institutions, discourse, and ritual are used by indigenous communities, peasants, workers, the urban poor, unemployed and minimally employed, and professional classes collectively experiencing economic exploitation and political domination to oppose inequitable processes in society.[2] In other words, cultural actors excluded from larger economic and political structures use popular religion to mold social ideas and political action structures aimed at projecting their purposes in society.

The study of the relation of popular religion and politics in Salvadoran society requires analysis of popular religious culture in relation to class dynamics and capitalist development, state hegemony in local political processes, and struggles for local political and economic freedom. Within this analytical framework, I refer to the following concept of popular religion,

> religious or ritual activities consciously practiced outside of or in opposition to dominant institutionalized religion or those religious activities which, although carried on within the framework of institutionalized religion, offer a critique of that framework and of larger political and economic inequities.[3]

Salvadoran popular religion informed by liberation theology conveys cultural meaning as a critique of the contradictions of capitalist relations. Although popular religion is a pervasive societal practice, here the definition applies to Salvadoran refugees in the barrio.

Several important studies of Hispanic popular religion or the beliefs and practices of subdivisions of society outside the internal power structure of the privileged classes are worth reviewing. For instance, a seminal work is Roger Lancaster's ethnography of the Nicaraguan revolution that defines popular religion as the process "whereby the poor assume interpretations and meanings of religion from their own point of view, as distinct from the elites with whom they share a general system of meaning."[4] Catholicism molds the general system of meaning undergoing a series of transformations in the movement from the elite to the poor end of the social class spectrum. Lancaster's reasoning behind popular religion blends with the "folk religion" notion of Redfield understood as part of the folk-urban continuum; however, he places classical peasantry among the popular classes.[5]

Working out of the context of five poor working-class eastern Managua barrios, Lancaster explores religion as a cultural system that reveals how the dominant social order mediated by the state is opposable. The structure of popular consciousness can be found in popular religious practices related to the *santos populares* and the *fiestas patronales*. This traditional popular religion is the springboard for liberation theology and revolutionary politics. For instance,

> The traditional beliefs of the people are shaped and codified, consciously and unconsciously, in the popular religious practice. Indeed, it is in the *santos populares* and the *fiestas patronales* that we seek out . . . the language of the people . . . the essential structures of the *habitus*. To interpret those symbols, to read those messages, is to read the consciousness of the popular classes, as typically and traditionally constituted; it is also to discover the starting point of popular consciousness that, in this case, provided the springboard for a systematic and revolutionary class consciousness.[6]

Thus, Lancaster argues that class consciousness is first encoded in traditional popular religious activities related to the cult of saints and patron fiestas.

For example, the fiesta of Santo Domingo celebrated in Managua lasts just over a week. The festival consists of the arrival of the Saint on the first of August whose image is placed in the Santo Domingo church. On the tenth of August, the image of the Saint is returned to its village location in a small church outside Managua. The fiesta was organized just before the turn of the century to celebrate an herbal doctor who in earthly life "eschewed monetary rewards and material gratification of his profession and class status, and pursued instead a life of service to the poor."[7] Ritual behavior and costumes express devotion and esteem for the Saint.

Lancaster reports that adolescent boys and young men dress as *las vacas* (the cows) and perform the "dance of the cows" involving crowd charging. Women less frequently assume this ritual role. Older men play the ritual role of *El Toro* (the bull) who is also referred to as *El Diablo* (the devil) appearing in loincloth and covered in black grease. Other men and boys, bodies covered in black grease, wear Hollywood-style Indian dress. *La Gigantóna* (the Giantess) is a twelve-foot-high marionette figure of a woman controlled by a youth. In the procession, she dances with men and boys and rushes the multitude, threatening males by goring them from behind or charging their genitalia.

Lancaster contends that certain "prevocal" or "subconscious" social meanings are embedded in the fiesta of Santo Domingo. For him the "logic of the poor" is vocalized by the fiesta of Santo Domingo that displays the social order challenged by its contradictory aspects. The poor and reversal of the logic of the established order constitute the subject of the fiesta. Thus,

> Every symbol in play in the fiesta for Santo Domingo represents a reversal or inversion, a world turned upside down, an established order challenged by its contradictions. Domesticated and usually docile animals turn and charge their human masters. Specifically, female animals charge male humans. Women tower over adult men, who appear as mere infants beside them, and likewise rebel against male authority. Youth run amok, blackening their elders' faces and engaging in acts of petty vandalism against property. Primitive Indians reemerge from a vanquished history, and walk about the streets to assert their challenge to civilization. And in anarchy, the Devil himself is loosed . . . seemingly out of place in a procession designed to commemorate the life of a saint, but very much in keeping with the nature of that commemoration, which is the metaphoric device of transgression, inversion, and revolt.[8]

Functionalist readings that would stress the "cathartic" dimension of the fiesta or a strict Marxist interpretation based on class paternalism are dismissed; instead, the fiesta represents traditional popular religion expressing the class commentary and resistance of the poor.

The wealth leveling and inversion values of traditional popular religion contest the capitalist order by presenting a "moral paradigm" which gets articulated as a freshly developed class consciousness. The new religion of the poor defined by the teachings of liberation theology and lived in the popular church directly clarifies this new class consciousness. The new religion rationalized, organized, and mobilized familiar popular class themes of inversion and leveling into a reading of the Bible and human action that constructed an imagined community of equality.

Specifically, the revolution in Nicaragua developed from a synthesis of traditional popular religion, liberation theology, and Sandinismo. Liberation theology acquired the widest following providing the overarching ideology of the Sandinista Revolution. Traditional popular religion with its wealth-leveling practices and accompanying cognitive structure provided the basis for the purposive construction of an identifiable self open to liberation theology's anti-capitalist discourse of social equality and economic distribution. Revolutionary Christianity was joined to the new political state to counter capitalist hegemony.

Another important study is that represented by June Nash's (1979) *We Eat the Mines and the Mines Eat Us*, which presents a symbolic analysis centered on the self-identity and class ideologies of the Bolivian tin miners of Oruro. Nash shows how popular religion understood as a cultural knowledge system interprets symbols of subordination and expresses ritual processes that foster social solidarity and political critique. Tin miners held socialist-communist ideologies and pre-conquest beliefs in primordial mythic forces exclusive of native identity alienation. Pre-conquest beliefs bolstered tin miner aboriginal identity supplying an ideology of resistance to capitalist penetration and external domination.

Bolivian tin miners equate the mines with a cannibalistic name, thus the statement "we eat the mines and the mines eat us."[9] Nash reports that working conditions are "inhuman," giving rise to feelings of extreme oppression and exploitation in workers reflected in the naming of mines such as *Moropoto* (Black Anus); *Veta Dolores* (Vein of Sadness); and *El Tambo Mata Gente*, among others. Nash's study of peasant ritual and cosmology shows how marginal groups use cultural belief systems to fashion ideologies of resistance and protest to interpret the political-economic order.

For Nash popular religion is an adaptational mechanism that confirms and reinforces tin miner indigenous identity and guides their action on the external environment. Rituals associated with Tio—a belowground pre-conquest deity controlling mine wealth—inside the mines were "part of communal gatherings that collectively enable the miners to overcome the alienation in their lives."[10] Bolivian tin miners' ritual practices, in the political economy setting of the dialectic between metropolis and satellite societies, show a social and cultural logic that facilitates a process of community formation that resists domination and oppression.

What these two major studies show is that popular religion constructs meaning for groups excluded from the power structure of the elite with which they contest the dominant social order. This in part means popular religious beliefs are expressed as a material social force in the practical behavior of community formation that constructs a self-identity opposed to a world of oppression. In other words, popular religion metaphorically expresses the social field of conflict and plays a role in the cultural, political, and economic liberation of dominated classes.

## Popular Religion as Liberation Theology

As liberation theology, popular religion expresses the behavioral norms and values of the Latin American poor who relate their view of Christianity to justice struggles and values. Indeed, popular religion represents the excluded classes' language of resistance and protest against marginalizing political and economic social structures. As a liberative form of religion, popular beliefs give voice to the values of protest, resistance and liberation. Gutiérrez, known as the father of liberation theology, observed:

> it is from within the people that the culture of oppression is being abolished. . . . One of the values of the people of Latin America is popular religion. Popular religion is something beyond comprehension, and beneath the contempt, of the "enlightened" bourgeois mentality. . . . the religious experiences of the people are . . . charged with values of protest, resistance, and liberation.[11]

In the 1960s, the concept of liberation was used by social scientists in Latin America to direct attention to the reality of dependent capitalism. The term liberation theology was coined by Gutiérrez in a talk in Chimbote, Peru in 1968. Liberation theology links traditional popular religious themes to a commitment to change the economic and political conditions of the poor in the context of larger society. Growing awareness of expanding poverty caused by capitalist misdevelopment along with authoritarian regimes' disregard for human rights gave rise to a theology of liberation.

Liberation theology voices religious belief from the perspective of the poor; it offers a critique of society's sustaining ideologies; and it critically reflects on the role of the church in the public order in light of efforts that promote a radical restructuring of social relations favoring exploited classes.[12] Liberation theology's source of originality is the popular religious awareness of the poor who as a social class emerge as agents of history with alternative values and action for building a new moral community. Thus, liberation theology critiques the structure of present society while offering a basis for new community.

The central popular religious metaphor of liberation theology refers to the idea of a liberator God who proffers life. Jesus, identified with those who suffer historical oppression, is believed to reveal this God of life. The central metaphor of life is articulated by an ideology of martyrdom which contextualizes the poor's decision to narrate their life stories in light of current struggles for justice and the acquired traditions of popular faith. For the popular faith of Latinos/as in this study it is belief in the "God of life," who raised the first martyr Jesus from death, that awakens the ethic of struggle and individual sacrifice (social martyrdom) for the sake of a renewed society.

El Salvador's context of political repression and the experience of social persecution ("martyrdom") structures the protest culture expressed in popular religion. A number of central themes are at work here: (1) the biblical "God of life" who sides with the poor and oppressed is against the organized oppression of the state that causes human death, and (2) belief in the "God of life" means engaging in action that contests the "idols of death" named dependent capitalism and national security ideology.

The discourse of Salvadoran popular religion critiques larger social and political processes with the Biblical idea of the "God of life." For instance, the late Archbishop Oscar Arnulfo Romero understood that faith in the "God of life" demanded awareness and struggle against political realities (idols) or social structures that enable men to kill with impunity. Romero reports in the Fourth Pastoral Letter of August 6, 1979:

> The absolutization of wealth holds out to persons the ideal of "having more" and to that extent reduces interest in "being more," whereas the latter should be the ideal for true progress, both for the people as such and for every individual. The absolute desire of "having more" encourages the selfishness that destroys the communal bonds among the children of God. It does so because the idolatry of riches prevents the majority from sharing the good the Creator made for all. . . . Absolutizing wealth and private property brings about the absolutizing of political, social, and economic power, without which it is impossible for the rich to preserve their privileges. . . . in our country this idolatry is at the root of structural and repressive violence.[13]

In the same pastoral letter, Romero viewed national security ideology as another idol justifying the state's use of security forces to kill and violate human rights.

In light of its belief in a "God of life" opposed to a life without political order, Salvadoran popular religion posits that genuine human identity comes about when responding to the world of those who suffer inhuman poverty and political oppression. Consequently, the Christian notion of martyrdom viewed as offering one's life for the cause of the poor among other things is a "root paradigm" that directs those under its guidance to change the system. Root paradigms define existing or unfolding social relationships with reference to patterns of thought and behavior capable of generating cooperation or conflict between socially related actors.[14]

The root paradigm of martyrdom in Salvadoran popular religion means Christians and their allies opposed to the politico-structural violence of the wealthy, the military, and the government embrace "real and symbolic death—to be in true social relation" to human beings whose affliction is perceived as produced by the dominant social forces and structures of society.[15] In Salvadoran popular religion, martyrdom is a contestational blueprint that functions as a collective representation ordering social experience that demands that human beings become more human by rejecting the repressive political order.

In El Salvador, popular religious culture sways people to accept the root paradigm of martyrdom understood as death for the neighbor on behalf of the substance of faith, life. Thus, the death of each committed Christian gives life to others and draws nearer a new society of freedom, justice, peace, human rights and equality. *As this new religion of martyrology evolved, a theology of life became the characteristic discourse of liberation. The theology of life consists of faith testimonies through which God's people proclaim that God helps them in life.*

## Popular Religious Testimony

I define popular religious testimony as discrete units of talk that unite self-identity to the political setting of the civil war and the post-war Salvadoran community. Memory in the testimony discourse I will share below depicts an aspect of social history as it is now, recalled, relived, and represented from the past in a purified and reconstructed way. Indeed, popular religious testimony invites hearers and readers alike to a new experience of the sacred.

Life-story testimony reflects the cultural centrality of popular religion in Latino/a lives. As a knowledge system life-story testimony is a way to meaningfully integrate social experiences and historical events in lives that are ongoing and always raising questions about the role of God in human affairs. As a popular religious expression Salvadoran life-story testimony tells us theology issues forth from concrete experiences and relationships. Life-story testimony is a reminder to take seriously the thought and life-struggle of Latinos/as.

The popular religious expression found in the Salvadoran life-story testimony below refuses to let us forget the suffering and struggle of the Latino/a community. Words are here used as a mighty weapon to break the silence of North American society and confront dominant culture and white society with the social reality it consistently refuses to see.

As a popular religious discourse, Salvadoran life-story testimony here blends into a single voice of cultural resistance the story of Exodus, Jesus who is viewed as poor and martyred for politically defying the political regime, and present justice struggles for Latino/a human and civil rights. Popular religion in the testimony discourse informs the belief that personal identity demands a commitment to political action and social change. In other words, the idiom of popular religion and its contestational symbols constitute a critical commentary on social relations and portray what are considered meaningful aspects of social reality.

## *Alberto*

Alberto is sixty years old, has short black hair and a moustache. He always wears a Christian cross around his neck made of wood. He was raised in poverty in the Department of La Libertad and completed nine years of education. Although separated from his wife, he supports nine children living in El Salvador. Six of his children are in school depending on his monthly remittance of two-hundred dollars. In December of 1990, Alberto came to Washington, D.C. after a four-month sojourn north during which time he crossed several national borders. He only held temporary jobs in Washington, D.C., thus it was not possible to send money to El Salvador on a regular basis.

Alberto found community at the edges of an already marginal Salvadoran community in Washington, D.C. Although he considered himself Roman Catholic, he associated with a Lutheran Church out of a sense of solidarity with the life-struggle of the gathered community. In his words, members of the small Lutheran church are "suffering the same and understand each other." For Alberto popular faith did not arise from the interpretations of religious officials; instead, it grew directly out of the experience of oppressed and suffering Salvadorans seeking social change through God.

Let us hear from Alberto about what is important in faith. Alberto's popular religious belief equates the gospel with justice and conflict:

> The Christian has to be a person, when I say a person, I refer to having character, being honest, and not perverted; who knows what his [sic] obligations in the world are to be. God gave liberty to humanity and came to take humanity out of slavery. If we really know our role, we have to take the good news [Christian gospel], organize others, proclaim justice and denounce injustice. This is where it gets difficult and serious. This is *compromiso* [commitment], you have to proclaim justice and denounce injustice. This brings danger and cowardice reigns in the majority of people.

> Danger comes because those who commit the injustice disagree. The Lords of this world do not like that those on the bottom should have other ideas than those that exist. Some suffer more than others and this is the weight of the cross that we take for the love of God. We suffer with patience but not with crossed arms. Everything is done in light of the Word of God. All people are equal because all are children of God and all are equally oppressed and suffering before the powers that be. Popular faith is not a religion that comes to finally close people's eyes. It helps everyone know where they stand and what they must do for themselves.

Alberto draws on the symbols of popular religion to name the class struggle:

Jesus carried a heavy cross. The cross is a symbol of struggle. We must remember that God said "blessed are the poor." God is not like the rich who want one to be poor. No! This is where one takes the cross and begins to organize the people. Soon you are hated and persecuted for this and it is hard. You are always with the thought that you may fall at any moment and your very friends may betray you; though you speak the truth about how things should be. The worst of this is that it is the same class, the poor, who denounce you, although you are trying to help them to defend their rights as the poor.

For Alberto struggle, conflict, and the sacrifice of martyrdom (personal life) means bearing witness to the gospel with a vision toward the ultimate transformation of history as the end of competing forces and the fulfillment of life:

We see it in the gospel when Jesus said, "It is good for the seed to fall to the earth, germinate and give much fruit." Jesus was saying it is good for me to die because without my death the Spirit would not come. Whatever occurs in the course of life has to be examined in light of what is said in the gospel. Romero's death was difficult, but the process continued to develop. The Jesuits were left. They were killed. We needed these voices. But this did not discourage the process. Anyone who falls in the struggle that takes place in God's name helps the struggle; their blood will flourish like the grass. When the Spirit of God is forging the struggle and someone falls, another takes over and the struggle continues.

We have to preach a religion that gives people all their rights as a people. The people's religion helps everyone know where they stand and what they must do for themselves. Everything is done in light of the Word of God. It understands that all people are equal because all are children of God and all are equally oppressed and suffering before the powers that be. Salvadorans [in Washington, D.C.] who are waiting for help and have no work spend time thinking about things, drinking and abandoned. They don't think of useful things or in organizing. Thus, in this regard we at the Lutheran church [*la comunidad*] want to work and go out and find these people.

### *Marisol*

Marisol is twenty-three years old and from Zacamil, San Salvador. She is a single mother of a boy whose father is still in El Salvador. She is expecting a second child from a Salvadoran male she met in Washington, D.C. Because Marisol was identified by government security forces as a FMLN combatant in the November offensive (1989), she fled out of fear for her life. In May of 1990, she left El Salvador bound for the States. Her father had migrated to the States over twenty years earlier. She acquired a "green card" or documented status through him without difficulty.

Marisol sharpened her popular religious faith in the base Christian communities:

> I was very involved in the life of the communities [BCCs]. The work of the communities originated in the Zacamil parish and had the support of Monseñor Romero. The communities have been running since 1968. They are my age. Today, it appears there are problems . . . they [official church] want to dismantle the BCC work. The method of the communities is based on the sharing of experience. The method consists of feeling like equals; there is no preference. The environment of the community is very fraternal and dominated by a communitarian spirit. You feel like you have a family in the community.

For Marisol popular religious experience not only means religion and politics are inseparable, but the essence of faith is the promotion of life and human rights in situations of injustice:

> Whenever religion favors the people, the oppressed, those who suffer the most, as it states in the Beatitudes [Matthew 5:1–12; Luke 6:20–23], then it fulfills its role. Involvement in this kind of religion implies entering into politics. We should not take these things as political but a Christian duty. Jesus took many actions that were viewed as political. He entered the Temple and accused those who were conducting business. People saw that as a political act, but Jesus was revealing the project of God, the project of His Father, and not the project of human beings.

> I think that while we are involved in fulfilling the project of God the Father, we will take action that will cause people to accuse us of engaging in pure politics. But we must be clear it is God's will that we are obeying in this life. I feel that is a *compromiso* [commitment] for this life. I define God's project with a simple prayer: It is a project of life. Only that which gives life helps God, and all that gives death goes against the project and reign of God.
>
> Monsenor Romero is one of the great persons of our people. Being the Archbishop of San Salvador did not make him great; instead, it was his personhood. He was a person who was capable of giving, as we say, a complete turn to the tortilla. He made a profound change in lifestyle. I think that most of us already know that Monseñor Romero in the past was very different in his way of thinking. He did not want the base communities. The death of Rutilio Grande with whom he had shared thoughts and studied in seminary caused him to have a thorough and deep conversion. In light of this, I think that he is a person of great importance because he admitted being wrong and changed.

> Most people are not like that, but prefer to guard their little pride and ego. One day he came to Zacamil and left very angry; indeed, in front

of the entire community he said the priests, nuns and the whole community were guerrillas. He left very angrily without even finishing the service. This was long before the death of Rutilio. On the day Rutilio was killed, we had invited Romero and had prepared a fiesta and all; he came but with deep humility asked the community for forgiveness for his previous behavior. I really feel that what distinguishes him is this capacity for change.

Afterward, all of his support for the people, his proclamation of the reign of God, and denunciation of everything against that reign brought him closer to the people. He became a prophet of our land that cried out the truth to the four winds. While announcing the reign of life, justice, peace and love, he denounced the government. For me he is really a prophet, martyr and a saint. Many times we think a saint is that person that from childhood comes with the crown of sainthood. Monsenor Romero's life has a greater sense of sainthood because life itself showed him his error and made him change. This gave a great deal more meaning to what he then lived.

For Marisol God's project brings change to Latino/a lives anywhere; Moreover, one joins that project understanding that struggle is one sure way to defend "the right to life given by God."

What do we learn about Salvadoran popular religion influenced by liberation theology from the life story testimony of Marisol and Alberto? First, this testimony addresses how under the contradictions of class situations, God, Jesus, and the social martyrs symbolize the oppositional struggle that negates the social system by those who rule. Second, when the poor are referred to in the testimonies it is an articulation of collective identity molded by the experience of suffering in the context of politicized belief. Third, both Marisol and Alberto use popular religion as a system of belief and analysis that contests the capitalist state and its ruling social forces.

### Conclusion

Popular religion is expressed by people outside or against hegemonic religious patterns or inside dominant institutional religious structures offering a critique of wider social and economic issues. Liberation theology, as a salient form of popular religion, is a form of protest culture that originates in the action of the poor existing on the lowest level of society. Liberation theology interprets Christian tradition from the perspective of the poor who are its source of originality. Salvadoran popular religion achieves articulation as a liberation theology conveyed by the symbols of a new religion of martyrology.

Life is the ultimate value expressed in the message of Salvadoran popular religion through the form of the BCC movement and life-story testimony. Indeed, in life-story testimony the received Christian tradition as represented by the Bible, standard symbols like the cross or specific texts about Jesus are given subversive power in relation to particular hegemonic social contexts. When the poor are referred to in the testimonies it is an articulation of collective identity molded by the experience of suffering and oppression in the context of politicized belief.

Salvadoran popular religious belief shaped by liberation theology is an expression of the internal relations shaped by society's political economy responsible for molding the experiential framework of daily life, labor, and struggle. Whereas death is imaged as structural injustice and institutionalized violence in popular religious belief, the ideology of life (resurrection) permeates political consciousness.

The sacrifice of life by those who follow the social martyrs is believed to lead to the end of exploitation and social injustice. I think the Salvadoran case tells us that Latino/a popular religion evolves in relation to its historical context. Indeed, a cultural subsystem and form of social conduct it adapts to psychological and social reality while it also shapes these aspects of human experience for itself.

Through the popular religious traditions of struggle-laden peoples like Latinos/as and African Americans a deep message is sent to culturally established religion—popular religion shows us that humanity through its cultural practices and invention is in a state of constant revolt.

# Response

## by Dwight N. Hopkins

Recinos's approach to and definition of popular religion is very similar to my understanding. What connects our positions very closely is the tight interrelationship between the popular in religion and the role of liberation theology. For him, liberation theology localizes within the context of Latin America and Christian refugees from Latin America who now reside in Washington, D.C. For me, my paper focuses on liberation theology which originated independently within the enslaved black community in the United States of America (1619 to 1865). This particular faith community stands as a foundational genealogical moment or cornerstone for contemporary black theology of liberation (1966 to the present). On several levels, we discover similarities.

Like the informants in Recinos's paper, enslaved African Americans experienced their religion as embracing, re-interpreting, and deploying Christian symbols for political effect. Black folk knew that God did not create them to be slaves. On the contrary, the guiding light of the good news of Jesus, in the mind's eye of poor blacks, opened up a belief and ethic that inspired the enslaved to organize for the overthrow of the slavery system. Therefore, popular religion created a direct thread weaving Christian faith, moral practice, community organizing, and revolutionary structural transformation. Specific Christian symbols originated from the Exodus theme in the Hebrew scriptures and the parables throughout the Christian scriptures depicting Jesus' sole mission as the salvation (i.e., eradication) from human poverty. Consequently, metaphors and images from the Bible gave black folk the power, vision, and justification to pursue a new life on earth as it was in heaven. At the core of this faith was the compelling vocation of the gospel of God revealed by Jesus and fortified daily by the Holy Spirit. Key to the liberation theology in the popular religion of slave faith is the priority of religion over politics and economics. Black chattel employed Christian symbols because this faith of the ebony poor gave them life which took them into the political and economic realms. Faith preceded politics and gave substance to politics.

The popular religion of enslaved black workers also exhibits what Recinos calls a value inversion and wealth leveling dynamic. For instance, black Christians, in their own popular religiosity, knew that they were not receiving a fair share of the wealth and products of the labor which they expended in the plantation political economy. They recognized, likewise, that the white over black hierarchy cut against the grain of the good news of the Bible. That is why a popular common wisdom during their day spoke of black workers making and white owners taking. To combat this sociological asymmetry, black folk drew on the theological level. Reversal permeated the theology of enslaved African Americans. They felt at home with Mary's Magnificat theme of bringing down the mighty from their thrones. They resonated with Lazarus and the rich man narrative. Daniel in the lion's den and the three little Hebrew boys in the fiery furnace permeated their worldview. The Spirituals (i.e., the religious songs created uniquely by enslaved black workers) offer abundant evidence for the wealth leveling and value inversion underscored in Recinos's paper.

Black Christian workers, moreover, pursued this leveling and inversion through new ethics and language. They crafted a practice of solidarity and an ethics of liberation. Solidarity practice showed itself in the lifestyle of not telling on other enslaved workers. Various interviews from former enslaved blacks speak to this idea of maintaining solidarity within the family and community of oppressed black folk. If a black person pursued the illegal choice of running away for freedom, most blacks tried to keep silent. Regarding the ethics of liberation, the perspective of taking-not-stealing gave content to this ethic. Blacks perceived "liberating" chickens, hogs, and other daily necessities from the white man's plantation storehouse as taking and not stealing. From their cosmological belief and disdain for white Christianity, they saw no contradiction in "taking" from white Christians. Indeed, black workers had labored for all of the products on the white plantations. So they were taking what was rightfully theirs. In contrast, black folk called "stealing" the act of removing a possession from another enslaved worker. If a person did not ask for permission, then that African American was stealing from another member of his or her race.

Recinos also points to how popular religion in his ethnography created a double coded language. Likewise, we discover multi-layered meanings in slave statements. For instance, the Spirituals contained various meanings. With the song "Steal Away to Jesus," we detect the obvious surface meaning of a possible compensatory role of popular religion. That is, one focuses not so much on this earthly world, but one longs for heaven by and by after one dies. However, ample slave testimony documents how this song meant that at times, but it also meant stealing away to a secret meeting of black workers, or stealing away to the northern United States or even to Canada. Furthermore, for black workers in Virginia, their phrase "weevils in the wheat" denoted, to other blacks but unknown to whites, the presence of whites who could potentially discover a secret organizing meeting of blacks. Consequently, when black workers heard this coded language, they knew not to show up at the planned clandestine gathering of ebony people.

Black theology of liberation as a major influence in African American popular religion attempts to understand popular religion as an inclusive life style. It first of all agrees with Recinos's insightful depiction of Latin American popular religion's accent on the macrodimension of social relations, especially the political economy of monopoly capitalism. Enslaved black workers stated explicitly their wish that God would step in and cause a civil war that would alter the political and economic status of black and white relations in North America. Indeed, when the violent war did arrive in the form of the Civil War or war between the States, freed African Americans declared that God had become tired of the white folk's "mess" and had abolished slavery. Thus the expectation and summation of engaging political economy (i.e., macrosystems and structures) are integral to enslaved popular religiosity.

In addition, black popular religion, informed by black theology, sees the need to implement liberation and the practice of freedom in, at least, three additional areas. One is the terrain of language. Language in popular religion is not simply a transparent medium carrying content neutrally from the speaker to the spoken to. Language embodies and, to a certain degree, creates identity, thought, and reality. Thus more attention should focus on the language employed by working people in their living out their popular religion. I am very curious about the creative and vibrant use of metaphors in Latin popular religion, for instance, the phrase "complete turn to the tortilla." What revolutionary and empowering messages exist in this phrase for those indigenous to the popular religiosity?

In addition to macro and language levels is the micro. Micro pertains to how people live out their lives in ways that might not seem directly tied to the macropolitical economy. How does popular religion speak to the liberating dimensions of laughter, fun, sorrow, walking, rituals of intimacy, and so on? And finally, racial culture speaks to a fourth possible area of further exploration in popular religion informed by forms of liberation theology. Within the most progressive movements of the popular, history confirms the creative possibilities that a racial cultural analysis can bring to marginalized peoples' efforts at survival and liberation. The God of liberation concerns herself or himself with the gift of racial culture as one component of the people's faith in a better world for all.

Finally, popular religion informed by liberation theology, as seen in enslaved black workers' stories, concerns both external and internal demons and structures. The people from the underside of history (i.e., black folk and el pueblo) know the dangers of both the external structures of the demon called monopoly capitalism and all of its attendant subdemons (such as commodification of life and putting profit at the expense of people). We must continue to deepen our understanding of the tentacles of this demon. How does it manifest domestically within the U.S.A. and how does it thrive on workers and consumers in other lands? What are the specific contours of the positive new vision for a new society which is offered in popular religion? In a word, what new political economy do particular communities of popular religion offer to the world?

At the same time, popular religion engages the internal demons of psychological and emotional pariahs inherent among the people themselves (such as feelings of abandonment, low self-esteem, lack of self-love, self-hatred, and so on). What type of theoretical disciplines can aid in this process—a liberative psychology, psychiatry, or a liberation theology pastoral counseling? What intentional rituals do we find within popular religion that facilitate attending to internal demons? What do the people offer us from their own experiences that will help them and us in the process of healing the wounded children within us.

In sum, to appreciate popular religion further, we might want to look at various dimensions of this phenomenon of faith and witness among the least in our diverse societies. That calls for probing the sacred life aspects of macro, micro, language, racial culture, external, and internal realities of the people. The God of life is truly the one who is present and sovereign in all the nooks and crannies of everyday people's faith.

# PART IV

## Women's Experience and Theology: Reflections on Womanist and Mujerista Theology

# 7

# *Preoccupations, Themes, and Proposals of* Mujerista *Theology*

ADA MARÍA ISASI-DÍAZ

$M$*UJERISTA* THEOLOGY, A THEOLOGY elaborated from the perspective of Hispanic/Latina Women living in the U.S.A., is a liberation theology. Liberation is central to our theological work, a holistic liberation that has political, personal-psychological, and spiritual dimensions. These three areas of liberation are interrelated in such a way that they not only influence each other but cannot be even conceptualized, much less understood, one apart from the others. If we talk of them separately it is only because of human limitations and not because they can be comprehended in isolation. It is around liberation that we have organized *mujerista* theology, and that will become obvious as we unfold the main preoccupations, themes, and proposals of our theological endeavor.

## *Preoccupations*

For us Latinas, the main preoccupations of liberation in the political sphere are the marginalization we suffer and the exploitation we endure due to the liberal, neo-colonial, and globalizing schemes that are being imposed on the world today.[1]

Marginalization is one of the most dangerous forms of oppression. By marginalization we refer to the situation we Latinas live, which places us at the border of what is desirable or possible, which endangers us constantly for who we are and what we do is considered of very little value to society at large. Without any doubt marginalization causes rampant poverty in most Hispanic communities. What is worse, however, is how marginalization diminishes our capacity to participate in society in a positive way. Latinas in the U.S.A. as a marginalized group not only do not have adequate representation in

135

the political structures of the country. We also suffer from a lack of processes that allow and encourage us to participate in society in a constructive way. Marginalization leads to our values and customs being ignored or, at best, they are viewed as something exotic to be commercialized and exploited. The injustice we endure because of marginalization makes us feel useless and leads us to a paralyzing sense of boredom and to a lack of self-respect. This, in turn, results in an oppression that makes personal fulfillment difficult if not impossible.

Oppression for Latinas extends to the economic aspect of the political sphere—and we do understand the economic as an integral element of the political. In our U.S.A. communities the powers-that-be practice the same exploitative mechanisms that they use in Third World countries. Hispanic women in the U.S.A. are in reality Third World people living in a First World context. Latinas are exploited economically. We are paid less than others are paid for the same jobs, we do not have access to jobs that pay more, we cannot demand just working conditions, medical insurance, retirement benefits for if we do, we are easily dismissed.

Very worrisome for us Hispanic women is the way in which the materialism of this society corrodes our souls and our families. The value of the person is linked so closely to material goods that, even if we fight to maintain a different perspective, we know we have little chance of being successful. Unbridled materialism and its concomitant consumerism eat away little by little at our sense of family and community and result in what is called "the easy way out" and "the individualistic way out." These are stances which lead our people to seek participation in existing societal structures at the expense of others, instead of struggling for radical change that might indeed make liberation possible.

Our principal preoccupation at the personal-psychological level is the lack of self-worth we feel because of our powerlessness. The negative way in which we see ourselves results from the lack of autonomy we experience in our jobs; the lack of opportunities to be creative instead of having always to follow orders given by others; the lack of appreciation and recognition from those with whom we work for who we are and what we do. In this area we struggle too with issues of personal as well as group identity. It is a fact that the dominant group defines "others," and though we Latinas bravely try to resist, little by little we internalize the negative definition attributed to us. We come to see ourselves in the disparaging way the privileged ones in this society see us.

At the personal-psychological level gender oppression is particularly demeaning and we women suffer it not only at the hands of the dominant group but also from the men in our own communities.

Violence in the lives of Hispanic women is real, tangible; it can be indexed! In our own communities we suffer domestic violence and sexual abuse. Our bodies are further exploited when we are not paid what our work is worth. All of this leads us to pay insufficient attention to our bodies. As a Puerto Rican woman said when asked how she dealt with her body, "I ignore my body. I do not have time to think if it hurts me or if my body feels tired. I have to keep working no matter what: working at home and at the factory. There is no way around it!"

At the spiritual level—and I want to make it very clear that in *mujerista* theology we do not understand the spiritual as something separate from the corporal, just as we do not understand the religious apart from the cultural, or the history of salvation as something different from human history—at this level what we are most concerned about is how religious teachings and institutions affect us. We are deeply concerned about the glorification of abnegation, which continues to be demanded of women, particularly of mothers, to the point of destroying their self-esteem. And we are concerned with the negative perspective of the body and sexuality, with which women are identified, ignoring of our capabilities in the spiritual-intellectual sphere.

## Present and Future Themes

Given the reality of Latinas in the U.S.A., what are the main themes of *mujerista* theology?

First of all *mujerista* theology insists on the fact that all theology is contextual theology. Our theological enterprise is not a matter of saying in a different way what the churches have always said about God and about our relationship with God. Theology has to facilitate and address the questions and preoccupations that arise from the reality in which we live. We insist in demystifying theology by saying clearly and plainly that theology, as all human discourse, is a mediation. It has to do with what we humans believe about the divine. At best it is nothing but a very limited way of referring to who God is and what God is like. Following an ancient Christian tradition we consider theology as "faith seeking understanding." It is a way of articulating and explaining what we believe. This is to say that *mujerista* theology recognizes as its source the faith of Hispanic women, faith that is intrinsically linked to our struggles for liberation. Other theologies claim to be objective when in reality they all reflect the experiences and way of thinking of those who write them. We, on the other hand, faithful to the centrality of liberation in our theological enterprise, make explicit that *mujerista* theology is a contextual theology, a subjective theology.

We do not understand the subjective in an individualistic and isolated fashion. On the contrary, in the Hispanic culture the real person
is the one that is in relationship with others, who is a member of the
community fully embracing responsibilities. This is why our theological enterprise struggles to be a community process committed to
listening to and articulating the beliefs of the communities of Latinas
who struggle for liberation. These communities whose experiences are
the source of *mujerista* theology have a long history of Christian belief
and practices. They are communities with a long religious tradition
which is central to our culture. In other words, because present-day
Hispanic women communities continue the traditions and religious
beliefs of our ancestors, we are provided with an important way to
evaluate contemporary theological elaborations. However, tradition is
not the main criterion of *mujerista* theology. A holistic liberation is
our main criterion.

Our insistence on the experience of grassroot Latinas who struggle
for liberation as the source of *mujerista* theology has led us to insist
on the fact that Hispanic women are capable of elaborating their own
theological reflection. We have repeatedly experienced grassroot Latinas as admirably capable of explaining their religious beliefs and practices, explanations that we gather and use in *mujerista* theology. Our
experience with grassroot Hispanic women leads us to recognize
them, using Gramsci's term, as "organic intellectuals." Our claim in
turn rescues the intellectual enterprise from being merely academic.

In other words, intellectual pursuit and ability have been limited
erroneously to academics—those with high degrees of formal education. Unfortunately this has led us to consider those who have little
formal education as less capable of understanding and explaining
even their own ideas. In *mujerista* theology we have insisted on bringing to the theological world the perspectives of grassroot Latinas,
using their own words as much as possible, using the narratives that
they elaborate when weaving together their own experiences. We
have tried to make them present not by representing them, which in
a way would continue to make them invisible, but by identifying
ourselves as *mujerista* theologians with the struggles of grassroot Hispanic women, struggles which we also experience as Latina women.
This is how *mujerista* theology struggles to make available the voices
that have been excluded hitherto from the theological enterprise. I
believe that this has been our major contribution to theology; we
certainly have tried to be faithful to this task at all times.

This perspective has led us to see theories not as abstractions or as
universally valid, never-changing statements but as true elaborations
of the concrete and particular experiences that are part of *lo cotidiano*,
the everyday. It has led us to see theories not as generalizations but as
ways of knowing, as a valid epistemology that guides us and helps us

to deal with reality. Because they are ways of knowing, theories for us are always in process, they are always being developed and we have to take responsibility for them. This way of thinking has also led us to see, embrace, and elaborate the importance of *lo cotidiano*, the everyday.

*Lo cotidiano* refers to the horizon of our daily lives, of our common, ordinary lives. *Lo cotidiano* is enmeshed in the materiality of our lives, this blessed materiality that is an intrinsic element of God's creation, and that God embraces in a most unique way in becoming incarnate in Jesus. *Lo cotidiano* is the main arena of our struggles and our knowing. It constitutes the place, the moments, and the occasions when we come to understand reality. *Lo cotidiano* makes us face reality; it makes us face the need to apprehend reality and not have merely an idea of reality. This apprehending of reality has three moments or phases that are important for us to consider. To know reality we have to be in the midst of reality, we have to take responsibility for reality, and we have to change reality.[2]

To be in the midst of reality means being enmeshed in its materiality, being affected by it. We understand how this is so for Latinas when we hear in the narratives they construct about their lives how their struggle to survive in situations of oppression absorbs much of their daily lives. This not only places them in the midst of reality but also leads them to take responsibility for this reality, a moral responsibility that makes very clear that there is an ethical component to knowing reality. Day after day Hispanic women change reality by making themselves responsible for it in the midst of neighborhoods full of drugs and of violence. They provide shelter and food for themselves and their families; they take care of the elderly of the community. Latinas seem to draw from thin air what is needed to take care of those in their communities who are most vulnerable.

The struggle for survival that occupies so much of *lo cotidiano* radically changes the hierarchical order of needs of the powerful ones for whom survival is at the bottom of the ladder.[3] One of the reasons why Hispanic women are not considered to be strong moral agents is because the struggle for survival is not considered to be something for which much intelligence and creativity is needed. This is also why Latinas are rarely regarded as capable of contributing to a future from which all peoples can profit. However, the struggle of Latinas makes it very clear that the common good cannot be conceptualized apart from their *cotidiano*. Quite the contrary. The common good has to be related to and spring from *lo cotidiano*.

The value that we ascribe to *lo cotidiano* and the struggle for liberation of Hispanic women has many theological implications that we have only begun to elaborate. The first one to consider is the understanding and re-elaboration of the "kingdom of God." In *mujerista* theology we speak of the kin-dom of God, of *la familia de Dios*. The image of kingdom has little relevance besides maintaining and strengthening understandings and structures that oppress us. The image of kingdom in the twenty-first century reinforces a hierarchy of privileges, a patriarchal concept oppressive to women. We believe it is much more relevant to speak about the kin-dom of God, the family of God, from which no one is excluded, in which relations are horizontal and not vertical, in which priority is given to the most vulnerable and the neediest. In *mujerista* theology the family of God's kin is not something of the next world, no matter how we understand such a world. The kin-dom of God belongs to this world. It is something concrete. We have to struggle to make it tangible in the midst of our communities. It needs to become a reality and it flourishes when we struggle for justice, a struggle the gospel message demands of us Christians. This perspective is in no way based in a false belief that we accomplish our own salvation. What it does affirm is that the doctrine of creation calls us to embrace responsibility for establishing justice and peace as realities in this world because they are the central elements of the gospel of Jesus. We believe that even being able to recognize our responsibility and to be able to embrace it is possible only because of the grace of God, a God that became incarnate in Jesus and is present in our world today. If God is present in this world then we have to become the family of God in this world. In *mujerista* theology the centrality of the struggle for justice does not negate the necessity of faith in God nor the fact that we depend on God's grace for everything.

*Lo cotidiano* and the struggle for survival make us turn to a second theological theme: sin. We recognize sin as essentially social. Sin involves not being responsible for our families, for our communities, and not being responsible to them for who we are and what we do. Sin involves postponing or not facilitating or opposing the inclusion of all in the family of God where all are loved and where everyone's rights and responsibilities are recognized. We see sin linked to prejudice, in establishing practices and institutions that do not recognize each and every one as a moral subject capable of contributing to the good of the community. In *mujerista* theology we consider sin as the anti-liberation forces that sustain the well-being and privileges of some at the expense of the majority of the people in the world. And sin has to do with organizing and/or maintaining social mechanisms based on beliefs or ideologies that do not take into consideration *lo cotidiano* of Latinas.

A third theological theme in *mujerista* theology is that of justice. Our delineations of justice are guided by the understanding of the kin-dom of God, of the *familia de Dios*. The insistence of Jesus of not differentiating between his family and his disciples (Matthew 12:46–

50) leads us to consider Matthew 25:31–46 as the basis for elaborating our understanding of justice. This explanation has three main ideas. First, it starts with the reality of the injustice that Hispanic women suffer. Second, it revolves around establishing just relationships—family-type relationships—at the personal as well as at the structural level. Third, justice is a process and, as such, different elements will have to be emphasized at different times.

In *mujerista* theology our starting point in our elaboration of justice is to listen to Latinas who struggle for liberation so we can understand the oppression—the injustice—they suffer. We have to understand the particularity of our oppression as fully as possible in order to be able to devise effective strategies for our struggle. We have used a schema that examines five kinds of oppression: exploitation, that is, misappropriating the work of others; marginalization, denying others the possibility to contribute to what is normative in society; power-lessness, keeping Latinas at the lowest levels of society; ethnic and racial prejudice, causing the dominant group to treat us as if we had a diminished humanity; and structural violence, making our lives cheap and dispensable.

The centrality of just relationships to justice makes us insist on three perspectives. One, we see reciprocity as a "must," not only emphasizing what society owes Hispanic women but also what we owe society. Two, we have a responsibility not only for others but particularly for who we are, who we become, an intrinsic link to our relationship with our community. Finally, we have to be accountable and we have to hold each other accountable; we have to find concrete and effective ways of keeping power from being in the hands of a few.

At present, we believe that justice seeking has to emphasize solidarity and reconciliation. Elsewhere we have elaborated more fully an understanding of solidarity that centers on commonality of interest as human beings and recognition of the interconnections of the privileges of a few and the needs of the many.[4] Conciliation/reconciliation is a basic need today to work in a constructive way with the various Hispanic communities in the U.S.A. and with other marginalized groups in this society. Conciliation/reconciliation is also a perspective that helps us to re-conceptualize differences as not exclusionary and confrontational but as indicative of great richness.

A fourth theological theme of great importance in *mujerista* theology is that of divine revelation. We insist on an understanding of revelation that is ongoing and not one that was completed and closed when the canon of Christianity was determined. We insist on an understanding of revelation that recognizes that it happens in *lo cotidiano*, that it takes place through the faith and religiosity of the poor and oppressed of this world. Here, as well as in other theological themes, we have to privilege the vision and way of knowing of the oppressed, their way of thinking and understanding. We have to apply to divine revelation what we know from our own experience: it is at the margins that the pilgrimage towards the fullness of being for which we were created really happens.

A fifth and last theological theme we have started to elaborate is that of Christology. We insist on the fact that Christology follows ethics, that we cannot say anything about Christ that does not contribute to justice and peace. We need to develop a Christology that is related to the historical Jesus more than to the ecclesial Christ, that is not so much related to the past but rather is grounded in the present. In other words Christology is not about a Christ who was but who is. Our Christology, then, has to be open to present and future elaborations. Here we have to take very seriously the fact that each Christian is an *alter Christus*, another Christ. Christ today refers not only to Jesus of Nazareth. Christ today also refers to Oscar Romero of El Salvador, to Dorothy Day of New York, to Cesar Chavez and Dolores Huerta of California, to the multitude of women and men who relentlessly struggle for liberation day after day.

## *Proposals for the Future*

We face the future convinced that the struggle for liberation must continue and that religion will continue to have an important role in the daily lives of Hispanic women in the U.S.A. *Mujerista* theology, therefore, will continue trying to contribute to the work of conscientization and enablement of Latinas just as it will continue to advocate by making their voices present at the ecclesial and academic institutions. But, since religion is something alive, theology will never be just a repetition of the past. Because it is a contextualized theology, *mujerista* theology will have to face new situations and will have to engage in new challenges. Those that seem to us to be most urgent right now involve the sociological and anthropological mediations used in theology, that is, the sociological and anthropological information that theology depends on for its elaborations. It is also imperative for us to continue to work on theological methods as well as on the theological elaborations that are derived from the ethical challenges of Hispanic women.

The sociological mediation is important since it is the one that helps us to understand the context of our communities and the reality in which Latinas are situated. We need new sociological schemas to better conceptualize and understand our world. We need a schema that brings together an analysis of class, of economic status, of gender, of ethnicity and race, and other elements that determine how society is organized and also determine who has access to material goods and other resources. Special attention has to be given to power, how power is understood and how it is used.[5]

Sociology has to help us understand reality not according to dialectic propositions that favor confrontation but according to dialogic proposals that favor solidarity and responsibility for all of humanity. The economic analysis (included in a general way within sociology) has to realize that capitalist markets are not going to disappear. The important thing, therefore, is to see how we make the market behave in reasonable ways, how we construct a world in which the market is at the service of all people. Such an understanding requires a radical change from the thinking that insists that market forces cannot be controlled and need to be left alone.

The sociological mediation has to give us a more comprehensive analysis of globalization, separating it from globality. The latter refers to the reality in which we live that makes the whole world our neighborhood, how quickly we learn what happens in the farthest corners of the world, how what happens everywhere affects us directly, as is the case, for example, with ecology and economics. Globality opens possibilities and can without doubt open possibilities for the good of all. Globalization, on the other hand, is a worldview as well as a neoliberal schema of power—mainly of economic power that controls the political and military powers—in which the majority of the world becomes an instrument for the benefit of no more than 10 percent of the human race. We need sociology to help us not to confuse globality with globalization so we can judge them according to the liberation criterium that is central to *mujerista* theology.[6]

We also urgently need to work on the anthropological mediation. I consider theological anthropology to be in greatest need of development and theologians cannot do this until work is done on anthropology per se. We need to understand the principal characteristics of the human person better. To do that we may well need to abandon rigid definitions and be open to fluid concepts that will make it possible for us to accept that, as happens to all of creation, human beings are not static.[7] Of great importance is the need to prioritize our corporeal reality. To embrace the centrality of the materiality of our beings opens us to appreciate the sexual-erotic component in a way we have not done up to now. We need to understand much better the role the emotions and the imagination play in our lives and their relationship to the rational. This has been one of the greatest contributions of feminist theology and theory that insist in the importance of feelings not only for women but also all men.

We also need a strong analysis of what it means to be social beings. Our sociality is not something that we can take into consideration after we have established our anthropological understandings but it is essential for us to understand what a human being is. Identity, relationships, our capacity to decide and act—all these are elements that cannot be considered derivatives of what is essentially human but need to be understood as central to our being human persons.

Besides continuing to develop the sociological and anthropological mediations, *mujerista* theology needs to continue elaborating our theological method which responds to central values of our work and vision because it contributes to the liberation of Hispanic women. We need to continue to struggle against liberal individualism, which often seems to be the goal of certain postmodern thought. This is a struggle which concerns us greatly not only because we think that individualism betrays the social-communal sense of humanity and makes impossible true solidarity, but also because it impedes the development of a world in which peoples will not be considered superfluous. Considering all vision of the future as an invalid meta-narrative that obstructs personal realization, postmodernism tends to cloud all concept of the common good without which we cannot have a true understanding of the kin-dom of God. This is why our theological method has by necessity to be a community-centered method, a method enmeshed in *lo cotidiano* of the great majority of the peoples of the world, the poor and the oppressed.

We also have to insist on a method that considers praxis as embodying a practice that includes reflection and action. The understanding of reality we have proposed above demands it. This is why we must embrace a narrative theology that emerges from the stories of grass-root Hispanic women, from how they see and understand their lives, from how they see and understand their faith and the religious practices that are central to their struggle for survival.

The future elaboration of *mujerista* theology will continue to be a subversive enterprise that has as its source the reality of Latinas in the U.S.A. and that contributes to our liberation.

# Response

## by Chandra Taylor Smith

The critical discussions in these essays highlight how both Womanist and *mujerista* theologians share the two-pronged self-defining process of establishing: (1) the characteristics of women's oppression, and (2) the distinctive disclosures of the divine power in women's lives that is their strength to survive and transform their oppression. This twin consequence of the endeavors of Womanist and *mujerista* theology is affirmed by Ada María Isasi-Díaz as she acknowledges that "*mujerista* theology needs to continue elaborating our theological method which responds to central values of work and vision because it contributes to the liberation of Hispanic women." The mandate of this self-clarifying process of the theological method in *mujerista* theology is akin to the critical self-interpretive framework of Womanist theology. For example, the roundtable discussion on "Christian Ethics and Theology in Womanist Perspectives"[1] represents just one of the ways that Womanists also continue the dynamic process of carefully elaborating their theological method. However, this similarity between these two theologies resides primarily in the pursuit of their methodological task, because the dual self-defining process itself necessarily discloses their differences. In other words, both Womanist and *mujerista* theologies maintain similar critical objectives in their construals of women's God-talk. But, their interpretive methods result ultimately in theological expressions of specific personal and communal struggles and particular witnesses of emancipating divine-human encounters.

The history of both African American women and Latina's confrontation with the early reductive and essentialist ideology in Euro-American feminist critiques of women's oppression provokes the critical analysis of Womanist and *mujerista* theologies. Womanists and *mujeristas* both have endured critical journeys of inheriting their own mother's gardens and defying being relegated "to weeds or exotica" in some illusionary, generic garden planted by white feminists. It has been over fifteen years now that Womanist theologian Delores S. Williams asserted that, "Afro-American women's oppression is distinctive from that of Anglo-American women," and she began to delineate methodically several ways that assaults against African American women differed from the sexist abuse experienced by white women.[2] The preoccupations of *mujerista* theology, described by Isasi-Díaz, further establishes the distinctiveness of Latinas' experience of oppression from that of both white and African American women, as well as other women of color.

When considering these essays together, what becomes apparent is that acknowledging and honoring the differences between them is a critical affirmation of being Womanist and *mujerista* theologians. To be clear, the differences between Womanist and *mujerista* theology does not emerge in opposition to each other's experiences or theoretical and practical expressions. Together, their distinct theological constructions powerfully attests to the destructive attacks on the lives of women of color by institutionalized and internalized poverty, sexism, racism, and classism among other abuses. However, each theology strives to articulate their subjectivity in the face of the comprehensive denigration and exploitation of the lives of non-white women. Their direct and indirect self-identification as contextual or subjective theologies exemplifies their calculated sensitivity to the significance of their differences relative to others, as well as among themselves. Stressing the centrality of relationality and the commitment to and support of community for women, both Womanists and *mujeristas* reject the enactment of subjectivity as individuality.

The principal Christian liberationist commitment to the poor, powerless, and voiceless women of their racial/ethnic communities is evident in the way that both Womanist and *mujerista* theologies honor the lives of grassroots women by retrieving their personal narratives. But, the different assertion of or emphasis on the language of liberation and the varying expressive elaborations of their methodologies are influenced in part by the predominate heritage of Womanists' and *mujeristas'* Protestantism and Roman Catholicism, respectively.[3] However, the formation of the Protestant and Roman Catholic heritages out of which Womanist and *mujerista* theologies emerge is extremely complex. Moreover, both Womanist and *mujerista* theologians are critically aware that African American women and Latinas have maintained faith beliefs and practices that have not been limited to either Protestant or Roman Catholic traditions, but have been influenced by various Spanish, Amerindian, African, and Caribbean religious expressions, as well. Therefore, historical descriptions that limit Womanists to monolithic understandings of Protestantism and *mujeristas* to generalized descriptions of Roman Catholicism would be reductionistic and deny the multi-dimensionality that is discussed in the Womanist essay and that Isasi-Díaz also acknowledges, in another essay, as *mestizaje* and *mulatez* which affirms the racial and cultural mixture of Hispanics in the U.S.A.[4]

The concept of liberation is embraced as the central analytical framework around which Isasi-Díaz organizes *mujerista* theology. She specifically explains how the multi-dimensional manifestations of political, personal-psychological, and spiritual levels of oppression are critiqued through the lenses of liberation. Furthermore, Isasi-Díaz acknowledges that "these three areas of liberation are interrelated in such a way that they not only influence each other but cannot be even conceptualized, much less understood, one apart from the others." Accordingly, this process of analysis contributes to Latinas' struggle for a holistic liberation in their daily lives. Thus, there is a constant referral to the mandates of liberation in Isasi-Díaz's essay, as rhetorically the notion of liberation represents both the source and the norm of *mujeristas'* theological enterprise. The self-conscious, thoughtfully critical, and logical explications of the meaning and consequence of liberation in the method of *mujerista* theology evoke the heritage of the theoretical and practical praxis of Latin American liberation theologians such as Gustavo Gutiérrez, Juan Luis Segundo, and Leonardo Boff.

The Christian liberation commitment of Womanist theology has roots in the predominately evangelical Protestant tradition in America, as it has been culturally defined by the churches in African American communities and the interpretations of black faith in black liberation theology. Academically, the language and structure of the biblical and correlational theological critique of black and Womanist theologians are historically influenced by the existential thought of nineteenth-century continental Protestant philosophers and theologians like Søren Kierkegaard, Karl Barth, Martin Heidegger, Rudolph Bultmann, and Paul Tillich. This intellectual heritage accounts in part for Womanists' expressive use of more existential language in their critical analysis. The term Womanist itself provides a critical cultural framework of interpretation, which establishes how in African American culture, the political, personal-psychological, and spiritual dimensions of black women's lives are also thoroughly interrelated and cannot be conceptualized separately. Consequently, in the way that *mujerista* theology values the assertion of Spanish words for critical terms of theological import, Womanists value and emphasize words and expressions, like womanish, that come out of black folk culture and the heritage of the black oral tradition.

Finally, given the heritage of male-centered theological thinking that precedes both Womanist and *mujerista* theologies, they both consciously challenge the sexism and other abusive, exclusive practices of their respective traditions. The precedent of using as a theological source Latinas' *cotidiano* in *mujerista* theology and the real-lived experience of the daily lives of African American women in Womanist theology represents the significant ways that they have both confronted and expanded the theological method of their traditions. It is also important to note how in both the Womanist and *mujerista* analysis, the practical and concrete redefinition of traditional theological themes like sin as "social sin" is also stressed. Furthermore, the three elements in the systematic explications of "justice" in *mujerista* theology and the three issues that result from a Womanist critique of "demonarchy" all further illustrate the critical contributions of each theology as it has come to voice and at the same time transform traditional theology.

In summary, at the points where Womanist and *mujerista* theologies appear to intersect in similarity, at the same points they necessarily disclose and honor the distinct experience of African American women and Latinas' struggles toward liberation. What is most highly praised by this process is the disclosure of the particular emancipatory manifestation of God in these women's lives. This way in which Womanist and *mujerista* theology both share similarities and differences is the foundation for the continued mutual respect and admiration that each theology has for the other. Precisely because of their differences Womanists and *mujeristas* have much to learn from each other and must continue to work in solidarity towards the liberation of all women well into the future.

# 8

# Womanist Theology: An Expression of Multi-dimensionality for Multi-dimensional Beings

CHANDRA TAYLOR SMITH

B LACK WOMEN BEGAN INTRODUCING their history into formal, academic theological inquiry in the 1970s through the writings of figures such as Pauli Murray, Theressa Hoover, and Jacquelyn Grant. However, the "naming" of this theological model is historically tied to the development of African American literature during the 1980s. In fact, Alice Walker's *In Search of Our Mothers' Gardens* delineated the characteristics of young African American women and religious scholars took notice. Their attention focused on the definition of womanish offered early in the book:

1. From *womanish* (opp. of "girlish," i.e., frivolous, irresponsible, not serious). A black feminist of color. From the black folk expression of mother to female children, "you acting womanish," i.e., like a woman. Usually referring to outrageous, audacious, courageous or *willful* behavior. Wanting to know more and in greater depth than is considered "good" for one. Interested in grown-up doings. Acting grown up. Being grown up. Interchangeable with another black folk expression: You trying to be grown: Responsible. In charge. *Serious.*
2. Also: A woman who loves other women, sexually and/or nonsexually. Appreciates and prefers women's culture, women's emotional flexibility (values tears as natural counterbalance of laughter), and women's strength. Sometimes loves individual men, sexually and/or nonsexually. Committed to revival and wholeness of entire people, male and female. Not a separatist, except periodically, for health. Traditionally universalist, as in: "Mama, why are we brown, pink, and yellow, and our cousins are white, beige, and black?" Ans.: "Well, you know the colored race is just like a flower garden, with every color flower represented." Tradi-

149

tionally capable, as in: "Mama, I'm walking to Canada and I'm taking you and a bunch of other slaves with me." Reply: "It wouldn't be the first time."

Walker's description publicly disclosed and culturally affirmed the experience of many young African American women who were grown, responsible, in charge, serious, and asking pressing questions.[1] Thus, while Walker's introduction of the notion of "Womanist" was a novel expression for most of the dominant culture, it signaled a deeply familiar self-disclosure, especially for women religious scholars. Such intergenerational tongue-lashings about, "You trying to be grown," from black mothers, necks cocked, with hands on their hips was indeed familiar to the ears of many of these women. Therefore, Walker's literary depiction provoked a theological response developed in ever-expanding personal, spiritual, methodological, and theoretical dimensions.

In this essay, I critically reflect upon the (1) self-naming; and (2) the mandate of African American women's real-lived experience, which are the principal threads in the intricate fibers woven throughout the multi-dimensional design of Womanist theology. I consider how the characteristics of self-naming and real-lived experience as sources of critical revelation ground this theological approach while confronting new challenges. My method of review constitutes a descriptive analysis of the significance of these two dynamics that has nurtured Womanist theology.[2]

## I. Self-Naming

I simply feel that naming our own experience after our own fashion (as well as rejecting whatever does not seem to suit) is the least we can do—and in this society may well be our only tangible sign of personal freedom.

—ALICE WALKER, *In Search of Our Mothers' Gardens*[3]

When I first read Alice Walker's definition of "Womanist," it engendered the same joy and sense of good feeling within me that I felt that day, now twenty years ago, when I acquired my "Afro" (a hairstyle I still wear). It just felt good. It fit. It provided a way of stating who I was and how I felt about a lot of things.

—CHERYL TOWNSEND GILKES, *Round Table Discussion*[4]

### Identity Issues

There was something intimately recognizable about the truth of being womanish in the personal identities and life journeys of many

African American women religious scholars. For example, in several of the writings in her collection of essays, *Katie's Canon: Womanism and the Soul of the Black Community* (New York: Continuum, 1995), Cannon reflects on the ways in which the notion of Womanist was embodied in the experience of being ground-breaking scholars in the academy. Womanishness provided a source of inspiration for the various aspects of their personal and scholarly achievements. For, while being a Womanist designated a positive and wholistic identity,[5] it was foremost a necessary way of being in order to survive and in the face of what has been described as "multiple jeopardy."[6] Womanishness seemed to capture that strengthening quality of character that "girded them up" to name and challenge the multiple oppressive power configurations (e.g., race, gender, sexual orientation, class, age, education, physical ability). Accordingly, one of the most indelible characteristics that the appellation of Womanist has provided is self-naming.

The significance of the event of naming, according to Womanist theologian Karen Baker-Fletcher, is that it gives "rise to speech, which is to participate in the power of creating one's context."[7] Baker-Fletcher further explains that

> Black women who choose the name "Womanist" first presuppose the right of self-naming. Naming oneself from within oneself, refusing categorizations of self and community that come from dominant groups and persons, is the first and basic step in coming to voice.[8]

Womanist means, therefore, "being and acting out who you are and interpreting the reality for yourself. "Amplifying marginal voices" is the way Womanist New Testament scholar, Clarice Martin, describes the Womanist methodology of unearthing and validating the voices of women in biblical narratives.[9] Mary McCloud Bethune, Anna Julia Cooper, Jarena Lee, Amanda Berry Smith, Mary Church Terrell, Sojourner Truth, and Ida Wells-Barnett are among countless other women whose voices Womanists have amplified as well.

### Womanism and Multi-dimensional Love

This self-naming quickly emerged as a self-interpretive framework, established on the centrality of African American women's "love." To acknowledge that black women do indeed love was an unprecedented presumption of an important yet neglected cultural, spiritual, and theoretical identity. By transcending the stereotypical (i.e., over-sexualized and victimized) representations of African American women's love, Womanists named and claimed intentional, self-actualizing, un-abstracted ways of loving—including music, dance, the moon, the spirit, love, food, roundness, struggle, the Folk, and self.[10] Unable to become the illusionary generic woman which dictated the experience and agenda of the feminist movement, convictions of African American women turned on a fierce self-love to claim and affirm the necessity of their identity as comprehensively black women. Thus, the intimate physical and spiritual power of "love" in African American women's experience strategically became a source of theological and ethical revelation in the work of Womanist religious scholars.

The unapologetic power of this self-defined loving resonated, for many African American women religious scholars and ministers, with the power that drives Christian faith. In other words, to begin the self-naming and self-actualizing process out of "love" was also to start with the same core of African American women's spiritual connections with God through their relationship with Jesus Christ. The importance of this connection between Christ and self, framed by love, is undeniable. Jacquelyn Grant, for example, was among the first theologians to closely examine African American women's embrace of Jesus in her text, *White Women's Christ and Black Women's Jesus: Feminist Christology and Womanist Response* (Atlanta: Scholars Press, 1989). During this same year, Kelly Brown Douglas began a critical study of the significance of Christology in an essay entitled "God Is as Christ Does: Toward a Womanist Theology," in *The Journal of Religious Thought* 46, no. 1 (Summer-Fall 1989): 7–16.[11] For both Grant and Brown Douglas self-love and love for others captures the Christ-like dimensions of African American women's lived experience.

Furthermore, "Womanist" in its self-naming of African American women undermined and unfurled the historically flattened negative stereotypes imposed to describe African American women as either Mammies, Sapphires, Jezebels, or Mules.[12] Any essential claim of what it meant to be an African American woman was subverted in the terms descriptive of diversity and complexity, especially as it acknowledged African American women's love of other women, sexually and/or nonsexually.[13] The lesbian dimension of African American women's experience challenged African American women Christian scholars with the self-critical consideration of "difference" as it is manifest among even African American women.

Womanist ethicist Cheryl Sanders, in a roundtable discussion published in the *Journal of Feminist Studies in Religion* (Fall 1989), questioned the adequacy of Walker's term as a rubric for Christian ethical and theological discourse because of its affirmation of African American women's sexual love for women. As part of this, Sanders gave a critical analysis of Walker's understanding and personal appropriation of Womanist critique, especially Walker's exception to the Jean McMahon Humez suggestion that Rebecca Jackson was a lesbian in the text that Humez edited entitled *Gift of Power: The Writings of Rebecca Jackson, Black Visionary, Shaker Eldress*. Among the inherent discomforts with Walker's political preference for the term Womanist as an alternative to the term lesbian to capture the dynamic of women who love women in African American culture,[14] Sanders proposed that Womanist was "essentially a secular cultural category whose theological and ecclesial significations are rather tenuous."[15] Sanders concluded that "there is a fundamental discrepancy between the Womanist criteria that would affirm and/or advocate homosexual practice, and the ethical norms the black church might employ to promote the survival and wholeness of black families."[16]

Responses to Sanders from Katie G. Cannon, Emilie M. Townes, M. Shawn Copeland, bell hooks, and Cheryl Townsend Gilkes illustrated the critical power of self-criticism and the courage of African American women to face their own relativity. The continuum between liberal and conservative theological perspectives and social/political commitments represented by these scholars and their various faith expressions highlighted the multi-dimensionality of the discussion. Each response affirmed Womanist as an adequate category for referencing and framing the ethical and theological experience of African American women. Sanders's critique and each response represented a complex—internal and external—critical process. This is constitutive of what Copeland explained as African American women's struggle to define themselves and their experiences—to be definers.[17] For Cannon it is pragmatically constitutive of the moral reasoning that "enables black women to refuse dehumanization and to resist the conditions that thwart life."[18]

### Complex Community and the Location of "Being"

That each woman took a serious approach in examining the issues posed by Sanders exhibited the kind of courage that philosophical theologian Paul Tillich observed as an element of faith illustrating the "daring self-affirmation of one's own being in spite of the powers of 'nonbeing' which are the heritage of everything finite."[19] Tillich's perspective is helpful here because it stresses the idea that courage is indicative of a "critical principle" that is constitutive of human religious consciousness. For him the critical principle is namely the concern about "that which is really ultimate over against what claims to be ultimate but is only preliminary, transitory, finite."[20] Thus, the community of faith, according to Tillich, which was strategically represented by the sisterhood of those at the roundtable, must include their own criticism to assure that liturgical, doctrinal, ethical, and even cultural expressions like "Womanist" do not become the ultimate concern. The passionate focus on "liberation concerned with

human equality and the ever present, ever-sustaining, judging, and redeeming nature of God,"[21] as it was stressed by Townes assured that the
primary function of the term "Womanist" points to the "ultimate,"
which is beyond all of them. In other words, each of the women at the
roundtable argued from the critical principle rooted in their religious
consciousness. The affirmation of the presence of lesbian African American women in the critical self-interpretive framework of Womanist theology was recognized as constitutive of the transcendent openings in
Womanists' aims towards the ultimate concern. As long as the multi-
dimensionality of the term maintains what Townes further describes as
Walker's concern for the survival and flourishing of the African American community in its diversity—age, gender, sexuality, radical activity,
accomodationist stance, and creative promise—then Womanist theological scholarship will avoid idolatry and the ambiguity of the holy,
which occurs when penultimate concerns become ultimate.[22] Another
way to explain the multi-dimensional, self-interpretive lens of Womanist is that it connotes ways of being as opposed to prescribing ways to
be. This understanding establishes the philosophical dimension of the
self-defining framework that the term Womanist provides. Accordingly,
none of the ways of being in the definition are elevated to a monolithic
ontological status. Fundamentally, Walker and Womanist thinkers
place emphasis on a general state of "being." In this way, Womanist is
descriptive of "nature" or of "being natural," of being "natural African
American women," actualizing all of their possibilities. The meaning
and employment of the term "nature" in this analysis is from the root of
the word in the future form of the Latin, *nasci, nat-*, to be born.[23]

From this origin the extended meaning of nature, as the basic
qualities in a person that must be allowed for or as fundamental to
their being, is captured in Walker's notion of Womanist. Self-defining
is constitutive of these qualities as it is necessary to bring forth one's
natural beingness. Anything outside of one's self that enacts this defining of self is unnatural. The philosophical precedent of natural
being in the meaning of the term Womanist emerged as a foil to those
who sought to undermine the being of African American women,
including: (1) white men's rape and abuse of black women that
stripped away their agency and relegated them to an invisible existence; (2) the cooptation of African American women's identities by
white women, especially in first and second wave feminist agendas;
and (3) the sexist driven exploitation of African American women by
African American men, especially as it is institutionalized in the traditional black church and in the black theology project. In other
words, Womanist is a reassertion of being "natural" in opposition to
the way white women and white and black men subjugated black
women to being "unnatural."

## II. God in Women's Lived Experience

It is my mother—and all our mothers who were not famous—that I went in search of the secret of what has fed that muzzled and often mutilated, but vibrant, creative spirit that the black woman has inherited, and that pops out in wild and unlikely places to this day.          —ALICE WALKER, *In Search of Our Mothers Gardens*[24]

One day my professor responded to my complaint about the absence of black women's experience from all Christian theology (black liberation and feminist theologies included). He suggested that my anxiety might lessen if my exploration of African American cultural sources was consciously informed by the statement "I am a black WOMAN." He was right. I had not realized before that I read African-American sources from a black male perspective. I assumed black women were included.

—DELORES S. WILLIAMS, *Sisters in the Wilderness*[25]

### Lived Experience as Hermeneutical Resource

Walker comments that, "[w]hen the poet Jean Toomer walked through the South in the early twenties he discovered a curious thing: black women whose spirituality was so intense, so deep, so unconscious, that they were themselves unaware of the richness they held."[26] African American women are still presently unaware of the full richness of their spirituality, which constitutes their internal source of communion with God and informs their real-lived convictions. This impoverishment of self-understanding is why it became imperative for Womanist scholars to name and bring forth their internal source of divine power. Such a process must take seriously the lived experiences of black women. Jacquelyn Grant declared that "black women's experience must be affirmed as the crucible for doing Womanist theology."[27] Such is the case, concurs Womanist ethicist Katie Cannon, because, "[t]he real-lived texture of Black life requires moral agency that may run contrary to the ethical boundaries of mainline Protestantism."[28] Howard Thurman's story about the way his grandmother critically interpreted the Bible, as it is rehearsed by Womanist Hebrew scholar, Renita J. Weems, beautifully illustrates why and how black women's lived experience yields critical ethical and theological discernment which serves as a source of divine revelation and hermeneutics in Womanist thought. Emphasizing the heritage of the aural culture of African American slaves, Weems's critiques the following passage by Thurman as representative of how his grandmother's "experience of reality became the norm for evaluating the contents of the Bible":[29]

Two or three times a week I read the Bible aloud to her. I was deeply impressed by the fact that she was most particular about the choice of Scripture. For instance, I might read many of the more devotional Psalms, some of Isaiah, the Gospels again and again; but the Pauline epistles, never—except, at long intervals, the thirteenth chapter of First Corinthians. . . . With a feeling of great temerity I asked her one day why it was that she would not let me read any of the Pauline letters. What she told me I shall never forget. "During the days of slavery," she said, "the master's minister would occasionally hold services for the slaves. Old man McGhee was so mean that he would not let a Negro minister preach to his slaves. Always the white minister used as his text something from Paul. At least three or four times a year he used as a text: 'Slaves, be obedient to them that are your master . . . as unto Christ.' Then he would go on to show how it was God's will that we were slaves and how, if we were good and happy slaves, God would bless us. I promised my Maker that if I ever learned to read and if freedom ever came, I would not read that part of the Bible."[30]

His grandmother's selective retrieval of those biblical passages that were liberating for her is brilliant. While her decision to avoid the Epistles of Paul may be controversial to some, the way in which her lived experiences influenced this hermeneutical approach is distinctive. Indeed, the actions of Thurman's grandmother bear out Cannon's proposal that "black women live out a moral wisdom in their real-lived context that does not appeal to the fixed rule or absolute principles of the white-oriented, male structured society."[31]

Moreover, Delores S. Williams argues that methodologically the primary use of the Bible by Christian Womanist scholars is "to identify and reflect upon those biblical stories in which poor oppressed women have a special encounter with divine emissaries of God, like the spirit."[32] According to Williams, Walker's mention of black women's love of the spirit is a true reflection of the great respect they have always shown for the presence and work of the spirit, *wherever it may be manifested.*[33] For example, in Genesis, Hagar's experience "of bondage, of African heritage, of encounter with God/emissary in the midst of fierce survival struggles" is often expounded upon by Womanist religious scholars and preachers for its parallels with the contemporary experiences in the lives of African American women. Furthermore, Clarice Martin proposes that Womanist biblical interpretation epitomizes a "quadruocentric" focus where,

gender, race, class, and language issues are all at the forefront of translation . . . and interpretation . . . concerns, and not just a threefold focus, where gender, class, and language concerns predominate almost exclusively, as is often the case in white feminist biblical interpretation and translation.[34]

Maintaining this quadruocentric hermeneutical focus, Womanist theologians have critically extended black theology's traditional biblical/ theological sources by also including narratives, autobiographies, prayers, other non-fictional and fictional writings by African American women.

### God in Women's Experience

Williams claims that to devalue the diverse cultural elements through which African American women express their humanity is "to be guilty of sin."[35] She first supports this indictment of "social sin" by elucidating the self-expression Walker values as Womanist, including the way Womanist defines universality in terms of an array of skin colors, giving intrinsic value to all skin color: "brown, pink and yellow" as well as "white, beige and black."[36] Secondly, Williams turns to the theological principle of the *imago dei* to undergird the intrinsic connection that these expressions have to African American womanhood and humanity. She argues that African American women's humanity "is in the image of God as is all humanity."[37] As a result, it is the image of God that is devalued when the expressive ways of African American women's humanity is devalued. Thus, the critical value that Womanists place on the inherent diversity that exists within their own racial/ethnic communities is deeply spiritual and fundamentally connected to their love of God and their understanding that God dwells within them.

### Challenges to Theology and the Church

It is out of the privileging of the real-lived experience of African American women that Womanists challenge the church and traditional theology whenever and wherever they deny the full extent of God's liberatory presence, especially in women's lives. Part of the reason that Womanist theology came into being, explains Womanist theologian Kelly Brown Douglas, is because "neither feminist theology—done mostly by white women—nor black theology—done mostly by black men" adequately addressed African American women's theological concerns.[38] Consequently, African American women theologians "vigorously offered critiques of both feminist and black theologies for their apparent neglect of black women."[39] Moreover, Cannon further explains that Womanist pedagogy emerged out of the experience of "black women challenging conventional and outmoded dominant theological resources, deconstructing ideologies that led us into complicity with our own oppression."[40] Indeed, one of the biggest challenges has been right at home in black church communities. Womanist activist Frances E. Woods describes and critiques this internal problem in this way:

> Within the African American church community the silence about the
> realities of women's experience and how it differs from men's experi-
> ence has taken [on] the proportions of a version of the "big lie," and is
> a deadly yoke. This yoke consists of silencing, ignoring, degrading, and
> dismissing women's experience, especially those experiences that reveal
> the nature and extent of oppression perpetuated against them within
> the community. . . . The yoke of silencing, degrading, ignoring or dis-
> missing women weighs down the Black Christian community in a con-
> spiracy against its own total liberation.[41]

Womanists' challenge to white men, white women, African American
men, traditional African American churches, black theology, and all
other ideologies and institutionalized social constructions that would
deny their total liberation tangibly illustrates their commitment to
"survival and wholeness of entire people, male and female," as it is
expressed in Walker's definition.

The words to a song by the a capella ensemble, Sweet Honey in the
Rock, profoundly captures Womanists' commitment to the inclusive
stand that no oppressed community is free until all oppressed communities are free. The song's primary chorus is "We who believe in
freedom cannot rest." These lyrics and their philosophy resonate with
Williams's description of the three primary goals of African American
feminism that is signified by Walker's delineation of Womanist. Williams constructively outlined these goals in her essay, "The Color of
Feminism: Or Speaking the Black Woman's Tongue." The following
three issues are the consequence of African American women's experience of "demonarchy,"[42] according to Williams:

> These would be (1) liberation of women and the family simultaneously;
> (2) establishing a positive quality of life for women and the family
> simultaneously, (3) forming political alliances with other marginal
> groups struggling to be free of the oppression imposed by white-
> controlled American institutions.[43]

The emphasis on the simultaneous liberation of both African American women and families advances some of the criticisms and explicit
sentiments expressed by the Black Feminist Statement from the Combahee River Collective, dated April 1977, which declares that

> Although we are feminist and Lesbians, we feel solidarity with progres-
> sive Black men and do not advocate the fractualization that white
> women who are separatists demand. Our situation as Black people ne-
> cessitates solidarity around the fact of race, which white women of

course do not need to have with white men, unless it is their negative solidarity as racial oppressors. We struggle together with Black men against racism, while we also struggle with Black men about sexism. We realize that the liberation of all oppressed peoples necessitates the deconstruction of the political-economic systems of capitalism and imperialism as well as patriarchy.[44]

Walker's portrayal of a Womanist in her definition as, "[n]ot a separatist, except periodically, for health," fosters this profound sense of solidarity that Womanists have with African American men and others in their families and communities whose liberation is constitutive of their own emancipation.

## III. Womanism and the Critique of "Ontological Blackness"

Even though it has been well over fifteen years since African American women religious scholars have embraced the notion of Womanist into their nomenclature, there is still a critical sense that Womanist theological thought is continuing to evolve as it defies a monolithic idea or definition. The Reverend Dr. Teresa L. Fry Brown, a Womanist pastor and homiletician, puts it this way: "Womanist scholars are still in process, still defining themselves, still broadening the idea."[45] Brown further argues that Womanist thought needs a regular infusion of "reality and social relevance to deepen the richness of the discipline."[46] I agree. The precedent of the multi-dimensional dynamic of the self-interpretive framework and utilization of real-lived experiences are provocations for its scholars and practitioners to keep abreast of reality and to remain socially relevant. Moreover, these two comprehensive aspects of Womanist theology gird up a constructive response to critical challenges to Womanist theology like that posed by African American religious and cultural critic Victor Anderson.

Anderson recognizes that Womanist theologians, like Williams and others, acknowledge and sanction the inclusive and non-essentialist vision of African American women's self expression and understanding of community and commitment, which includes "an affirmation of black lesbian love and relativizing of race and color."[47] Such reading and employment of Walker's notion maintains, according to Anderson, the openings that Walker's definition connotes which move black liberation theology beyond its parochial allegiances to "ontological blackness."

Succinctly, "[o]ntological blackness is a covering term," proposes Anderson, "that connotes categorical, essentialist, and representational languages depicting black life and experience."[48] As a religious and cultural critic, Anderson maintains a prophetic pragmatist view that is "rigorously iconoclastic in its attempt to track the ways that

cultural activities [which includes religion for Anderson] threaten individuality, novelty, and moral agency."[49] Womanist ethicist, Emilie
Townes, assures that "[m]uch of what Womanist thought seeks to
debunk is the notion of universals and absolutes."[50] However, Anderson's concern is that Womanist theological thought binds itself to the
totalizing tendencies of ontological blackness in its hermeneutical
emphasis on exceptionalist claims of black women's suffering and
resistance. Such emphasis, which corroborates the essentialist catego-
rization of black identity in black oppression, belies the non-
essentialist mandate of Walker's Womanist, suggests Anderson.
Moreover, this contradiction inherent in Womanist theology, Anderson argues, leaves unanswered questions: "On what does transcen-
dence depend in Womanist theology?" "At what point do thriving
and flourishing enter the equation of suffering and resistance?" Sur-
viving represents the minimal requirement of a fulfilled life, Anderson
proclaims, and "we all want more than to survive."[51]

The human drive to flourish and thrive encapsulates the basic
pragmatic ends of the emancipatory goal of Womanist theology. It
is precisely in Womanists' continued self-naming and focus on African American women that such flourishing is both theoretically
and practically manifested. These multi-dimensional dynamics in
Womanist theology appropriately shift African American women
theologians from the insular, ontological categories of black oppression, in which "the binary matrices that have driven prior racial
discourse in African American religions and theology,"[52] according
to Anderson, are no longer adequate to describe what are the "*real
interests* that structure black life."[53] In other words, the traditional
oppositions between whiteness/blackness, oppressors/oppressed, and
community/personality in black theology, including Womanist theologians' additional preoccupation with the bipolar categories of
male/female, explode in their binary contrasts to open up to
the multi-dimensions of racial/ethnic/social/economic/gender/sexual
and religious identities representative of African American women's
real-lived experiences.

In summary, ontological blackness becomes moot in the emerging
mandates of Womanist theology if it remains grounded in both the
complexities of its self-naming and pragmatic resourcefulness. Thus
in answer to Anderson, Womanist theology from this standpoint transcends the aporias of ontological blackness and, at the same time,
holds to the transcending openings that Walker's Womanist connotations commend.[54] Fully naming the suffering and resistance as well
as the points of flourishing and thriving among the myriad of African
American identities that represent the multi-dimensional reality of
the real-lived experience of African American communities is an undeniable self-interpretive process in Womanist theology. This process

is so deeply rooted in the origins of African American women religious scholars' self-embracement of the term Womanist, that Womanist theology will continue to blossom and make a critical contribution as it produces and endures the coming challenges of the new millennium.

# Response

## by Ada María Isasi-Díaz

One of *mujerista* theology's main dialogue partners has been Womanist theology. We, *mujerista* theologians, have carefully read and studied Womanist ethics and theology and have learned much from them. I personally have been blessed with the friendship of many of the Womanist theologians. I went to school with several of them. Sometimes at conferences where I have been the only Latina theologian, Womanist theologians have welcomed me in their group and offered me their support.

Given the fact that we are women, we share the same socio-political-economic circumstances as marginalized groups within the U.S.A., it is not surprising at all that there are many similarities between *mujerista* and Womanist theology. These similarities do not do away with the distinctiveness of these two theologies, distinctiveness that emerges from the particularities of our oppression, from the historical realities of our two communities of accountability, from the role that religions and churches have in our cultures and from the role of women in our different cultures and struggles for survival.

Like Womanist theology, *mujerista* theology has worked at naming itself. For us there were and continue to be two main reasons for this. First, to name oneself is one of the most powerful acts a person can do. A name is not just a word by which one is identified. A name also provides the conceptual framework, the point of reference, the mental constructs that are used in thinking, understanding, and relating to a person, an idea, a movement. So, we named ourselves *mujeristas* and our enterprise *mujerista* theology as a way of coming into our own power, as a way of being self-defining, as a way to stop being an adjective in the theological enterprise of women of the dominant group here in the U.S.A.

This points to the second reason why we have named our enterprise *mujerista* theology. We needed and still need the specifics of our oppression and of our vision of liberation to be known. As long as we were but an appendix to Euro-American feminist theology, we did not believe we could make much headway in this complex and all-embracing task. *Mujerista* is the word we have chosen to identify the struggles of Latinas and to name our devotion to the liberation of Hispanic women.

In *mujerista* theology we have stayed clear of prescribing any kind of litmus test for being a *mujerista*. Avoiding any tinge of essentialism we have instead insisted on accountability and solidarity as key issues in the identification of our theological enterprise. We have likewise been concerned with the centrality of praxis in our theological work, claiming that doing *mujerista* theology itself is praxis, for it works to uncover and dismantle the network of privileges that keep Latinas absent or, at best, marginalized in the women's movement, in Latino/a communities, in the academy, in churches, and in society. *Mujerista* theology is a praxis because it contributes to creating a voice for Latinas, not the only one but a valid one; and *mujerista* theology is about creating public spaces for the voices of Hispanic women.

Praxis is at the heart of *mujerista* theology. In our view doing theology is a liberative praxis, and we have insisted that to see theological reflection as a second moment in the doing of theology denies the intrinsic link that exists between thinking and doing. We declare this separation to be a false dichotomy that often works against Hispanic women. Often considered intellectually inferior because of our limitations with the English language and because many of us have had limited access to formal education, Latina women have been seen as valuable only insofar as the physical work we can produce. However, *mujerista* theology insists that grassroot Latinas are organic intellectuals, people who day by day face choices and make choices, who day by day engage reality in very specific ways and that by doing so, make and re-make themselves, their families, their communities, and society at large. We have gone further than privileging the experience of Latinas. We have insisted at all times that the lived experience of grassroot Hispanic women who struggle for liberation is the starting point and the source of *mujerista* theology. It is their hopes and dreams coming out of their struggles for survival—coming out of *la lucha*—that constitute a singular quarry out of which to fashion the building blocks for a just society, for a just world order. Yes, this insistence on the centrality of the lived experience of Latinas gives concrete expression to the preferential option for the poor and the oppressed to which *mujerista* theology is committed. We do not claim moral superiority for Hispanic women but rather know that the fact that they are excluded and do not profit from the present societal structures—including church structures—frees them to dream dreams and see visions for the building of a future in which no one will be excluded.

One of the first articles of *mujerista* theology to be published dealt with the necessity for solidarity. We have worked insistently and consistently to build bridges between our Latina communities and other oppressed women's communities. We have done so by developing at length a lens which makes clear that among oppressed people, and between oppressed people and "converted oppressors" (people who consciously use their privileges to struggle against oppression), there has to be an operative mutuality that goes well beyond working in coalitions. Though in no way do we downplay the importance of coalition-building, solidarity outdistances it by insisting that there exists a commonality of interest that makes it absolutely necessary for all of us committed to justice to establish, maintain, and make flourish a strong and ongoing praxis of mutuality. We have stressed the fact that in any and all liberative praxis one needs to go beyond particularities and engage the particularities of others. There is much work that we need to do along these lines but this is indeed an area on which we have always insisted and which we have asked Womanist theologians to take into consideration. Succinctly, we believe that one cannot do Womanist theology without taking *mujersita* theology, Asian American women's theology, and Native American women's theology into consideration.

Finally, without in any way minimizing the need for focusing on our different communities of accountability and while continuing to denounce assimilation, *mujerista* theology has turned its attention to the work that needs to be done on issues of difference. Using the category of *mestizaje/mulatez* we have insisted on the need to conceptualize differences not as absolute otherness, mutual exclusion, and categorical opposition. As long as this is the prevalent understanding there is no possibility of having just personal relationships, and it will be impossible to create just societal structures that will not benefit some groups at the expense of others. As long as this is the prevalent understanding of difference we will always be oppressing those who are outside our group, threatening both them and ourselves with destruction. Instead we have proposed that we need to understand that differences are relative so that those who are different will not be seen as "other." In *mujerista* theology we emphasize the importance of embracing the partiality of all human perspectives and of admitting others' point of view as a possible corrective lens to our own. To understand differences as enabling relationality and solidarity we have to de-center ourselves so as to be able to become cognizant of what connects us as much as if not more than what separtes us. This will make it possible for us to unlock subjectivity and move to a social ontology that emphasizes non-opposition and non-exclusion. It will also make it possible for us to work on reconciliation among and within our communities in ways that, while not ignoring injustices, look to the future instead of to the past.

I am proposing that Womanist theology as well as *mujerista* theology, and all theologies arising from marginalized communities, need to take on the task of reconciliation so as to move beyond the divisions and prejudices that keep us oppressed. We need reconciliation among ourselves as communities often pitted against each other by those in power. We need reconciliation with those who have oppressed us. For that to happen they have to understand and acknowledge that they are oppressors and repent in a radical way. I am not in any way going soft; I am not in any way trying to fabricate an easy way out for oppressors at the expense of Hispanic women, black women, Asian American women, Native women, and all the poor and oppressed, who constitute more than two-thirds of the world population. Reconciliation is not possible or understandable apart from justice. Reconciliation, I am saying, is an intrinsic element of justice in our world today. This is the clear teaching that has come out of South Africa at the close of the twentieth century that we have to heed. If not we will perish.

The work of reconciliation is a humble process, a road to be traveled together, one step at a time, by those seeking to be reconciled. Reconciliation is not a matter of making known preconceived answers to a given situation. Instead, the work of reconciliation projects itself into the future, opening up and concentrating on possibilities. It is not a matter of repeating or of limiting oneself to the past. Reconciliation understands that there is a plurality of truths and that this plurality is precisely what is at the heart of possibilities, that it is what makes choices possible. It is what roots human freedom. It cannot be understood apart from responsibility to others. The richness of possibilities that demands choice is precisely what makes reconciliation a moral virtue, a way of being and acting that requires responsible choice. Responsible choice is not a matter of controlling situations. It is not a matter of being absolutely certain that what one chooses is the most effective choice or one that guarantees success. Responsible choice recognizes that this is but one way to proceed, that given the present situation and the understanding one has, it seems the best possible way to proceed.

Reconciliation makes it all the more obvious that moral responsibility has to focus on responding to others and establishing and maintaining mutuality. This in turn redefines the concepts of autonomy, self-reliance, and self-definition. The work of reconciliation focuses on responsibility as "participation in a communal work, laying the groundwork for the creative response of people in the present and the future. Responsible action means changing what can be altered in the present even though a problem is not completely resolved. Responsible action focuses on and respects partial resolutions and the inspiration and conditions for further partial resolutions . . . [by ourselves] and by others."[1] The work of reconciliation has to recognize that those who have been apart and opposed to each other need to move together, one step at a time, willing to accept that risk, ambiguity, and uncertainty are part of the process. The work of reconciliation asks above all for a commitment to mutuality, to opening possibilities together even if one may never see them become a reality—this over and above a desire for tangible changes. Reconciliation has to be guided by a sense that the results of much work and commitment may be only a list of shared desires and possibilities. Even that outcome, if it is the result of mature ethical commitment, has value because it will allow and oblige one to sustain a reconciling attitude and reconciling behavior.

Reconciliation is a moral choice. It makes one remember that all persons have been, at some point in their lives, oppressors and exploiters, and that good intentions are not enough. Moral action requires the risk of taking steps together, of being accountable to each other, of participating in a process that concentrates on the future precisely by working to alter the present. Reconciliation as moral action makes it clear that healing the rifts that divide people cannot be incidental to one's life for the work of justice; that it is essential to being a human being, a responsible person, a person fully alive.

This is the life-giving task ahead of us, *mujerista* theologians. It is a task that by its very nature we cannot do alone. It is a task for which we need not only brown hands but also black hands and yellow hands and red hands and white hands. It is a task for which we seek to be in dialogue with Womanist theology and with all liberation theologies.

# PART V

## *On Pain and Suffering: Theology and the Problem of Evil*

# 9

## Christian Doctrines of Humanity and the African Experience of Evil and Suffering: Toward a Black Theological Anthropology

### Dianne Stewart

AFTER THIRTY YEARS OF BLACK theological discourse there still remains a paucity of scholarship on theological anthropology and its relationship to African/black people's experiences with evil and suffering.[1] With this in mind my chief aim here is to examine theological doctrines that have fostered Christian beliefs about the evil nature and characteristics of Africans and their providentially ordained low ontological and social status among the human creation.

Beginning with an examination of orthodox Western Christian anthropology, I argue that racist and anti-African doctrines of humanity, promoted later in popular Christian thought by missionaries and pro-slavery advocates, derive theological legitimacy from Augustinian theological anthropology. Although Augustine's ethnicity as a continental African cannot be taken for granted in Augustinian studies, his theological anthropology was notably influenced by Western philosophical thinking, which poses problems for contemporary formulations of black theological anthropology. Secondly, black Christian responses to the evil characterization of black humanity in the Christian tradition are all too often no less inimical. Black theologians, while uncovering radical and liberating traditions in black religious history, must be willing to expose and critically analyze problematic material that can be used as authoritative black Christian sources to support anti-black and anti-African theology.[2] Finally, in coming to terms with Christian doctrines of humanity and the African experience of evil and suffering, black theological anthropology should be

169

structured to account for the Original Violation of dislocation, exile, and enslavement in the African experience.

## Saint Augustine's Doctrine of Humanity

St. Augustine anchored his theological anthropology in biblical narratives, the sacred legacy of church testimony, and the philosophical pursuit of wisdom. From the Genesis creation story he developed a theological anthropology, thereby determining the moral history and nature of the human being, the stages of human moral development, and the purpose of human life. Augustine maintained that, since the fall of Adam, humanity has had the capacity to know and to choose what is good or evil. The ability to choose evil (*posse peccare*), however, is the essential moral quality of human existence distinguishing human beings from God who cannot choose evil. Augustine identified pride (*tolma*) as the cardinal human sin, giving rise to a plethora of desires and emotions that impel human beings to disobey God.[3] However, he concluded that the underlying cause of all human sin is not a human quality but a human condition called *concupiscence*. According to Augustine, *concupiscence* attacks the will, making it frail and susceptible to sin; and it is the perversity of the will that qualifies humanity's fallen state in the world.

Augustine argued that everything in the universe, although not perfect like the Christian God, is essentially good, including the souls and bodies of human beings.[4] He conceived of the soul as the source of all agency in human activity while the body merely cooperates with the soul's will. Generally speaking, Augustine defined the soul as the essence constituting all life forms; that is, the animating force that qualifies a plant, animal, or human being as alive.[5] Human beings, however, possess the highest intelligent soul form, capable of vegetative, perceptive, and rational states. Given the human soul's powers of perception, reason, and desire, Augustine especially valued and advocated for the place of knowledge in human fulfillment. Departing from Neoplatonist philosophers, he insisted that the pursuit of knowledge as an end could not yield happiness. Rather, human happiness is necessarily contingent upon knowledge of absolute truth (i.e., God), attained only through the faculties of the soul.

In *De Trinitate* Augustine argues that the human soul is actually an integration of three main faculties—understanding, memory, and will, and is invested with the inferior (yet necessary) capability of knowing all that is corporeal and mutable. This type of cognitive knowledge Augustine terms science (*scientia*), the outcome of which is action or accomplishment. Most important, however, the soul possesses the superior capability of knowing God, who is immutable and incorporeal.[6] Contemplation or knowledge of God (*sapientia*) is the *telos* of Christian life and furthermore, everything in the created world exists to assist human beings in pursuit of love of God, including the inferior powers of the rational soul.[7]

Augustine did not espouse a soul/body dualism within his theology. He concluded that the human being is a "rational substance composed of body and soul."[8] Technically speaking, if there is any dualism within Augustine's anthropology, it begins and ends with the faculties of the soul and the specific workings of the will, which directs human beings toward or away from God. Augustine did, however, conceive of the human soul and body hierarchically; he classified them respectively as a greater and lesser good, rendering the soul a permeable immaterial agent and the body a perishable, passive participant in the soul's activity.

### Implications of Augustine's Anthropology for Racially Oppressed Africans

Augustine's stratified classification of the soul and body and their respective attributes has contributed to the type of hierarchical thinking in Christian theology that readily collapses into menacing dualisms with crippling social consequences. In the context of slavery, Africans had to come to terms with Manichaean or dualistic anthropologies that are ostensibly traceable to Augustinian metaphysics. From his study entitled *Dark Symbols, Obscure Signs: God, Self, and Community in the Slave Mind*, Riggins Earl determines that Europeans generally viewed African people as "bodiless souls" or "soulless bodies;" and both anthropological views were used to justify the evil conditions under which Africans survived the Middle Passage and chattel enslavement.[9] In the first case, African bodies were insignificant and could be devalued or destroyed for the greater purpose of saving African souls. Thus, slavery was a means of exposing heathen Africans to the way of redemption via European Christianity. In the second case, whites purported that Africans had no souls, and that they were the most inferior beings among the various human races. It was believed that African bodies were naturally suited for slave labor. Salvation, then, was not an option for Africans because they did not have souls.

Whether white people viewed Africans as "bodiless souls" or "soulless bodies," the dichotomy has conceptual roots in the theological anthropology of St. Augustine in that it privileges and values the soul over the body. To be sure, a careful evaluation of Augustine's anthropology actually shows that he did not support intentional acts of bodily denigration or destruction. Nevertheless, his characterization of the soul as the locus of the will, sense perception,[10] and knowledge, closer to God than the body, and ruler of the body[11] implies that "[t]he truly valuable experience, religious or worldly, is one which takes place in the privacy of the soul."[12]

Augustinian anthropology also supported the type of docetic soteriologies, especially imparted to enslaved Africans by European Protestant missionaries, that corresponded well with the institution of slavery.[13] Many Protestant missionaries accepted the myth that Africans were the cursed descendants of the biblical figure Ham and were therefore destined to serve as slaves on plantations owned by whites, who, some even went as far to claim, were the blessed descendants of Ham's brother Japheth. Their dark or "black" complexion indicated African people's moral and cultural inferiority when compared with the light- or "white-" complexioned ruling class.

The missionaries maintained, nonetheless, that, while African people's external features, physical, and cultural traits invited slavery and an inferior existence "naturally" suitable for the cursed descendants of Ham, their interior souls, although black and evil with sin, could be redeemed, and no less so than the souls of their white rulers. They believed that the equality of souls across racial groups was of ultimate value and deserved more consideration than the inequality of bodies across racial groups. They complemented this dualistic anthropology with a stratification of human experience that was concordant with Augustinian anthropology and functioned in consort with white supremacist, anti-African values and practices in the context of slavery. Instructing African converts to tolerate temporal corporeal experiences of physical, emotional, and psychological suffering humbly with the anticipation of post-death soul salvation, the missionaries promised them due compensation for their suffering in an eternal life of heavenly bliss. African converts traded in their fixation upon alleviating their suffering and improving their social condition for a fixation upon the suffering Christ who redeemed their souls from eternal damnation.

Although missionary records show consistent evidence that white missionaries sympathized with their enslaved converts and disapproved of the brutalities inflicted upon them in the slave plantation system, they were often vulnerable to censure by plantation authorities. Thus they accepted and cooperated with slavery to protect their evangelical privileges on the plantations.[14] What is more, they taught African converts that the Christian virtues of obedience, humility, docility, and dependency, when internalized, would equip them with the appropriate moral attitude and spiritual armor to withstand their oppressors. With this type of Christian consciousness, Africans could think less about their concrete social predicament as undernourished, underclothed, brutalized captives as they thought instead about the suffering, crucified Christ who paid the ultimate price for their personal sins and made salvation possible for them.

In the end, the missionaries placed the greatest emphasis upon condemning personal offenses against white enslavers such as stealing from one's master; lying to one's master; running away from one's master; disobeying one's master; and so on.[15] The Eurocentric missionary Christian understanding of morality and suffering made Jesus Christ (who suffered unjustly) the paragon suffering servant for Africans to emulate by obediently enduring, if not embracing, their own unjust suffering as enslaved exiles. Africans realized that Jesus suffered *like* they did; that is, he was tortured by means that were familiar to them.[16] This realization undoubtedly facilitated an existential identification with the missionaries' incarnate Christian divinity. They simultaneously learned that Jesus suffered *for* them, for the absolution of their sins and the redemption of their souls if they would just accept Christ as their personal redeemer and discard heathenism and fetishism forever. Enslaved African converts, brutalized in their bodies and cleansed in their souls, became acceptable candidates for eternal life with the Christian God.

Indeed, far too many enslaved African converts internalized Manichaean anthropologies that privileged soul salvation over bodily emancipation and allowed for popular constructions of Africans as "soulless bodies" or "bodiless souls." Consequently, they adopted *docetic* soteriologies, thereby ignoring their actual bodies and the burdens they bore.[17] This pattern in the black Christian experience points back to Augustine's hierarchical division of knowledge within the soul's dual rational powers. The missionaries evangelized Africans with a pre-understanding that the soul's superior knowledge of God (*sapientia*) leads to contemplation while its inferior knowledge of the world (*scientia*) leads to action or accomplishment. Thus a number of enslaved Africans, prepped for conversion, complied with missionary instructions to: (1) develop a Christian piety that corresponded with their knowledge of God (contemplation) and the redemption of their souls; and (2) ignore their material bodily conditions toward the end of minimizing their knowledge of the world and the resultant likelihood of social praxis (action/accomplishment) in the form of rebellion.[18]

The encounter between Africans and European missionaries provoked an interior experience of duplicity within black Christians. Duplicity characterizes the black Christian experience because adherents have never been able to reconcile the positive value they have been conditioned to assign to *both* the *painful* human experience of physical bondage, corporeal suffering, material poverty, emotional and psychological abuse, and the ecstatic *joyful* human experience of spiritual redemption. The soul/body dualism and docetic soteriologies, in one way or another, continually resurface as challenges to the notion that people of African descent are equal in worth to people of

European descent. It follows then that Augustine's hierarchical conception of the soul and body is not an adequate source to which people of African descent can turn for a theological solution to their anthropological dilemma.

### The Doctrine of the Hamitic Curse and the Predicament of African Enslavement

Converting Africans to embrace a god and religion that showed no regard for their earthly bondage was reasonable to many white missionaries because they relied upon the doctrine of the Hamitic curse to establish that African enslavement was divinely ordained. Although some version of the Hamitic curse was generally propagated by white missionaries wherever they encountered Africans, the doctrine held particular sway over Christian slaveholding culture in the southern United States. Taken from Genesis 9:18–27, the doctrine of the Hamitic curse was the most important theological construction reinforcing the negativity, promiscuity, and immorality of African people and became popular in the United States during the antebellum period, especially between 1831 and 1861.[19] In the biblical narrative, Noah's son Ham observes him drunk and naked, neglects to cover him, and thus incurs Noah's curse upon his son Canaan. Euro-American Christians interpreted this passage as a divine curse against Ham and his African progeny. Although containing no reference to race, through allegorical substitution, the doctrine of the Hamitic curse justified the creation of a white supremacist worldview, especially within the plantation South.

White Christian authorities erroneously taught Africans that they were enslaved because it was sanctioned by God through Noah's curse of Ham and his descendants. Simultaneously, they were taught that they were sinful by nature (original sin) and that the only way to salvation was through the Christian faith. The doctrine of the Hamitic curse was central because it impacted the self-perception of enslaved African Christians at a time when they were being socialized to view themselves as one black *race*. Prior to their experience as enslaved "blacks," they knew themselves to be identified with specific ethnic societies and civilizations in Africa. The doctrine of the Hamitic curse became the new-world myth superseding all old-world African myths about the origin of diverse African ethnic groups. It was thought to explain the specific "origin" of the black race, in the same way that the Adam and Eve story was thought to explain the origin of the human race *qua* the white race.

While abolitionists—both white and black—denounced the claim that Africans were destined through providence to be enslaved by the white race, it was generally accepted that Ham was the progenitor of the African race. In his book *Ham and Japheth: The Mythic World of Whites in the Antebellum South*, Thomas Virgil Peterson documents how (1) the doctrine of the Hamitic curse was widespread in antebellum America; (2) it reinforced and perpetuated racist ideology; and (3) during the antebellum period, when white enslavers were consolidating biblical teachings with ethnological theories "proving" black inferiority, both free blacks and enslaved blacks accepted the theory that Ham was the progenitor of the African race.[20] Despite the reality that many blacks did not go as far as concurring with whites who popularized the myth that slavery was a curse upon the black race, the ideology of race denoting moral and intellectual superiority or inferiority, through constructs like the Hamitic curse, has influenced black people's perception of their blackness and their African heritage.

The internalization of "black" inferiority and "white" superiority by African Americans through Christian traditions does not discount the presence of oppositional indigenous African religio-cultural retentions; nor does it negate the radical tradition of resistance within the African American religious experience. What it does reveal, however, is that Africans in exile were forced to renegotiate their identity within the psychological and linguistic boundaries of a racially constructed culture. Africans influenced by Christianity were consistently indoctrinated to accept white supremacy and simultaneously reminded of their inferior, base, and especially "sinful" nature symbolized by their "black" skins: for the Bible records that God had eliminated all human sin from the earth with the flood. According to many antebellum mythmakers, Ham, then, is the first symbol of sin, the *original sinner*, in the new post-flood world. Through sexual misconduct, Ham becomes cursed with black skin, which would forever be a constant reminder to his descendants of their deviant sexual mores, evil disposition, and diminished status. Consequently, for persons of African descent, blackness is inextricably linked to their progenitor's (Ham's) original sin, or what George D. Kelsey calls a "second fall." Thus "while the Negro shares the universal condemnation of the human race in Adam, he [sic] also bears the added condemnation of God in a special racial fall. Since no promise of renewal and redemption is ever correlated with this second, special, racial fall, the Negro is a permanent victim of history and ultimately without hope."[21]

The history of black religious experience in the United States bears out Kelsey's thesis. The double fall, and especially the second "racial fall," has impacted the African American Christian tradition so negatively precisely because of its inability to distinguish "blackness" as a human identity from evil, shame, sin, guilt, and other self-abnegating experiences known by many practicing Christians. Religious groups like the Nation of Islam and Rastafari have attempted to respond specifically to the problem of evil and blackness in Christian doctrines of humanity by proclaiming the divinity of African people. Their twentieth-century anthropological responses to anti-blackness and anti-Africanness in Christianity come on the heels of nineteenth-century Pan-Africanist responses from prominent black clergy. These men embodied the paradox of opposing African enslavement but promoting and participating in African colonization due to their acceptance of doctrines that only reinforced Christian beliefs that Africans are naturally evil in body, soul, character, and culture.

The paradox is seen most conspicuously in the theological reflections of Alexander Crummell, a significant nineteenth-century African American clergyman and Pan-Africanist. Crummell, a distinguished figure in African American and African religious and socio-political history, responded directly to popular theological understandings of the doctrine of the Hamitic curse by advancing a doctrine of "redemptive providence." By redemptive providence I mean the view that the Christian God is controlling the events of history toward the specific end of redeeming non-Christian people. Unfortunately, Crummell's doctrine of redemptive providence contributed to the theological controversy initiated by Euro-Christian formulations of Manichaean anthropologies, docetic soteriologies as well as the doctrine of the Hamitic curse.

## *Alexander Crummell's Doctrine of Redemptive Providence*

During the nineteenth century many African American religious leaders were at the forefront of abolitionist activities and were instrumental in providing refuge to fugitives and formerly enslaved Africans. Alexander Crummell (1819–98) was one such leader. After tremendous struggles with institutional racism in the Episcopal Church, Crummell was ordained in 1842. Following his ambition to serve as an educator and administrator in an institution where blacks could be properly and indiscriminately instructed, Crummell emigrated to Liberia in 1853 and spent the next twenty years of his life as a missionary and educator in the North American colony. His decision to live and work in Liberia stemmed from a passionate understanding of *God's providential design for Africans.*

Crummell's interpretation of God's providential design is expressly related in his 1862 publication *The Future of Africa*.[22] The work is a collection of Crummell's papers presented at public forums mostly in Liberia. The concluding essay entitled "The Negro Race Not Under a Curse" is a categorical refutation of the Hamitic curse doctrine. Crummell constructs an exegetical counter-argument to disprove the widespread notion that Africans are the cursed descendants of Ham. He points to the fact that in the Genesis passage, it is actually Canaan, one of Ham's four sons, who is cursed and uses the table of nations passage, from the tenth chapter of Genesis, to show that Africans are actually direct descendants of Ham's son Cush. According to Wilson Jeremiah Moses:

> It was of great importance that the black race be descendants of Cush, rather than his brother, Canaan, since the defenders of slavery often cited Noah's curse as proof of the destiny of the black race to be "servants unto their brethren" . . . As descendants of Cush, the contemporary Africans could claim kinship with the founders of Ninevah and Ethiopia. . . . The status of black people in biblical times, the validity of Noah's curse, and the mutability of human affairs were ever present topics with black writers of Crummell's generation.[23]

While Crummell did not subscribe to the standard theological interpretation of the Hamitic curse doctrine, he did accept the typological structure of the doctrine; for Crummell, Africans *were* the descendants of Ham. Although not cursed directly, the figure of Ham is problematic in black religious history because he is connected to undesirable behavior in Scripture and a constructed myth that problematizes black humanity as evil and inferior. Given the historical polemic over the "curse," the simple association of the black race with a controversial progenitor runs the risk of lending some credence to the doctrine. Furthermore, his interpretation of providence, shared by many black contemporaries, was flawed theology, for it provided an alternative reason for black suffering and enslavement and, like the doctrine of the Hamitic curse, honors God for designing the master plan. By advancing a Eurocentric notion of providence, Crummell implied that it was absolutely imperative that some of Ham's progeny undergo slavery in order to receive the blessings of European Christianity and culture. Subsequently, those estranged from Africa had a moral obligation to uplift and mediate the redemption of their "heathen" siblings through various political, religious, and cultural enterprises. One example is Crummell's promotion of the Anglo-Saxon language in Liberia.

The spread of the English language was an essential part of Crummell's program for uplifting the African race. He categorized West African languages as "tongues" and "dialects" having "definite marks of inferiority connected with them all, which place them at the widest distance from civilized languages."[24] Teaching the English language in Liberia would liberate the African consciousness from "lowness of ideas," "brutal and vindictive sentiments, and those principles which show a predominance of the animal propensities."[25] Crummell especially believed that West African languages were devoid of virtuous ideas and moral principles, contributing to the low and depressed condition of the race. Africans, emigrating to the continent from America, were equipped to introduce new concepts about liberty, civilized government, and religion to their kinfolk by training them to speak the English language.

Crummell's doctrine of redemptive providence enabled him to downplay the "sorrowful history" that accompanied the socialization of enslaved Africans in America. Thus, he could denounce the context of coercion and subjugation in which African Americans adopted their enslavers' language and in the same breath assert that "this fact of humiliation seems to have been one of those ordinances of Providence designed as a means for the introduction of new ideas into the language of a people; or to serve as the transitional step from low degradation to a higher nobler civilization."[26] Here and elsewhere, Crummell harmonizes the tension between slavery and redemption, or rather, a certain type of liberation from degrading African ways of life. In applying a redemptive providence doctrine to the African experience, he acknowledges slavery as the evil situation that eventually brings about the good results of preparing African Americans to Christianize and civilize the African continent. The assumption Crummell makes is that the latter "good" outweighs the former evil; the eventual good results are greater than the precipitating evil event. For example, in his speech "Progress of Civilization Along the West Coast of Africa," Crummell declared that

> the whole of Negroland seems, without doubt, to be given up to the English language, and hence to the influence of Anglo-Saxon life and civilization. It is a most singular providence that that very people, who have most largely participated in the slave-trade, should have been brought, by the power of God's dealings, and in the workings of His plans, to bear the weighty burden of lifting up this large section of humanity to manhood and of illuminating them with Christian light and knowledge. Does any one here doubt this providence? Do any of you question the obligation?[27]

Crummell's speeches, letters, and sermons are replete with the idea that God's redemptive providence, which is always necessary and good, determines the events of history for African people.

A proper analysis of Crummell's ideas also places him in the evangelical Christian context of nineteenth-century America where it was assumed that God controlled all unfolding events of history. Not only was Crummell a pious Christian and educated minister, he was also burdened with the dilemma of rationalizing the historical experience of African enslavement. As an African in America, his answer to the questions all human beings ask about the meaning of life had to include some rationally acceptable explanation for the systematic black suffering and subjugation that had been occurring for centuries before his time.

Crummell vehemently opposed the doctrine of the Hamitic curse because it was biblically unfounded and overtly racist; it was not the destiny of Africans to *serve* the white race. Crummell did not accept for one moment that the Christian God *desired* black suffering. He attempted instead to advance an argument that would de-emphasize any divine sanctioning of black suffering and thus, he emphasized divine sanction of black redemption in America and later in Africa. The problem with Crummell's understanding of redemptive provi-dence is that it functions rationally only to the extent that one ac-cepts the view that African culture is ignominious while European culture is redemptive.

In the end, Crummell's internalization of white supremacy and a Eurocentric notion of progress, coupled with his doctrine of redemp-tive providence, create an inadequate basis for developing affirming doctrines of humanity from a black theological perspective. It can be inferred from Crummell's argument that the causative factor of Afri-can enslavement is not a curse but the inferior status of Africans. The question remains: Why is one race (white) blessed with the resources to mediate the salvation of another (black)? While Crummell rejects the doctrine of the Hamitic curse, he is not able to find a just answer to the causality question, and ultimately to the theodical question of black suffering, with his doctrine of redemptive providence.

### *Implications for Contemporary Black Theological Discourse*

Since the advent of academic black theology in the late 1960s, both black male and Womanist theologians have developed theological perspectives that emphasize the connection between a God of libera-tion and the black experience of oppression. In this vein, their reflec-tions upon Christian doctrine pertain more to christology than to any other doctrine. James Cone makes the case that only through reflec-tion upon Jesus Christ do black theologians proclaim God's concern for the black oppressed. God's incarnation in Jesus (a politically op-pressed first-century Palestinian Jew from humble parentage) is the most concrete demonstration of God's solidarity with poor and op-pressed blacks. In addition, Jesus' ministry to the afflicted, oppressed, and outcast is more evidence of God's will to liberate blacks from earthly forms of oppression, especially sociopolitical oppression.[28]

Although black male and Womanist theologians have not consid-ered the doctrine of humanity as extensively as they have christology, their analyses of black people's experiences of dehumanization entail specific remarks about black theological anthropology and related themes of suffering, sin, chosenness, power, freedom, and servanthood. Jacquelyn Grant, for example, confesses her personal inability to claim servanthood as an essential aspect of her Christian identity. Calling servanthood "a theological dilemma," she links her discomfort with the term to a critical analysis of black people's bondage in America and the particular exploitation of black female domestic servants in post-emancipation America.[29] Grant does not attempt to reconcile her discomfort with "servant" terminology. Rather she argues against the devaluation of people who perform stigmatized roles of service in the social order. In the end, Grant maintains that all Christians, including women, are called to a life of discipleship, which she correlates with the experience of deliverance from the sin of servanthood so often imposed upon black women and the black community.[30]

In his early work, James Cone defined sin as a communal notion and noted its significance for the black community as "a loss of identity." Cone's analysis of the demonic impact of whiteness upon anomie within the black community and the estrangement between the black community and the black God of liberation makes clear the social nature of sin and black theology's rejection of any exclusive preoccupation with personal sin and redemption.[31]

James Evans explores the theme of anomie more deeply in his narrative theology, associating the African experience of dislocation and exile with "the Fall." He maintains that "the expulsion of the first woman and man from the garden of Eden is as much the evidence as it is the consequence of the Fall."[32] Referring to the experiences of Gustavus Vassa, an eighteenth-century African who was kidnapped into slavery from the modern-day region of Nigeria, Evans argues that physical location and social location are intertwined in the African American experience and thus deserve substantial consideration in black theological anthropology. Evans's outline for a black theological anthropology and reinterpretation of the Fall accommodates: (1) an examination of the relationship between African people's exilic status in colonial America and Western Christian doctrines of anthropology, (2) a critical engagement of black theological responses to dislocation and dehumanization in the American experience, and (3) an examination of classical African theological and philosophical ideas as an important source for a black theological anthropology.[33]

My scrutiny of Western Christian doctrines of anthropology and nineteenth-century black responses to enslavement and dehumanization supports Grant's critique of servanthood as sinful. However, it also engenders a rejection of other terms like "the Fall" and "deliverance" in that they carry too much negative theological baggage for black theological construction. The Fall indicts each individual for offending God and is associated with Jesus' deliverance from sin as the only means to reconciliation with God. Evans's interpretation of

expulsion as a *"consequence* of the Fall" in black theology also implies
that exiled and enslaved Africans/blacks were personally culpable for
their experience of dislocation and bondage in the American experience. His use of the term "expulsion" is more consistent, however,
with the African experience of exile, and involuntary servitude in
America when viewed only as *"evidence* of 'the Fall' " (that is, as evidence of dislocation). Interpreted as dislocation, the Fall symbolizes
the Original catastrophic Violation of human community. Taking into
account the social and psychological significance of Christian theology in its reinforcement of black people's dehumanization, the Fall as
a catastrophic and irreversible Offense against persons of African descent by persons of European descent is an indispensable category for
any constructive black theological anthropology.

In connection with this, it is theologically misleading to conceive
of blacks as born with original sin and as candidates for reconciliation
with God through the redemption offered by Jesus Christ. What is
primordial about black people is suffering, not sin. Blacks are born
with a Primordial Suffering caused by the Original Violation of avarice
egregiously expressed in the institution of slavery and attendant ubiq-
uitous forms of racist aggression against people of African descent by
people of European descent. The truth is that, after four centuries of
relating to Jesus Christ, blacks have not found "deliverance" from the
immoral Original Offense against them nor from their resultant Primordial Suffering. Furthermore, in line with Delores Williams's Womanist theology, standard orthodox doctrines of redemption reinforce
black people's Primordial Suffering by sacralizing their identification
with suffering.[34]

My approach to constructing a doctrine of anthropology for the
African American community begins with accepting the reality that
the Original Violation or Original Offense has happened. It is both an
irreversible event and an ambiguous yet concrete condition.[35] But
while irreversible, it is a most condensed, peculiar, and particular
expression of greed. Ultimately, greed is a universal immoral desire[36]
which disrupts and violates human community but can be controlled
toward the end of alleviating Primordial Suffering by promoting normative African values of good character,[37] hospitality, and abundant
life.[38] Laurenti Magesa maintains that, "in African religious ethical
thought . . . greed constitutes the most grievous wrong." It is "the
antonym of hospitality and sociability, or . . . good company . . .
greed destroys the 'communitarian' purpose of the universe and is
immoral."[39] My position is that greed—the root cause of African people's dislocation, enslavement, and disorientation in America for the
past four centuries—is also the "most grievous wrong" for the African
American community. Greed is the Original Condition provoking the
loss of identity among exiled Africans and their descendants' struggle

to find meaning in being human while perpetually unfree. The struggle is especially observable in the pattern of associating human worth with Primordial Suffering in African American Christian consciousness.

Historically, black Christians have tended to derive human worth from Primordial Suffering as they attempt to make their daily experiences, organized responses to oppression, and their relationship to God meaningful and purposeful. Alexander Crummell's nineteenth-century theology of redemptive providence and Martin Luther King's twentieth-century theology of redemptive suffering are two examples of this tendency in black religious thought. As discussed above, Crummell valorized the suffering endured by enslaved Africans as a necessary component of God's redemptive providence. King, on the other hand, valorized the suffering blacks were encountering in their organized protests against racial oppression as socially and spiritually redemptive for African Americans and the larger American society. Indeed, the positive value associated with multiple forms of human suffering in Christian theology, hymnody, iconography, and popular culture provides a spiritual context and rationale for the self-inflicted violation that takes place when Africans confuse human worth with Primordial Suffering.

Black theologians have tried to address the problem of Primordial Suffering in the African American experience through their interpretations of the cross. In their reflections on the significance of the cross for African Americans, black male theologians and some Womanist theologians distinguish between the experiences of suffering caused by social oppression and the suffering endured when resisting social oppression.[40] They denounce the former as enslaving and consistent with white oppressive theology and affirm the latter as consistent with the liberating cross of Jesus. The distinction, though, is apparently too subtle to overcome the tendency in black Christian culture of collapsing the two types of suffering in the comforting symbol of Jesus' redemptive cross.

In constructing a black theological anthropology, the incipient task then is to develop theologically competent terminology and symbols that distinguish between human worth and Primordial Suffering. Potential resources for this task might be appropriated from pragmatic post-Christian theological anthropologies of the Nation of Islam and Rastafari that emphasize the divine nature of black people, and from continental African understandings of hospitable community and its significance for personal human worth and identity formation. In their complete departure from orthodox and popular Christian anthropologies, the Nation of Islam and Rastafari together suggest that any attempt to retain traditional Christian symbols and categories in constructing a black theological anthropology is counterproductive.

Traditional notions of the Fall and redemption offer no tenable resources for alleviating Primordial Suffering because they seek to explain how humans have offended God through pride and disobedience rather than how humans violate and offend human community through accumulated acts of greed. They also identify a foundational offensive impulse in every human being and attribute to it a congenital condition of original sin, which obscures the orthodox claim that human beings are essentially good. My understanding of greed as a human desire and expression is pragmatic rather than essentialist and is specifically related to my postmodern theological analysis of black people's dehumanizing experiences with evil and suffering. It is not spurred by the need to provide generic explanations for universal human evil, which is the starting point for Augustine's pre-modern theological anthropology.

Given the dehumanizing experiences of people of African descent since the Original Violation, I reject the Western Christian essentialist preoccupation with nature and origins and would decline to make any judgments about African people's human nature. I am most compelled by the transformative potential for alleviating Primordial Suffering and the opportunity for human fulfillment found in classical African ethical approaches to community, and would instead emphasize what black human beings can *become* when empowered to develop good character through hospitable virtues that celebrate and sustain abundant life.

## *Conclusion*

From a black theological perspective, addressing the dehumanizing anthropological predicament that qualifies black Christian identity necessarily involves critical assessments of anthropological doctrines in the history of Western Christian thought and black people's responses to those doctrines. As we enter a new millennium, Christians of African descent are still struggling with lingering anthropological issues that problematize black humanity in orthodox and popular Christian theologies. Black theologians interested in anthropology will have to define a postmodern theological orientation for applying a "hermeneutics of suspicion" to the construct of the Fall (of original sin) and redemption and for pondering the moral and spiritual consequences of the Original Violation for black people.

# Response

## by Nancy Pineda-Madrid

A number of similarities and differences emerge in the approaches used by Dianne Stewart and myself. In our essays, we both center our attention on the impact of theological reflection on our communities; therefore, we begin with the questions: What is the most life-giving way to understand ourselves as both Christian believers and subjugated peoples in the throws of undeserved suffering? How do we make sense of this dilemma in such a way that values our human fullness or wholeness? Our essays bear the mark of liberationist discourse. This may seem a rather obvious beginning place, yet much contemporary theological discourse begins elsewhere with questions such as: What is the most credible argument for reconciling belief in a good and powerful God with the reality of evil? Rarely is this question explicitly examined from the perspective of a specific cultural, racial, socio-political location. Second, both of us are well aware of the powerful role of narrative in creating a compelling worldview, one that shapes imaginations. Narrative stimulates not only our cognitive faculties but also our creative and emotional abilities. Stewart's examination of the Genesis account of Ham, along with her analysis of its varied interpretations, and my analysis of Sandra Cisneros's *Woman Hollering Creek* as a reinterpretation of the age-old legend of La Lloróna, both exemplify this critical awareness. Yet our approaches differ in some important aspects. Stewart grounds her work in a historical and critical assessment of Western Christian anthropology's interpretation of black suffering, illuminating its inadequacies. I, in contrast, ground mine in an interpretation of contemporary Chicana literature, illuminating some of its possibilities for theological insight. In other words, we turn to different kinds of resources to clarify the experience of our communities. Additionally, we look at suffering through different lenses. Stewart examines suffering through the lens of racist and anti-African systems of belief, and I, on the other hand, explore suffering as the composite of various sources.

While these and other similarities and differences deserve further reflection, I want to address one particular, shared concern. What is the relationship between suffering and human nature? Is suffering

184

itself essential or integral to being human? In what sense, if any, does the experience of suffering enhance human nature? Is it possible to live both a full life and a life void of any serious suffering? Or, is suffering distinct from human nature, in other words, not essential to humanity, but an unavoidable dimension of human life fully lived? Whether one claims either that suffering is essential to human nature, or that suffering is an existential part of the human condition, makes a world of difference.

Stewart and I both conclude that suffering must be understood as a dimension of human existence but not as essential to human nature. If one identifies suffering with human nature, then one's operative anthropology tends to become human-as-victim. What is wrong with this anthropology? People whose central self-definition is victim, predominately see themselves as their sufferings, as people whom life has dealt a raw deal. Hence, these individuals become objects and not subjects of their own lives. Any people who routinely experience institutionalized injustices (racism, sexism, classism, heterosexism, and so forth) may feel tempted to slip into a human-as-victim anthropology. However, the doctrine of *imago dei* invalidates such an anthropology. *Imago dei*, namely that God made human beings in God's own image, means that God gave humans the capacity to co-create their own lives and the world. (Co-create means that ideally humans in cooperation with God forge their lives and their world.) People who fundamentally define themselves as victims abdicate their God-given capacity and birthright. Even in the most oppressive of life circumstances, human beings invariably possess some potential to shape their own self-understanding. The movie *Life Is Beautiful* illustrates the realization of this human capacity. Within the confines of a Nazi concentration camp, a Jewish father creates a world for his son (and perhaps for himself as well), such that he may continue to believe in the utter gift of life and the basic goodness of humanity. Over time the human-as-victim anthropology will result in the destruction of the human spirit and soul because suffering itself takes possession of the human soul and snuffs out any possibility of hope, leaving only despair.

On the other hand, if one holds that suffering is a dimension of human existence, then one's operative anthropology can become human-as-made-for-freedom. By freedom, I mean the capacity and possibility to co-create one's life by means of the life-decisions one makes. The creating of one's life occurs not only externally in the readily observable life-decisions one makes, but also interiorly in the way one understands oneself as an individual, as a member of society, as part of the whole of creation, and as in relationship with God. Sojourner Truth's famous soliloquy *Ain't I a Woman* powerfully illustrates the difference between her understanding of herself as *woman* and the operative white definition of *woman*. While the freedom to shape one's life outwardly can be severely limited (e.g., the life experience of Latino/a farm-workers) or even all but eliminated (e.g., the life experience of African Americans during the institution of slavery), the interior freedom to choose one's self-understanding can never be taken away without one's cooperation. Even in the context of extreme suffering, how one chooses to interpret one's suffering can either enhance or reduce one's freedom. Nonetheless, the very capacity of human beings to step back and offer some account of their suffering, some interpretation of their affliction provides a warrant for the human-as-made-for-freedom anthropology. While an understanding of suffering as part of human existence, not human essence, is implicit in both of our essays, Stewart and I arrive at this claim by different means.

Stewart situates her work within the arena of suffering as part of human existence when she asserts that black theology needs to draw a sharp distinction between human worth (essence) and Primordial Suffering (human existence). She criticizes theologians and Christians who blur the lines between human worth and Primordial Suffering either by suggesting that the former derives from the latter or by confusing the two. For African Americans to find meaning in their humanity, the greed that leads to Primordial Suffering must be subverted by a recovery of classical African communal values and virtues. In other words, she issues a clarion call to African American Christians to seek abundant life through African resources that underscore "human worth and identity formation." In so doing, I believe that Stewart implies that the essence of African American humanity, while marked by suffering, invariably transcends it. Ultimately, African American humanity is other than suffering.

My own work presumes that suffering is part of human existence, not essence. From the onset, I put forward various potential interpretations of suffering through my analysis of both Cisneros's and Moraga's work. My presumption here is that Latinas (and all human beings) have the capacity to choose how they will interpret their experience of suffering. In the very act of stepping back from the experience of suffering, taking account of it and assigning some meaning to it, human beings exercise their God-given capacity as subjects of their lives, which includes their experiences of suffering. Latinas define their suffering; it does not and must not define them. Moreover, if one believes, as I do, that God wills justice in *this* life, then God incessantly calls Latinas to, and supports Latinas in, their struggle against all suffering precipitated by injustices and all suffering that is destructive of humanity. Absent such a struggle, despair takes possession of the human soul. Suffering in and of itself does not enhance Latinas' humanity, but how Latinas choose to interpret their suffering has a direct impact on their humanity.

# 10

## *In Search of a Theology of Suffering,* Latinamente[1]

### NANCY PINEDA-MADRID

T HE EXPERIENCE OF SUFFERING can push us to the edge of belief
and consequently functions as a primal font of theology.[2] Suffering brings us face to face with our failures, and with the stinging
effects of life's stubborn limits. When we face our child's alcoholism,
the loss of our employment, or the growing problem of hunger world-
wide, we confront the wide chasm between life's limitations and our
desire for more. Such leads us to question the meaning of life and
therefore to the cornerstone upon which theology rests. This essay
explores this question from a distinctive cultural perspective, namely
the perspective of Latinas.[3] A Latina cultural lens can enable us to
glimpse that which is universal in the experience of suffering. This
essay offers an account of the theological significance of suffering[4]
based on the lives of Latinas as represented in selected works by two
Latina literary artists, Sandra Cisneros[5] and Cherríe Moraga.[6] Accordingly, this essay focuses on how Latinas deal with and interpret their
suffering rather than on how Latinas address the causes of suffering.
In their drive to make sense of their lives, Latinas inevitably interpret
their suffering. Any interpretation betrays a particular life orientation.
For example, for many Latinas, a liberative, God-centered orientation
necessarily means that their suffering must be understood in light of
the redemption of all people.

The first section of this three-part essay consists of a summary of
selected works by Cisneros and Moraga in which each explores different manifestations of suffering. Why use the work of Latina artists?
Meaningful art enables participants both to explore the depth of experience and to tap into the unconscious underpinnings of their reality, and thereby know themselves more fully. Even though Cisneros
and Moraga are exceptional artists, their work does not yield defini-

tive nor universally valid statements about Latinas' experience—an impossible task—but their work does provide the raw material from which some insight into the lives of Latinas can be gleaned.[7] In the second section, based upon the portraits put forward by Cisneros and Moraga, this essay examines *how* Latinas engage suffering, and *which* strategies support their search for wholeness. In the final section, I present a theological interpretation of suffering based on two essential themes: the virtue of courage and the redemption of all people.

## Suffering Through the Eyes of Cisneros and Moraga

In her short story, "Woman Hollering Creek," Cisneros's central character, Cleófilas, becomes increasingly aware of the complexity of her own suffering. Cisneros draws her readers' attention to the tale of Cleófilas's physically abusive marriage and she artfully portrays the unraveling of the life threads that keep Cleófilas's abuse in place. She also depicts Cleófilas's re-weaving of her life toward greater well-being and flourishing.

"Woman Hollering Creek," which reinterprets the legend of La Lloróna, begins in the hubbub of Cleófilas's wedding plans. As her father Don Serafín tells Cleófilas goodbye, he hugs her, saying *"I am your father, I will never abandon you."*[8] Cisneros quickly flashes forward to the present in which Cleófilas sits by the creek's edge with her young son Juan Pedrito, painfully ruminating about "how when a man and a woman love each other, sometimes that love sours. But a parent's love for a child, a child's for its parents, is another thing entirely." This scene foreshadows the painful disintegration of her marriage and the return to her father's house. In a sharp break in her train of thought, Cleófilas recalls her adolescent years, a time when through *telenovelas*[9] like *Tú o Nadie,*[10] she grew to anticipate a marriage "full of happily ever after," one filled with "passion in its purest crystalline essence." These recollections set up the story's pivotal dramatic tension. This tension contrasts Cleófilas's dreams and fantasies about married life with the cruel reality of her circumstances. In her musings, Cleófilas relays her curiosity about the creek named *La Gritona,*[11] speculating about whether the creek hollers from "pain or rage." Cleófilas's curiosity leads her to ask her neighbor ladies, Soledad and Dolores,[12] about how the creek got its name, but they do not remember. Sharply intruding into her placid recollections is the horrifying memory of the first time Juan Pedro struck her, splitting her lip. Cleófilas's subsequent series of flashbacks discloses her own ongoing experience of physical abuse and growing isolation. The fantasies and dreams she held for her marriage are now fully shattered, mirrored in the *telenovela* title, *María de Nadie,*[13] which she contrasts with her own name *"Cleófilas de . . . "* For the sake of his second child, which she is carrying, Cleófilas pleads with and finally convinces Juan Pedro to take her to the doctor. During her doctor's appointment she meets Graciela and Felice,[14] who, seeing her "black-and-blue marks all over," respond to her cry for help. Cleófilas's transformation is marked by an escape in Felice's truck across *La Gritona*. Thus begins the first leg of her journey back to her father's home. During this ride, for the first time, Cleófilas experiences "a gurgling out of her own throat, a long ribbon of laughter, like water."[15]

Well aware of how different forms of suffering reinforce one another and create a web which it is difficult to break, Cisneros emphasizes Cleófilas's overwhelming trauma and physical abuse at the hands of Juan Pedro to stress the complexity of Cleófilas's situation. Not only does she communicate Cleófilas's shock at the discovery that she is in an abusive relationship, but Cisneros links this discovery to the anticipatory terror of unpredictable yet inevitable future beatings.

> The first time she had been so surprised she didn't cry out or try to defend herself. She had always said she would strike back if a man, any man, were to strike her. But when the moment came, and he slapped her once, and then again, and again; until the lip split and bled an orchid of blood, she didn't fight back, she didn't break into tears, she didn't run away as she imagined she might when she saw such things in the *telenovelas*.[16] . . . Cleófilas's distress intensifies when she learns through the daily newspapers of women badly beaten, some even killed by their husbands, lovers or fathers.[17]

Cleófilas's experience of abuse is further complicated by a related but distinct form of suffering, her sense of powerlessness expressed in her silence. In other words, she lacks the imagination to see herself speaking (much less acting) on her own behalf. The initial shock of being beaten silences her instantly. Early in the story, Cleófilas does not choose to be silent, which would necessitate her agency, but instead she is silenced, her voice taken from her. Through much of the narrative Cleófilas seemingly lives a *self*-less life, one defined almost exclusively by her deference to Juan Pedro. As Cisneros discloses Cleófilas's inner thoughts, her diffuse sense of self becomes more apparent.[18] Cisneros suggests that there is no self who can respond. Cleófilas's silenced self is continually juxtaposed with the creek's name, *La Gritona*. It is as if Cleófilas is *La Gritona* suppressed and muted. Thus remains Cleófilas until the end of the story when she releases a joyous laughter from her depths.

Finally, Cleófilas's isolation and the limitations of her role models likewise contribute to her suffering. Raised with powerful social expectations, Cleófilas, prior to the time of her marriage, exudes much hope about her future with Juan Pedro. Her parents' blessing suffices.

She quite confidently and willingly steps into the role of wife and mother as it is defined by others, family and neighbors. Yet her experiences of physical abuse, her *telenovela*-informed marriage fantasies and her internalized, but externally defined, models of "good wife and mother," create a deepening isolation. She has not created the kind of marriage which she so eagerly idealized. Cisneros conveys Cleófilas's isolation in part through the symbolism of the two women neighbors, Soledad and Dolores, who together represent the world that circumscribes Cleófilas. These neighbors validate the idea that Cleófilas's life is unavoidably defined by painful limitations. Interactions with Juan Pedro's friends affirm the same message. Through a series of sketches, Cisneros sharpens the picture of Cleófilas's isolation. In one sketch, Cleófilas compares her life to the lives of *telenovela* women: only hers appears relentlessly and increasingly despairing. "And there were no commercials in between for comic relief. And no happy ending in sight."[19]

In the selected works of Moraga, taken from *Loving in the War Years* and *The Last Generation*, she employs a memoir genre through which she prods her readers to reflect on suffering in their own lives. Moraga's autobiographical vignettes not only encourage self-awareness but also disclose her perception of the eternal, richly present in day-to-day experiences. Moraga explores suffering precipitated by the angst of being caught between two languages and by the undervaluing of female humanity.

Moraga conveys her sense of loss and anguish as she struggles with the limitations of the English language. For her, English words cannot sufficiently disclose who she is nor what she feels. Even though fluent in English, Moraga finds that unless she breaks through her English-dominant world the deepest part of her will remain silenced.

> I am "born American." College English educated, but what I must admit is that I have felt in my writing that the English was not cutting it. ¿Entiendes?[20] That there is something else, deep and behind my heart and I want to hold it hot and bold in the hands of my writing and it will not come out sounding like English. Te prometo. No es inglés.[21]

Early in life Moraga became aware that being a female meant that she would be treated as a second-class human. Not only did this second-class status operate within her family but popular myths explaining the origins of her people also supported this idea. In her reflections, Moraga laments the pain and distortion these experiences and myths foster in female-male relationships. In her family, this painful norm persists.

> When my sister and I were fifteen and fourteen, respectively, and my brother a few years older, we were still waiting on him. I write "were"

as if now, nearly two decades later, it were over. But that would be a lie. To this day in my mother's home, my brother and father are waited on, including by me. I do this now out of respect for my mother and her wishes. In those early years, however, it was mainly in relation to my brother that I resented providing such service. For unlike my father, who sometimes worked as much as seventy hours a week to feed my face every day, the only thing that earned my brother my servitude was his maleness.[22]

Moraga recognizes that such distorted female-male relationships thrive, in part, due to the support rendered by ancient myths which explain and endorse a patriarchal world order. Rather than merely critiquing one such Mesoamerican Nahua (Aztec) myth,[23] Moraga chooses to reinterpret it. In her reinterpretation the myth no longer authorizes a patriarchal world order but becomes an explanation of the origins of distorted female-male relationships. At stake in this reinterpretation is nothing short of "misogyny, war, and greed." Will Latinas continue to participate blindly in a patriarchal world order and take on the suffering it fosters? Or might Latinas be able to imagine a different kind of world? Moraga begins her reinterpretation of the Nahua myth of Coatlicue's birthing of Huitzilopochtli by asking her readers to imagine

> la Mechicana before the "Fall," before shame, before betrayal, before Eve, Malinche, and Guadalupe . . . [female humanity] is more than the bent back in the fields, more than the assembly-line fingers and the rigid body beneath him in bed, more than the veiled face above the rosary beads. She is more than the sum of all these fragmented parts.[24]

Moraga queries: Can we imagine a whole female humanity, one that existed before the brokenness which we now know? How did woman become so wounded and broken? What led to the envious tension which characterizes our female-male relationships? Moraga reinterprets the myth,

> *Según la leyenda, Coatlicue, "Madre de los Dioses,"[25] is sweeping on top of the mountain, Coatepec, when she discovers two beautiful feathers. Thinking that later she will place them on her altar, she stuffs them into her apron and continues sweeping. But without [her] noticing, the feathers begin to gestate there next to her womb and Coatlicue, already advanced in age, soon discovers that she is pregnant.*
>
> *When her daughter, Coyolxauhqui, learns that her mother is about to give birth to Huitzilopochtli, God of War, she is incensed. And, along with her siblings, the Four Hundred Stars, she conspires to kill Coatlicue rather than submit to a world where War would become God.*

> *Huitzilopochtli is warned of this by a hummingbird and vows to defend his mother. At the moment of birth, he murders Coyolxauhqui, cutting off her head and completely dismembering her body.*
>
> *Breast splits from chest splits from hip splits from thigh from knee from arm and foot. Coyolxauhqui is banished to the darkness and becomes the moon, la diosa de la luna.*[26]

In exploring suffering in the lives of Latinas, Moraga insists that the struggle between patriarchal motherhood and the rebellious daughter continues to this day. Moraga identifies Coyolxauhqui with "la fuerza femenina,"[27] namely our efforts to pick up and mend the brokenness of female humanity. Chicanas, she claims, are about this task when they write their stories, draw and paint their world, dance to the music of their souls, in other words, in the manifold ways Chicanas interpret and reinterpret who they are. Each effort strives after the female eternal, the female divine.

By recognizing the complexity of suffering, Cisneros and Moraga point to the way in which we can inadvertently allow suffering to become entrenched, in other words the way in which our experience of suffering can shape how we understand ourselves. In their portrayals, suffering is not only physical but also psychological, not only multi-generational but also spiritual, not only externally provoked but also inwardly triggered. Suffering is not simple. Cleófilas's suffering results from the gestalt created by her physical abuse and by her internalized, rigid, social beliefs. This can either paralyze her or impel her to seek out something more.

Significantly, Cisneros and Moraga call attention to the stakes involved in attending to the experience of suffering. Their work suggests that when suffering is glossed over, ignored, or deemed insignificant, it becomes a dead fragment within us which not only endures from one generation to the next but also manifests itself in destructive patterns. Implicit in their work is the role of the imagination. It substantially determines whether suffering will become an occasion for transformation or for debilitation. After Moraga faces the reality that English will not adequately disclose who she is, it is her pain coupled with imagination which spurs her to create a language which will be ample enough for her desires.

What is not covered in the selected works of Cisneros and Moraga? Their works prod and push Latinas toward liberation, toward a more whole experience of life. But what is the character of the liberation they propose? Is it individual or social or both? Does it transcend the boundaries of Latina sisterhood and if so, how far does this liberation stretch? These are questions that the selected works of Cisneros and Moraga do not substantially explore. In the last section of this essay I will present a theological interpretation of suffering in light of these questions.

## Grappling with Suffering, Seeking Wholeness

Only when Latinas take their suffering, and their search for wholeness, seriously can they in turn contribute to the redemption of all
people.[28] Latinas do not take their suffering seriously when they
choose to resign themselves passively to it, seeking only to escape its
effects. Escape strategies typically take on forms such as addiction,
avoidance, suppression, or trivialization. Ultimately these strategies
lead to the deterioration of a person's spirit and soul because in the
process of escaping, the wounded, pain-filled part of their interior
hardens into numbness. Moreover, as a person continues to use escape strategies, they will increasingly respond to the sufferings of
society with apathy, illusion, and superficiality.[29] Second, Latinas do
not take their suffering seriously when they blindly seek to eliminate
suffering and its sources by any means necessary, without regard to
the consequences. Strategies aimed at the destruction of the cause of
suffering can and often do result in the destruction of some "good"
as well. The cause of suffering is rarely, if ever, purely evil. Suffering is
not only complex but its role in our lives is ambiguous.[30]

Cisneros and Moraga offer a third response to suffering, one that
values human flourishing. They each recognize that *we must come to
terms with what suffering means and how it functions.* For if the question
of meaning and function is not asked, there can be no possible pathos
in the face of the suffering of others, no vision to guide the struggle
against evil. Interpretation is pivotal. The interpretation of suffering
reveals not only an orienting vision for the engagement of suffering
but also a value-laden vision of humanity itself.[31] How Latinas discover meaning and seek wholeness in their suffering comes to light
when Latinas seek community, when Latinas struggle to find their
voice and when Latinas tenaciously discern truth.

### Seeking Community

Individuals and communities are fully interrelated in that they interpret and shape each other's experience. The communities of which
Latinas are a part interpret, via social ethos and mores, how Latinas
grapple with suffering. Conversely, Latinas interpret how their communities frame the experience of suffering. This dynamic, reciprocal
relationship of interpretation creates the space in which growth and
transformation can flourish, or be destructively undermined.

Cleófilas, aware of her own isolation and pain, seeks understanding
and companionship from her neighbors Soledad and Dolores. But,
they fail to be the community that she so desperately needs because
they exclusively define themselves in terms of their ability to fulfill
the social roles of "good wife and mother" assigned to them by a
patriarchal world order. Consequently, they fail to take much of their

own suffering seriously, and therefore cannot possibly support Cleó-filas's desire for more. In contrast, upon seeing Cleófilas's beaten body and hearing her story, Graciela and Felice immediately respond. In a moment which can only be described as grace-filled, this new trinity of women forms the community which enables Cleófilas's courageous steps toward her own wholeness.[32] These women provide not only the material resources but, equally if not more importantly, a vision of female humanity whose value transcends the roles Cleófilas per-forms. Thus, Cleófilas's suffering becomes the prod for her discovery of new life within herself. Cleófilas notices and admires the model of interior freedom so evident in Felice, which perhaps foreshadows Cleófilas's future self-understanding.

Moraga uses her personal narrative to illustrate sharply how heal-ing or further destructiveness weigh in the balance of the interdependent interpretations of individuals and communities. In her recollections of how females are treated as second-class humans, Moraga highlights the common practice of women waiting on men who "deserve" such treatment by virtue of their maleness alone. Moreover, within this worldview, "good" women do not resent their inferior position. Yet resentment simmers among some Latinas who ceaselessly observe and challenge the historically widespread interpre-tation of female as inferior. Do these Latinas seek each other out based on their shared disaffection, or do these Latinas seek relationships with one another based on a shared search for wholeness? Moraga's reinterpretation of the Mesoamerican legend of Coyolxauhqui re-minds us that Latinas are *more* than woundedness, *more* than the scars which mark their experiences of suffering. Wholeness necessitates that Latinas simultaneously seek each other out and seek a critical appreciation of this *more*.

### Coming to Voice

Suffering can propel Latinas to find their voice. Cisneros portrays Cleófilas as a woman who, prior to her marriage, lacks an authentic voice. Through her stream of consciousness we learn that Cleófilas's "voice" and those of the community are intermeshed, with no clear boundaries.[33] Even so, Cleófilas does not surrender her sense of self, weak though it may be. As the story progresses, Cleófilas moves from *being silenced* (during this period Juan Pedro is her voice) to *choosing to be silent.* Externally these two behaviors appear the same, but they are not. Her pregnancy signals her own coming transformation, her growing ability to voice her sufferings, to cry out for more from life. Suffering painfully affords Cleófilas an opportunity to develop her voice, to define more clearly who she is and what she stands for. Throughout, Cleófilas possesses enough self-appreciation to support the development of her respect for her own voice. Undoubtedly, Graciela and Felice's authority-filled voices stir her, awakening Cleófilas's own dormant dream of a self-possessed life, one of ever-deepening inner freedom. As Cleófilas crosses *La Gritona* she laughs, signaling the birth of a new self.

Moraga emphasizes one facet of the relationship between suffering and coming to voice in her vignette on the inadequacy of the English language. She calls attention to a subtle, but nonetheless real, form of suffering, a form exceptionally difficult to name. She recounts her struggle with "living Spanish" but "speaking English," unable to adequately express her deep feelings exclusively in either language.[34] If she had resigned herself to the use of proper English or even proper Spanish, she would have truncated her voice. Language inevitably both enables and limits our affective and cognitive patterns, but when a person is fluent in two or more languages, there are times when neither language fittingly captures their experience. Paradoxically, the language of greatest fluency may be woefully inadequate for expressing what is most deeply felt. Moraga knows this. Rather than allowing herself to be defined by and limited to the confines of English or Spanish, Moraga reveals a willingness to map out a space for herself at the chaotic crossroads of two languages. Not settling for a voice which does not suit, she creates one which will. Out of her pain, she creates a new "language." It will not sound like English but it will not sound like Spanish either.

As Moraga shares her account of waiting on her father and brother, she notes that the women of her mother's generation did not voice "a word of resentment." She invites readers to wonder: Did these women uncritically accept their socially imposed, subordinate position? Or did they recognize their position and knowingly choose to be silent? Was their silence one of oblivious acceptance or one of internalized pain? On this occasion, Moraga contrasts the silence of her mother's generation with her own decision to call critical attention to the inferior position relegated to female humanity. Suffering at times needlessly continues because of a casual and silent acceptance of the status quo.

### Discerning Truth

Through their discernment of truth, Latinas begin exploring the possible meaning of their suffering.[35] Cisneros, during her short story, intensifies the contrast between Cleófilas's marriage fantasies as portrayed in the *telenovelas* and the cruel reality of her life with Juan Pedro. Cleófilas neither minimizes the brutality of her experience nor becomes bitter with the recurrent beatings she receives. Late in the story, she realizes that her life with Juan Pedro will not end well. Of import here is that Cleófilas grows in her resolve to sort through the anguishing and embarrassing truths of her life. As she comes to terms with her situation and with her feelings of disillusionment, Cleófilas becomes stronger. In the process, she musters enormous courage. Through her courage she opens herself to transformation.

When we suffer, Moraga claims, the pain we experience, and often internalize, can lead us down a destructive path or a constructive one. The extent of our willingness to probe our pain and to seek healing determines which path we tread. The crux lies in discerning the truth, first and foremost about ourselves. In Moraga's recollections, she quickly strips away any and all rationalizations which might be used to impede or trivialize Latinas' pursuit of truth. Discerning the truth is essential, Moraga believes, because transformation occurs not only through our efforts to change the world around us, but by examining our own suffering and pain. The suffering experienced and the pain inflicted by oppression do not automatically enable us to love more or to care more. No moral superiority emerges as a simple result of experiencing more pain.

> What is hardest for any oppressed people to understand is that *the sources of oppression form not only our radicalism, but also our pain.* Therefore, they are often the places we feel we must protect unexamined at all costs. . . . Oppression. Let's be clear about this. Oppression does not make for hearts as big as all outdoors. Oppression makes us big and small. Expressive and silenced. Deep and Dead.[36]

For Moraga the decisive question is: Does our suffering become the source of further destruction, or does it lead to a search for greater wholeness?

When Latinas seek out relationships which support their journey toward abundant life, when Latinas dare to respect the strength of their own voices, when Latinas risk the grief that comes with sorting through the pain-filled truths of their lives, they search for greater liberation and wholeness. But this human search for greater liberation and wholeness is not an end in itself. This human search may become the occasion for our encounter with Divine Mystery. How do we behold Mystery in the context of our ordinary awareness? How might the suffering experienced by Latinas play a role in the redemption of all people? These questions mark the transition from human strategies aimed at greater wholeness to the wonder of Divine Mystery's irrepressible passion.

### *In Search of a Theology of Suffering,* Latinamente

To explore the theological significance of suffering we must ask: Where in the experience of suffering do we encounter the mystery of

God? Admittedly no definitive response can be offered; ultimately this encounter centers on the unfolding of our relationship with Divine Mystery, a relationship which invariably transcends the power of words to clarify. Even so, in these portrayals of suffering we can point to occasions in which we sense the presence of Divine Mystery. Two essential themes deserve our attention: acts of courage and an orientation toward the redemption of the universal community.

Far too often, "Christian" reflections on suffering have advanced the idealization of the passive, uncritical resignation to suffering. Unfortunately, this idealization and its corresponding distorted "theology" have long plagued Latinas. Cisneros, aware of how passive suffering kills the human soul, uses the characters Soledad and Dolores to symbolize the oppressive and destructive nature of this idealization. Her characters refer to *Nuestra Señora de la Soledad* and *La Virgen Dolorosa.*[37] We must make a crucial distinction. When Latinas (and others) elucidate God's will for women, such that the exemplar woman endures, silently and uncritically, all sorrows, and consistently disregards her own needs and desires, then such reflection ceases to be Christian. Too often devotional practices involving female images like *Nuestra Señora de la Soledad* and *La Virgen Dolorosa* are used to bolster an oppressive model of womanhood, oppressive in its idealization of woman as contained, as publicly mute, as long-suffering, as a pawn of (and not a producer of) history.[38]

On the other hand, when Latinas apprehend that God desires and seeks justice in *this* world; and when Latinas apprehend that God is not only present to them in their suffering, but more importantly suffers with them analogous to the God-human suffering of Jesus Christ on the cross; then their theology will embody the essence of Christian insight. Moreover, within this framework of genuine Christian insight, devotional images can and do strengthen the idea that God desires justice and suffers with us, and therefore that there is cause for hope.[39]

Even so, evil, and the suffering which results, ultimately take us beyond the power of words and ultimately frustrate our search for meaning. When faced with the problem of evil, theologians must acknowledge the unavoidable limitations of their insights.[40] However, to distance suffering (particularly the suffering of the innocent) from God, from Jesus Christ, and from Christian theology renders suffering utterly insignificant, void of any positive meaning. If God suffers internally with us, then God can and does, in the midst of suffering, create a higher good out of evil. In contrast, if we think of God as fully external to the problem of evil, then the problem of evil remains, in the end, unsolvable. In such a theological vision, evil operates outside any ultimate aim of the universe. But if our pain and suffering are included in the eternity of God, then our suffering is significant and meaningful even when that meaning is not fully clear to us. Indeed, through the suffering of the God-human, Jesus Christ, we know that suffering can attain meaning, that we can learn from it and grow through it.[41]

### Honoring Courage

A theology of suffering, *Latinamente*, honors courage. Courage is the ability to face what happens to us in life.[42] Latinas manifest courage in *lucha*[43] as well as *confianza*. *Lucha* or "vigilant struggle" signifies both the clarification of the causes of suffering and the effort to eliminate the conditions which allow pointless suffering to continue. *Confianza* or "hopeful confidence" signifies the effort to find meaning in suffering, to live in the trust and assurance that God will ultimately bring life from pain. While either *lucha* or *confianza* may prevail during a specific time in life or moment in history, through the course of our lives both are necessary in our relationship with God.[44]

The courage of Latinas, like Cleófilas, emerges time and again when they struggle against injustice and work to eliminate the conditions which needlessly and cruelly foster suffering, whether theirs or others. It is precisely in this struggle, in the fight against and the triumph over evil, that Latinas through their courage grow in their capacity to embody and incarnate the life of God. Those innocent of evil and those without fears bear a more limited capacity to embody God's life; courage has not been demanded of them. It is through the *lucha* that the spirit of God manifests itself ever more vividly among us.[45]

*Confianza* provides an orientation for the *lucha*. Moraga, when she offers a reinterpretation of Latina woundedness, incarnates and points to Latina courage. The act of reinterpretation demands openness to reliving the unbearable burden of suffering, and invites us to trust that in God our pain bears meaning. Some Latinas, like Moraga, recognize that the growth and integration of individuals and of communities require just such a reinterpretation of sufferings. In the end, we conquer the ills that intrude upon our lives only to the extent that we decipher and clarify them, only to the extent that we "take them up into the plan of our lives, give them meaning, set them in their place in the whole."[46] Through this reordering process, we trust that suffering ultimately has the potential to shape constructively and give meaning to our lives if we are willing to enter into its mystery. When we enter into the mystery of our sufferings, we enter into the pascal mystery[47] of Jesus Christ's death and resurrection.

### Seeking Universal Redemption

A theology of suffering, *Latinamente*, seeks the redemption of the universal community. How do Latinas imagine the transformation of their suffering into some greater good? Any explanation or interpretation of suffering includes some aim or orientation. To the extent that Latinas seek an interpretation of their suffering in light of the mystery embodied in Jesus Christ's death and resurrection, their suffering itself may become transformative beyond their own lives. Such an interpretation requires a discerning imagination, which means the ability to see former betrayals and ills in light of the wisdom of a lifetime, and in anticipation of a hope-filled future. Such an interpretation enables us to deepen our own fullness and wholeness.[48] The writings of Cisneros and Moraga disclose examples of Latinas who knowingly choose to touch the wounds of their suffering, who then recast their suffering in concrete, imaginative ways such that it enlivens the community, turning suffering into service. Redemption means adjusting one's personal will to the will of the Divine Spirit, who wills the fulfillment and liberation of all. Latinas' creative work, fashioned from the residue of suffering, a work rich in pathos, efficaciously calls those responsible for suffering to recognize the evil of their ways. In other words, through this creative work the Divine enters in, and in the process, those who have known suffering become the agents of redemption, the agents of liberation for others.[49] When Moraga implores Latinas to strive after the eternal through their creative work, it is redemption in the largest sense that Moraga longs for. Although Cisneros does not write about the impact of Cleófilas's departure on Juan Pedro, she provokes us to speculate. Did her separation jolt Juan Pedro into a heightened awareness of his abomination? Did he experience remorse? We do not know. Nevertheless, as a result of Cleófilas's departure the possibility of these outcomes increases.

By seeking to enter into the mystery of their suffering and thereby into the paschal mystery, Latinas live recognizing the profundity of the interrelationships of all humans and of all creation across the whole of time, past, present, and future.[50] Such a recognition sharpens our awareness of the common good. It clarifies our apprehension of the spiritual unity of the world. In the end, it lays the groundwork for the greatest good of humanity, the ethical transformation of communities along with individuals.

# Response

## by Dianne Stewart

Nancy Pineda-Madrid's essay "In Search of a Theology of Suffering, Latinamente," is a provocative analysis of suffering in the life and literature of Latinas in the United States. Her essay is not an investigation of the causes of suffering but of how Latinas respond to their suffering. Pineda-Madrid's examination of Sandra Cisneros's Cleófilas evokes Toni Morrison's Pecola from her novel *The Bluest Eye*, and Alice Walker's Celie from *The Color Purple*.[1] Pecola's and Celie's lives are encrusted within layers of suffering that are clearly "not only physical but also psychological, not only multi-generational but also spiritual, not only externally provoked but also inwardly triggered." Pineda-Madrid is correct; "suffering is not simple." The fictional characters of Latina and black women writers embody the struggles of women in both communities to acknowledge and respond to "the complexity of suffering" out of their own agency. With insight and imagination Latina and black women create characters that confront their suffering and muster enough strength and power to realize self-transformation. From her assessment of Latina literary traditions, Pineda-Madrid maintains that when Latinas "seek community," "struggle to find their voice," and "discern truth" their methods of "discover[ing] meaning and seek[ing] wholeness in their suffering" become apparent.[2]

Pineda-Madrid's transition from literary analysis to theological reflection compels me to ponder the significance of identifying different types of suffering and the various responses to each type that might contribute to black and Latina women's wholeness and abundant life. Since the rise of liberation and contextual theologies, much attention has been given to suffering as it relates to one's social location as a member of an oppressed group, and for valid reasons. Socially constructed suffering was virtually ignored before theologians from oppressed communities around the globe began to deconstruct standard theological approaches to suffering that undermine the empowerment and emancipation of the oppressed. Pineda-Madrid too discounts theologies that trivialize, tolerate, or basically ignore suffering. Ultimately, Pineda-Madrid contends that "suffering will become an occasion for transformation or debilitation," and, as the works of Latina artists indicate, imaginative power is capable of determining its longevity in women's lives.[3]

Her point is well taken. For me, analysis and imagination are critical tools for nurturing communities and relationships that foster hospitality and wholeness. The very nature of black people's suffering, which is complex and nuanced, presents black theologians with compounded issues as we consider the implications of our people's exilic presence, compulsory labor, and the trans-generational suffering caused by such oppression in the Americas and the Caribbean. Taking seriously the need for black professional theological responses to multiple forms of black dehumanization I argue against Christian theological perspectives and doctrines that assign any positive value to suffering. Indeed Christian theology has made meaning out of Jesus' suffering. But, do people without divine qualities and without a theological mission of redeeming others from sin really discover meaning in suffering? Is it the prophetic and priestly responsibility of theologians to encourage the oppresed in this type of discovery? As I reflect upon Pineda-Madrid's essay and the works of other Christian theologians, I struggle to reconcile suffering with meaning, that is, with value. The meaning of suffering as I see it is pain, arrested fulfillment, and compromised livelihood. Pineda-Madrid is correct; these indicators cannot be ignored or trivialized. They are necessarily significant to those who attempt to address their suffering toward the positive end of alleviating it. However, I maintain that the experience of suffering in itself should not be valued.

For me, discerning the causes of suffering is important in encouraging black people to "deal with and interpret their suffering." I remain interested in the complex causes of what I term black people's Primordial Suffering, as I struggle to provide sound theological analysis of the African experience with evil and suffering. Pineda-Madrid's essay provides reinforcement for this theological aim when she affirms the virtue of courage and the place of hope in addressing one's suffering. In the end, she finds hope and meaning in the Christian testimony that God and Jesus suffer with the innocent, and in the "mystery" of suffering, both divine and human.[4]

My investigation into black suffering, however, is most acutely affected by the profound insights into Primordial Suffering gleaned from W. E. B. Dubois's theories on being black; Malcolm X's celebration of black selfhood, rehabilitated from the ashes of a moribund, deformed, and self-destructive Negro-ness; Celie's Womanist transformation from torture and misogyny to courage, agency, and independence—that is, by personages and traditions in the black experience that either denounce or maintain distance from normative Christian perspectives on suffering. Even Cherríe Moraga's "reinterpretation of

Latina woundedness," which Pineda-Madrid evaluates as "incarnat[ing] and point[ing] to Latina courage," pertains to a non-Christian indigenous Mesoamerican Aztec myth. As Pineda-Madrid notes "Moraga begins her reinterpretation of the Nahua myth of Coatlicue's birthing of Huitzilopochtli by asking her readers to imagine 'la Mechicana before the "Fall," before shame, before betrayal, before Eve, Malinche, and Guadalupe.' " In terms of sources for theological construction, women from a variety of cultural contexts are increasingly turning to indigenous traditions to challenge orthodox Christian doctrines and ideas that reinforce female subordination. I am encouraged by this development, and I likewise suggest how classical African culture and post-Christian black traditions might offer alternative resources for rethinking the meaning of being human in the African experience.[5]

Pineda-Madrid also values Moraga's analysis of her own personal suffering, namely enduring voicelessness betwixt two known languages that are nevertheless alien to her emotions and visions. The problem of language and hybridity in the Latina experience discloses how concrete the interior suffering of the colonized can be. In my own emotional and intellectual wrestling with suffering the problem of Christian language, in particular, prohibits a desired comprehensive critique of constructed suffering. Hence I experience theological muteness, a dilemma of sorts that leaves me bereft and incapable of surmounting the void between Christian consciousness and Christian theology where I find no appropriate language to express my emotions about black suffering and my visions of emancipation from catastrophic suffering in the African experience.

This notwithstanding, I still hold that analyzing the causes of suffering is an important task for theologians who write in behalf of oppressed communities. My nascent assessment of black people's experiences with evil and catastrophic suffering parallels Moraga's concern with the "Fall," "shame," "betrayal," and the many manifestations of "Eve." The experience of blackness is at once intensified experiences of "Fallenness," "shame," "betrayal," and "Eve." My analysis of how this is so for people of African descent discloses that Christian doctrines of humanity place premium value upon soul salvation even to the detriment of the body. It also suggests that greed is the most offensive insult to human community and responsible human thriving. Excessive greed fosters feelings of entitlement at any cost and the impulse to transgress boundaries of respect for the sanctity life. This type of excessive greed creates the conditions for what I call the "Original Violation" (of African people) and makes necessary a doctrine of humanity that affirms that the dignity and sanctity of human life is sealed within each person's body and soul and is honored through hospitable communion with others.[6]

# PART VI

*Building Bridges: Reflections on Context, Identity, and Communities of Struggle*

# 11

# Building Bridges between Communities of Struggle: Similarities, Differences, Objectives, and Goals

## Luis Pedraja

A MYTH OFTEN ACCEPTED by scholars in theology is the mistaken assumption that so-called "contextual" or "special interest" theologies are only relevant within their respective contexts. The acceptance of this myth often fosters an attitude that hinders the development of meaningful dialogues between contextual theologies and more traditionally accepted theological perspectives. Yet, this need not be the case. By exploring common elements amid our diverse perspectives, we can enrich our respective theologies.

The belief that contextual theologies are irrelevant beyond their context stems from two incorrect assumptions. The first assumption is that a non-contextual theology with an unadulterated, objective, detached, and universal viewpoint is possible. This prevalent, yet false assumption, assumes that one can objectively know ultimate truths that are applicable to all circumstances, individuals, and situations without these truths being affected by one's context. Generally, theologies that claim objectivity ignore their contextual nature and assume normative status due to their participation in the dominant culture's power structure.[1]

The claim that one theology can be universal in scope is not only arrogant, but also untenable in a postmodern setting. We are inescapably enmeshed in our environment and in our cultural context.[2] Our use of language is in itself a testament to the contextual nature of our theology since languages are the prime artifacts of culture.[3] Ultimately, we must accept that all theology is inevitably contextual

205

through and through.[4] Our finite and temporal nature limits our theological perspectives, which are shaped by cultural norms, presuppositions, biases, and socioeconomic status. To assume that our perspective is objective and normative creates an idolatrous theology that falsely assumes that a given abstraction or perspective can represent the full reality of any subject.[5]

The second equally erroneous assumption is that contextual theologies are limited by their context in such a manner that they are completely incommensurable with anything outside their context. This assumes that the relevance of contextual theologies is limited to their respective context to the extent that they are utterly irrelevant and inapplicable beyond their cultural setting. This position radicalizes the contextual nature of theology, making it insular and valid only within its cultural realm, thus creating a radical relativism that limits the relevance and critical analysis of theology to those that are within that particular context. Precluding the possibility of criticism and exchange between theological constructs emerging out of different contexts leads to theological provincialism, preventing the richness of dialogue and theological enhancement that may come from these exchanges.

A more benevolent form of this position with roots in postmodernism aims to protect minority positions by positing the validity of all perspectives without the possibility of adjudication between conflicting views. Since meaning is ultimately derived from a given context, propositions become meaningless or are altered when taken outside of their original context or examined with the criteria of an alien context. However, the lack of a method for adjudicating between conflicting and alternate positions merely limits the ability of contextual theologies to impact and critique the assumption of normative status taken by dominant cultures. Hence, contextual theologies are rendered impotent, unable to posit a critique or establish a dialogue with any other theological perspective. While the intent of this position is to validate and safeguard the claims of minority positions, it can easily have the opposite effect. Thus, it can easily end up safeguarding the status quo by not allowing oppressed groups to critique and challenge dominant groups by virtue of being part of a different context.[6] In other words, in safeguarding minority perspectives, this position also safeguards dominant ones.

Contrary to the positions discussed above, contextual theologies often share common motifs and diverse themes that help clarify and enrich each other, as well as more mainstream theologies. In our global context we are living within an intercultural environment defined more by a state of intermeshed contexts than by insular cultural communities. While our cultural context influences our theology, we are not limited to one singular context. Rather, we inhabit many contexts that shape and influence us. Thus, it is both beneficial and essential to develop a dynamic methodology that provides a venue for the development and continuation of dialogue among diverse theologies—especially those that share a common struggle.

## The Dynamic of Dialogue

Most contextual theologies use a dialogical methodology that can adapt to the living flux of their communities. This dialogic methodology—present in both Hispanic/Latino/a and African American theologies—allows theologians to engage in an ever-expanding dialogue with their respective communities, as well as with the other traditional sources of theology.[7]

The dialogic method of these communities of struggle takes several forms. First, it is a dialogue between the theologians and their faith communities. Here, theologians bring to life elements of the communal faith articulated by the people within the communities, correlating them with similar themes and theological insights from both the community and the larger theological context. The insights of the theologian are also brought back to the community who can then appropriate, refine, or discard them in accordance to how well they reflect the reality of the community and their beliefs. Second, the theologian also engages in dialogue with other theologians from their community to clarify and refine their understanding of the community. Third, the dialogue extends beyond the particular community of faith, addressing other theological communities and engaging them by either critiquing their theology or helping them to see new perspectives that might have been previously ignored. Fourth, the theologian also engages in a dialogue with their respective tradition, as well as the broader Christian tradition and the scriptures, bringing their own hermeneutical twists to the tradition in light of their particular community of faith. As a result, the dialogue both occurs internally, within the community, and externally with other communities of faith and traditions.

The dialogues in which communities of struggle engage are continually expanding to include others within their folds by engaging different communities. The dialogic method that is common among theologians emerging from marginalized communities always transcends the particularity of the individual and the community through its engagement of others into an expanding dialogic process. Thus, because of their similar methodologies and their emphasis upon maintaining cultural ties to their respective communities, establishing a dialogue between communities of struggle is not a difficult task.

The dialogic method itself fosters the creation of bridges to communities other than itself. This is inherent in the nature of dialogic methodologies. Dialogic methods require the presence of three key elements. First, both parties must share a mutual willingness and ability to engage in dialogue as equal partners. Second, both parties must share some common elements or points of contact that make the dialogue possible. Finally, there must be sufficient differences between the parties entering in the dialogue to make it meaningful and rewarding to both parties involved in the dialogue.[8] Without the presence of these three elements, the dialogue would be impossible. If a dialogue partner assumes a dominant role, the dialogue would break down into a monologue, dominated by the stronger of the two. Similarly, if sufficient differences, challenges, and perspectives are lacking, the dialogue will simply become monotonous. Hence, all three elements are necessary to maintain the dynamic tension that constitutes dialogue.

In Hispanic/Latino/a theology, the dialogue partners themselves fall within a threefold pattern that includes the community, the academy, and the traditional sources of theology.[9] Thus, Hispanic/Latino/a theologians engage in dialogue with other Hispanic/Latino/a theologians in their attempt to fashion their theology jointly, as a community, rather than as detached individuals.[10] However, they also engage in dialogue with their community as a whole, drawing from the faith and experiences of the people. Finally, they place this dialogue in the broader context of the Scriptures, tradition, academy, and church. It is within this latter context that we can engage in dialogue with other communities that share some of our struggles and also with those who consciously or unconsciously oppress us.[11]

African American and Hispanic/Latino/a theologies share many of the same dynamics of dialogue and connections to their communities of faith. Hence, even in their methodology they share a common bond. Like Hispanic/Latino/a theologians, African American theologians also reflect upon the faith and experiences of their community and engage in fruitful dialogue with other traditional sources of theology such as the Scriptures, traditions, academy, and church.[12] As a result, our common methodological concerns facilitate the development of a fruitful dialogue between our theologies, as well as those of others.

Because rigid systems and categories of comparison are detrimental to fostering dialogue and because of their location within a living, hence, changing community, most contextual theologies also resist rigid definitions that tend to fossilize their theology. Often, strict definitions and rigid systems of interpretation hinder connections to the ever-changing reality of a living community by failing to adapt, expand, and accurately portray change. Thus, fluid and flexible points of demarcations are preferable over rigid abstractions in comparing and establishing a dialogue between African American and Hispanic/Latino/a theologies.[13]

In addition to a common methodology, Hispanic/Latino/a and African American theologies also share similar hermeneutical approaches to Scripture and theology. Like many contextual theologies, they apply a liberating hermeneutics, what some have called a hermeneutics of suspicion, to texts exploring and exposing hidden agendas, political dimensions, and structures of oppressions that might have gone unnoticed in more innocent readings of the text.[14] This hermeneutics of liberation examines the texts and theological traditions from the perspective of the marginalized, oppressed, and disenfranchised revealing new ways to understand the text that empower liberation from the structures of sin and oppression that pervade our world. Although each context, as we shall see, provides different perspectives that enrich our understanding of theology and the Scriptures, there are many shared concerns and concepts that emerge in their hermeneutical approaches.

## *Different Contexts and Shared Realities*

Establishing this dialogue between Hispanic/Latino/a and African American theologies is both facilitated and hindered by the diverse context that shapes the Hispanic/Latino/a community. The diversity of cultures, nationalities, and races that fall within the Hispanic/Latino/a reality is often staggering. While most Hispanics/Latinos/as share a partial heritage shaped by the Spanish language and the legacy of the Spanish conquest of the Americas, they are not a single race. The wide diversity defined by the artificial rubrics of "Hispanic" and "Latino/a" encompasses a myriad of people of African, Asian, Native American, and European descent. Likewise, these terms engulf a broad spectrum of nationalities, economic statuses, cultural styles, and political views. This diversity can fragment the development of community, but it can also create bridges between Hispanics/Latinos/as and other races and nationalities. In many respects, Hispanics/Latinos/as exist at the crossroads of cultures and races, enabling them to be mediators between them.[15]

In some respects, for instance, Hispanics/Latinos/as do not share the same legacy of slavery and oppression shared by African Americans. On the contrary, some Hispanics/Latinos/as of Iberian descent were actually involved in the slave trade and were slave owners themselves. On the other hand, some Hispanics/Latinos/as are the descendants of slaves—Africans brought here in chains to supplement the labor force of indigenous people decimated by disease and slavery. Even Bartolomé de las Casas, the defender of the Amerindians, originally advocated the import of African slaves, mistakenly believing them to be better able to handle harsh labor and slavery, to ease the strain of indentured servitude and slavery, placed upon the natives. It was not until later, upon seeing the suffering of the African slaves, that de las Casas repented and advocated on their behalf. Thus, Hispanics/Latinos/as share, at least partly, in the legacy of slavery—both as slaves and as enslavers.

Unlike many of the white settlers of North America, the Iberian settlers who came were often young single men or men who had left their families in Spain. Through intermarriage and rape, the *mestizaje-mulatez* became an integral, although sometimes denied, aspect of our being. Hence, most Hispanics/Latinos/as bear a share of the legacy of both the slaves and the enslavers in their family. Often, it is easy to forget or to even deny that many of the people subsumed under the rubric of "Hispanic" are the descendents of Amerindian and African slaves, it is a reality with which we must contend. While our heritage as enslavers can hinder the building of bridges, I believe that the shared legacy of slavery in our history can serve as a point of dialogue and the creation of bridges between our communities.

Today, many Hispanics/Latinos/as and African Americans in our respective communities find themselves living under unbearable socioeconomic conditions and under the slavery of inner-city violence, drugs, and crime. Our struggle is often against the same socioeconomic forces and prejudices as that of other minority groups. Thus, as communities of struggles, we both share the call for the liberation of our respective communities from oppressive conditions—conditions that often are rooted in the same societal causes and structures of oppression. Yet, rather than working together for a common cause, we often find ourselves at odds with one another. For instance, in the city of Dallas, Texas, Hispanic/Latino/a and African American civic leaders often find themselves in heated discussions and animosity directed against each other over appointments to the public school system and city posts. In this struggle, we are pitted against each other, attempting to coalesce what we perceive as a limited amount of power and resources. Instead of cooperation, we live in distrust and struggle with one another. In this respect, Dallas is but a mere microcosm of our nation. Often, discourse in the United States in terms of race are limited to black-white issues, seldom considering the presence of other people of color.

In this struggle, the church can take the lead toward unifying our communities and focusing our strength and resources upon common problems. In the disputes in Dallas, Hispanic/Latino/a and African American pastors came to the forefront to seek dialogue and to diffuse the tensions created by appointments to the school superintendent position. In our shared faith, we find a common strand that creates the space for dialogue and mutual support for one another. As James Cone wisely indicated in his book, *God of the Oppressed:*

> There is no truth in Jesus Christ independent of the oppressed of the
> land—their history and culture. And in America, the oppressed are the

people of color—black, yellow, red, and brown. Indeed it can be said that to know Jesus is to know him as revealed in the struggle of the oppressed for freedom. Their struggle is Jesus' struggle, and he is thus revealed in the particularity of their cultural history—their hopes and dreams of freedom.[16]

Although, in making this statement, Cone is arguing for the validity of using black experience as theological resource, he also is emphasizing a key aspect of most theologies that emerge from communities of struggle. To most of these communities, the understanding that Jesus shares in their own struggle is central to both their faith and to their theology. Hence, if we understand Jesus as one who not only shares our struggle, but also as the one who instantiates God's presence in the midst of our struggles and the promise of liberation, then we find a common bond between our communities. In this sense, our faith and our shared quest for liberation require that the church take the lead in our struggle and support all those who struggle under oppression, regardless of their color or status. In coming together, our churches can serve as the focal point for dialogue to occur between our communities and as the place where we are called to stand in solidarity with one another and with all who struggle against oppression.

Our shared struggles are not the only point of contact between our communities. Culturally, Hispanics/Latinos/as and African Americans share some common traits in their spirituality, expressive nature, and familial ties, as well as in their theological reflection upon these traits. Both Hispanics/Latinos/as and African Americans are specifically attentive to their cultural practices and the role they play in their religion and faith, while reflecting a more organic mode of relationship to each other and to their environment than the technocratic-utilitarian modes that seem to prevail in Western cultures. In addition, both pay considerable attention to the role of popular religion, innovations, and aesthetic practices within their respective traditions.[17]

Furthermore, Hispanics/Latinos/as are an amalgam of different cultures and races; a reality referred to by Hispanic/Latino/a theologians as *mestizaje-mulatez*. Both words basically mean the same, a mixture. *Mestizaje*, coming from the Latin, generally refers to the racial mixture of Iberians and Native Americans, while *mulatez*, coming from the Arabic, refers to the mixture of Iberians and Africans. In time, people of other racial and cultural origins that include Asians and Northern Europeans have augmented this mixture of races and cultures. Hence, I can say with confidence that I have Anglo, European, Asian, and African relatives, as well as others whose origins are impossible to know.

Even our traditions and religions have been influenced by the *mestizaje-mulatez* that predominates in our cultures. African religions, such as the Yoruba faith, have found fertile ground among Hispanics/ Latinos/as in the Caribbean, and most recently in other groups of Hispanics/Latinos/as from Latin America. In addition, our music and our food have been heavily influenced by the music and food brought from Africa, especially for those of us with roots in the Caribbean. A prime example of these roots can be seen in the movie *The Buena Vista Social Club*, which has brought forth a revival of Afro-Cuban music to the United States. The music featured in the movie, as well as many of those who play it, clearly has African roots. Yet, they are both Hispanic/Latino/a as well.

In my own country, Cuba, many of the traditional dishes we eat at our Christmas dinner originated in Africa and from our Moorish ancestors, many of whom also came from North Africa. Our shared heritage as Hispanics/Latinos/as with people of African descent is so extensive in some communities, that once a student from Africa, enrolled in one of my Hispanic/Latino/a theology classes, remarked that many of the elements of Hispanic/Latino/a theology were similar to those of traditional Native African religions.

When we add the influence of native traditions and religions from the Americas, it is easy to see why some have used the term coined by José Vasconcelos, *raza cosmica* ("cosmic race"), to refer to the broad mixture of races and cultures embodied by Hispanics/Latinos/as. As a result of these shared traits, it should not surprise us that a dialogue between African American and Hispanic/Latino/a theologies is not only possible, but that it is presently occurring. What should surprise us is that it has taken so long to occur.

However, the diversity that exists in Hispanic/Latino/a communities can also hinder dialogue in other respects. Our diversity often prevents the formation of coalitions and consensus between our communities, weakening our ability to present a united front in the same manner that our African American brothers and sisters have been able to do in the last part of the twentieth century. Often, the political views of different segments of the Hispanic/Latino/a population are as radically different as their nationalities, foods, and culture. Take, for instance, the activism of the fiercely right-wing anti-Communist segment of some Cuban leaders in Miami and compare it to the activism of the Farm Workers Union in California and Texas, and you will see a clear indication of our differences.

## *The Construction of Race: Similarities and Differences*

Even within a given nationality, there are elements of prejudice and differentiation. Hispanics/Latinos/as are not immune to racism, classism, and sexism. Within our own cultures racism exists as "white" Hispanics/Latinos/as often shun and discriminate against people with darker skin.[18] Similarly, class and gender discrimination also affects Hispanics/Latinos/as in the same manner that it affects other cultures and communities.[19] Hence, like many other communities of struggle, we must opt for liberation ourselves and not fall prey to the same paradigms and divisive structures of oppression that are perpetuated by the dominant classes. In this respect, Hispanics/Latinos/as have often been guilty of the same racism decried by many African American theologians. In many Latin American countries, discrimination against people who exhibit Amerindian or African traits, such as darker skin color or facial features, is fairly commonplace. Even within nationalities in Latin America that are predominantly African American or Amerindian in origin, as well as with mix racial groups, there are subtle preferences for those with lighter skin tones.[20] However, this does not eradicate the reality that most Hispanics/Latinos/as do have Amerindian or African lineage to some degree. Even those who are primarily of Iberian descent often have Moorish ancestors with African roots.

Yet, the danger of racism pervades all classes and races that might achieve a more normative or dominant status. Racial constructs are seldom purely physiological. On the contrary, most race theorists seem to agree that racial constructs are primarily socioeconomic in origin. Thus, racial traits are exploited to demarcate one group from another, and to justify the domination and oppression of the group that is different from how those who are in power define themselves. As a result, we create hierarchical structures that justify the supremacy of one group above the other. These tendencies go as far back as time, and are epitomized in Aristotle's hierarchies defining humanity in terms of the civilized Greek, while rendering barbarians and others to lesser status, barely devoid of humanity.[21] These same hierarchies would be used in ages to come to justify the enslavement of African and Amerindians in this continent. Yet, the underlying reality in these trends resided in the need for dominant groups, adept in waging war, to control other groups to work to perform the necessary labor that would sustain their society, economy, and leisurely lifestyle. Genetically and biologically, racial constructs have little scientific basis. Recently, geneticists have been able to trace a common origin for all homo sapiens to a very small group originating in Africa. Genetically, we are not that different from each other. However, racial constructs based on skin color or physical characteristics persevere, due to a variety of reasons among which power, economy, religion, and culture can be found.[22] Among these reasons, race and racial hierarchies were commonly used to justify the political power and economic gain of particular groups or nations.[23]

Yet, even when economy was the underlying reason for the creation of racial constructs, often theology and philosophy were willing

accomplices. The very basis of racism and the hierarchies that dominate racial discourse are themselves embedded in our theological heritage and in Christianity were the subjugation of one race by another
was argued as being ordained by God.[24] These arguments can be seen
in the papers of Spanish theologians trying to justify the conquest
and enslavement of the Amerindians, as well as the purchasing of
slaves. Often, enslavement was justified under the guise that their
treatment was more benevolent or that it was a means to civilize and
Christianize them.

Although slavery among the Amerindians was for the most part
outlawed by the Spanish government by the end of the sixteenth
century, it was not always effectively eradicated in many parts until
much later.[25] The enslavement of Africans continued until late in the
nineteenth century.[26] Generally, the reasons for the prolongation of
slavery for the African resided in theological arguments that understood Africa to be infidel territory, giving the Portuguese the right to
wage just war against the inhabitants and allowing for their enslavement as a condition of the war.[27] In addition, their enslavement was
seen as beneficial to the slaves in that they would supposedly receive
more lenient treatment and have the opportunity to be Christian-
ized.[28] Another rationale used by the Spanish was that they themselves were not doing the enslaving, but that it was done by other
Africans and by the Portuguese, thus the moral responsibility did not
fall upon them, but upon those who enslaved them. At no time was
the actual practice of slavery brought into question as being unjust
until the debates on the subject began in the eighteenth century.

Unlike Latin America, where racial mixture and the inclusion of
Amerindians in the question of race was commonplace, the American
paradigm of race has been primarily centered on the white-black distinction. The enslavement of blacks by whites in the U.S. still pervades the consciousness of Americans in many respects. Most lines
and racial divides were drawn along the black-white paradigm in the
U.S. and to some degree they still continue to dominate the agendas
of politicians and many theologians. Given the injustices endured by
African Americans, the issues that pervade black-white racial relations
in the U.S. should not be ignored. Yet, in creating this racial divide,
other oppressed groups have often been relegated to invisibility. Racism directed against Hispanics/Latinos/as who were seen as lazy,
dirty, and uncivilized existed in America since as far back as the
sixteenth and seventeenth centuries. The infamous "Black Legends"
promulgated by the British as propaganda in their wars with Spain,
portrayed the Spanish and, by default, those of Spanish descent, as
less than human, ruthless, ungodly, and unsophisticated. Many of
these images, often drawn along Protestant (Anglos)-Catholic (His-
panic/Latino/a) lines, still persist until these days and were a domi-

nant force in the formulation of the notion of Manifest Destiny in the United States during the nineteenth and early twentieth century. Currently, with the growing ranks of Hispanics/Latinos/as in the United States, many anti-Hispanic/Latino/a sentiments are growing within the United States, generally drawn around an outsider-insider paradigm driven by fear that Hispanics/Latinos/as will displace or take the wealth, work, and resources from the established working classes in the United States.

Because for many years most of the dialogue and issues related to racism in the United States and in our own theological circles have been defined in terms of a black-white paradigm that excludes other races and nationalities, we have failed to address many of these latent issues. This has left Hispanics/Latinos/as in a precarious place of ambiguity and displacement. I still hear stories told by many Hispanics/ Latinos/as that during segregation they were not allowed to use public restrooms, water fountains, and similar facilities marked for whites or those marked for blacks because they were neither white nor black.[29]

As a result of the demarcation of racial issues along black-white lines, Hispanics/Latinos/as, in the past, have often been shut out of many significant conversations and decision in politics, society, and the academy. This has left many Hispanics/Latinos/as disenfranchised, making them a hidden and often voiceless minority. In order to establish lasting bridges between Hispanics/Latinos/as and African Americans, the invisibility of Hispanics/Latinos/as must be overcome in public discourse. With the growing numbers of Hispanics/ Latinos/as in the United States, projected census numbers, and the growing awareness of the shared struggles among minorities, these conditions of disenfranchisement and invisibility are slowly dissipating. Although, often, too slowly.

In spite of our similarities and shared struggles, another radical difference between the African and Hispanic American communities is the reality of "black being" and "blackness."[30] According to Gayraud S. Wilmore, the symbolic meaning attached to blackness in the consciousness of both white and black Americans has many powerful dimensions that remain largely unexamined.[31] The respective symbolic meaning associated with blackness in American culture pervades much of the American psyche for both whites and blacks, serving as an identifiable reality that cannot be easily ignored. The negative connotations associated with blackness in our culture often bleeds into our perception of many African Americans, creating problems in our understanding of their own identity, as well as problematic theological and anthropological issues.[32]

The significance of "blackness" is difficult to understand for those who do not embody being black. Both the pride and the stigma that can be associated with it are difficult to understand unless you actually live it. Yet, in the essay, "The Fact of Blackness," Frantz Fanon provides a passionate account of coming to the realization of his own "blackness" in the face of the white other and its effects upon him.[33] For Fanon, the cry of a little girl shouting to her mother, "Look, a Negro, Mama, see the Negro! I am frightened!" makes him aware of his own "blackness" as a stigma, a source of fear and loathing.[34] The perception and attributions made by the white other upon his embodied reality forced to a certain degree an internalization of the projections of the white dominant classes upon his own sense of embodiment. Unlike others who can remain incognito about their ethnicity, Fanon remarks that he cannot hide his own, being a slave not just of the ideas others have of him, but of his own appearance which is irrevocably intertwined with those ideas.[35] Although Fanon argues that often black men and women find themselves locked into their own skin, unable to escape what is attributed to them, the answer is not to escape, but to help the perpetrator to escape their delusions of superiority and their projections upon blackness as unhealthful.[36]

Hispanics/Latinos/as of Iberian descent and those with lighter skin tones often define themselves racially as white. Yet, upon coming to the U.S. a metamorphosis occurs in our perception. There comes a time in our lives when, like Fanon, the white dominant class too confronts us with a comment or attitude that forces us to realize that we are not perceived as white in their eyes. For me that realization came when a dear friend said to me once that I was having problems with someone because I was not white. Other friends also would recall the moment in their lives when they realized that they were no longer white. Being Hispanic/Latino/a, although it is the result of an artificial racial rubric, lumps us all together into a different category that sometimes we can escape by the lightness of our skin, but not by our surname, accents, or culture. Thus, for Hispanics/Latinos/as, the struggle we face is not with "blackness," although some Hispanics/Latinos/as are indeed black, but with our non-whiteness, our being people of color in a world dominated by the standards of whiteness.

Nevertheless, although the symbolic power of "blackness" affects some Hispanics/Latinos/as, it does not pervade our reality as strongly as it pervades the African American ethos. The entrenched religious and cultural symbolism associated with white and black do play a role in our self-identity as an invisible mechanism of oppression and denigration.[37] In our shared Christian heritage, white still retains connotations of purity and goodness, while black, and even brown, maintain associations with evil and filth.[38] To those who must bear their skin color as an embodied emblem of who they are, the symbolism associated with these colors stigmatizes them in the eyes of others and often unconsciously devalues their own sense of self-worth.

Hence, the issues of color and color symbolism must be taken seriously within a theological setting that examines the value and dignity of humanity in developing shared views of theological anthropology. In this, we must become cognizant of the role color symbolism plays in our lives, while re-discovering new symbolic structures and ways of understanding our own identity beyond the color of our skins.

## *Theological Anthropology and the* Mestizo-Mulatto *Reality*

Issues of identity are paramount for our culture and theology, playing a significant role in the construct of our theological anthropology and praxis. While the *mestizo-mulatto* reality of Hispanics/Latinos/as facilitates dialogue with other cultures and races, it also displaces our identity. As a result, Hispanics/Latinos/as find themselves in an ontological reality defined primarily by negations: we are neither this nor that. Because Hispanics/Latinos/as exist in the borderland of cultures, we are often outsiders to both our native countries and to the mainstream culture of the United States. As a result, as the Hispanic theologian Virgilio Elizondo points out, our ontological status is one of "non-being."[39]

However, as disconcerting as this position may be, our non-being can become the source of a new being that can bridge our cultures and transform us into a people who embody and bridge diversity in our very being.[40] This transformation allows us to discover the value inherent in our identity. Where before we were defined by negation, dislocating both our identity and our intrinsic ontological value, we can now become the bearers of the promise and possibility of constructing a new reality that encompasses all humanity and finds intrinsic value in diversity.

Within the area of theological anthropology we encounter both a common struggle and a common vision. When we deny the intrinsic worth and value of a person based on their ethnicity or race, we deny their creation in the image of God and the value God places on all human beings. Racial constructs efface our common origin in God's good creation and our inherent value as creatures. The creation of hierarchies that privilege a given set of people based on their ethnic or racial origin goes against the Christian message and the Scriptures which regard us as having equal worth in Christ (Col. 3:11). Not even our sinful state can justify the creation of hierarchies of value. Yet, even unwittingly, those who have a dominant place in society tend to assume their normative anthropological character. Hence, they view themselves as the bearers of the *imago dei* and those who are unlike them as inferior.

Hispanics/Latinos/as and African Americans often encounter social structures that demean their value as human beings and deny them dignity, respect, and their just place in creation.[41] African Americans struggle against those who equate "blackness" with evil and oppressive structures that view them as inferior human beings. Hispanics/Latinos/as struggle against their marginalized status in society and against those who view all Hispanics/Latinos/as as "illegal," interlopers, dumb, dirty, worthless, and lazy. In a sense, both Hispanics/Latinos/as and African Americans struggle against dehumanizing forces that deny the *imago dei* present in them.

Traditionally, theologians argued that sin effaced and even destroyed the image of God that was present in humanity. In a sense, they are right, but not in the way that it is usually interpreted. Sin does rob humanity of God's image, but not because it was lost in some prehistoric or mythic fall into a sinful state. Rather, our sin obscures the image of God in two ways. First, because of our sin, we deny that some are created in God's image to justify our oppression, subjugation, and exploitation of them. Thus, we blind ourselves to the *imago dei* manifest in them. Second, in dehumanizing other human beings and not acting out of love, we cease to bear God's image ourselves. Hence, sin does rob us of the image of God, because we do not act in accordance to God's will.[42] Thus, we efface our own *imago dei* by failing to bear God's image in loving others.

Contrary to theological and social notions that would deny the value and worth of Hispanics/Latinos/as and African Americans, we must affirm that all human beings were created in the image of God and hence are valued by God. That God created all human beings is sufficient in itself to warrant the ethical treatment of all persons as worthy of dignity and value.[43] Even if this was not sufficient, God's love for humanity in itself imbues us with value, making us worthy of respect, dignity, and care.[44] Ultimately, in the affirmation of the *imago dei* in humanity, Hispanic/Latino/a and African American theologians find common ground for affirming the worthiness of all human beings and the value bestowed upon them by God's love.[45]

This shared belief in the worth of all human beings before God provides a common vision for the liberation of all those who struggle under oppression. In both theological perspectives we are called to oppose the forces and socioeconomic structures that dehumanize and enslave human beings wherever we may encounter them.[46] Thus, as people of faith, we must live in solidarity with those who exist at the margin of society and under the power of systemic oppression, sharing their interests and common responsibilities.[47] As black and Hispanic/Latino/a theologians make gains in establishing their academic positions within the mainstream culture, it is imperative that we continue to be in solidarity with the people and cultures from whence our theologies have come, with each other, and with all those who share our struggle against oppression.

### Prophetic Vision and Eschatological Dimensions

The ultimate bond between Hispanic/Latino/a and African American theologies comes not from their past or present, but from their prophetic vision of the future. Their shared eschatology is not characterized by a passive waiting. Rather, it is forged by a teleological vision of the Kingdom of God that calls us to transform our present reality through our actions. Hispanic/Latino/a theologians often speak of a "new ecumenism" that is born not out of compromise and doctrinal agreement, but out of a shared struggle and a common goal.[48] Yet, this new ecumenism also extends beyond the bounds of our denominational divisions to include cultural, racial, and socioeconomic diversity in its folds.[49] It is a call toward a shared vision of the Kingdom of God as a liberating catalyst toward transformation of our present structure.[50]

In this sense we are called jointly to hope in God's liberating grace and embody the liberating power of God's Kingdom in the present by acting in accordance to what is envisioned in God's future.[51] This shared vision of the Kingdom of God is the establishment of an inclusive diversity that empowers human agency and enriches our mutual understanding through our celebration of difference. It is also a vision of a world constituted by love in which we value all creation and seek the well-being of all humanity.[52] In a sense, our liberation not only frees the oppressed, but also the oppressors from the sin that dehumanizes both oppressed and oppressors, without forgetting that the burden of oppression has been borne by the poor, the weak, and the marginalized.

The ties that bind us are the chains of enslavement and the bonds of oppression. Yet, these ties that come from our shared struggle join us in our resolve to break all the bonds of oppression that deface God's image in humanity and dehumanize us through exploitation and sin. And in this struggle we find ourselves building a bridge not just for ourselves, but for all who will join us. We find ourselves building a bridge to God's Kingdom.

# Response

*by Lee H. Butler, Jr.*

The old cliché, "easier said than done," seems to be very true as it relates to the topic "Building Bridges between Communities of Struggle." I agree with Pedraja, the theologies of Hispanic/Latino/a Americans and African Americans are presentations that represent the lived experiences of the people. But I also think that our theologies are intended to push and encourage the people to become more and to do more in life. Rather than theology merely serving the task of restating, theology also serves to inspire. To wit, while we each have identified a theological position of our respective communities, our hope has been to provide a basis for mutual relationship between our two communions.

Although our hopes are similar, our approaches to bridge building differ. Emphasizing the dialogic component between person and scholar, Pedraja articulates the similarities between our theological methods. Here, our difference is related to the point of departure. Much of Pedraja's presentation concentrated on the work of the theologian. My focus is on the life and experience of the Christian faith tradition of African American people. While he connects theology to the lived experience of the people, theology as an enterprise is not presented by the grassroots person in the pew. His theological overview was void of the person in the pew speaking in the first person. Quite often, the grassroots person is a secondary resource for the theologian. His theological approach was not as descriptive of practice as I attempted to be in my presentation. My focus was on the church work done by and on behalf of the grassroots person in the pew.

The optimal word from my presentation was not dialogue but survival. African American Christianity has been concerned first and foremost with the survival of African American people. From this perspective, the dialogue between our two communities will have to participate in African American survival efforts. This is the case in part because of the two different ways we have had to struggle to retain traditional expressions of religion. Our religion, spirituality, and faith are what kept us together and resistant. I agree with Pedraja that there are similarities between Hispanic/Latino/a Americans and African Americans on the usage of Scripture for liberation, however our favorite text and guiding myths differ. Whereas he considered Scripture and its interpretation, I emphasized faith as a sustaining force of the people. Our faith in God and the myths encouraged our survival more than biblical reflection and interpretation.

Due to the significance of race in America, Pedraja spent time exploring the racial/ethnic heritage of Hispanic/Latino/a Americans. This history, combined with a discussion of racism, was used to express the similarities of experiences among Africans and Hispanics/Latinos/as in America. The same thematic exploration was also used to point to our common West African heritage. Whereas I spoke of our West African heritage as what distinguishes African Americans and promoted our survival in America, Pedraja explained that the racial landscape of America in black-and-white relegates Hispanics to "invisibility." Yet, even the ideal of invisibility is not unknown to African Americans. The color-consciousness of America has historically denied the humanity of African Americans. Our black skin causes us to stand out in sharp contrast but our humanity has remained invisible to racist American eyes. I wonder to what extent our similar experiences of invisibility in the United States have made us invisible to one another?

In addition to invisibility, Pedraja explored the theological anthropology of our communities. He declared that we both struggle against non-being. While this remained a theological presentation for him, I attempted to present the ways the African American church has struggled against non-being through its ministries. This is clearly a place where the resistance activities of the African American church declares the black identity in America. Pedraja spoke of being defined by negation and the idea "we are neither this nor that." The African American church rearranged that negation to say: "Thank God, we are neither this nor that!" The terms that declare non-being for each of us may be similar but their oppressive impact differs. We have each experienced non-being differently, and those differences have stimulated us to resist in different ways. Although we both have resisted accepting non-being as definitive for our reality, the spiritual resources we have called upon make our self-understandings and experiences different. Unfortunately, this, perhaps, also stands as one of the inhibitors to our bridge building. Our differing presentations of these similar issues may be illustrative of this point: one a theological emphasis and the other a ministerial emphasis.

Finally, Pedraja declared the similarities of between our eschatological visions. He identified our common experience of enslavement and oppression in America as our meeting ground. We both maintain the hope of God's liberating power and justice and look forward to the coming of the Kingdom of God. I resisted identifying this as our meeting ground because that is the ground where many want to meet African Americans. I attempted to say that our meeting ground needs to be based on a new story with a common purpose rather than looking to declare a common past. To that extent, an eschatological vision is an appropriate approach, that is, we look forward to the building of a new kingdom together.

# 12

## African American Christian Churches: The Faith Tradition of a Resistance Culture

### Lee H. Butler, Jr.

W HILE HAVING A CONVERSATION with a Baptist pastor who was to be the revivalist at a church where I was a member many years ago, I was startled by his division of African American culture and Christianity. The revivalist asked me what courses I was teaching during that particular semester. Of the courses I identified, the one that caught his attention was "African American Christianity." He asked if there is such an entity. I went on to say that our faith experience and religious history differed radically from European Christians. Even our worship style differs from mainline white Christians. To this, he responded, "Let's just call it an Afrocentric approach to Christianity." Not wanting to argue him down, I allowed the conversation to end.

For him, African American culture and Christianity influence one another, but they are independent enterprises. As we talked, it became clear that he believed Christianity to stand outside African American culture in a superior way. His closing comment implied that Christianity had come straight from Heaven, bypassing any cultural norms or influences. His implications further suggest that African Americans are to be transformed by a pure Christian faith making us African American *and* Christian. Such a suggestion stands in complete contradiction to my own position which says there is a religious tradition, with its own faith history, known as African American Christianity. This pastor, in his pulpit robe adorned with kente cloth, expressed a theological position which declared his preaching garments to be a fashion statement rather than a faith and identity statement.

As I revisit that conversation, in some ways it resembles the position articulated by Joseph Washington, who identified theology as a

European enterprise unavailable to black believers.[1] Our religious experience, faith history, and spiritual traditions, however, did not begin with our captivity by Europeans. Furthermore, Christianity as it has been inculturated in America is not the sole repository of truth. The Africans who came to America integrated the Christianity that was being practiced in America into their being. They did not become Christian as much as Christianity became a part of them. Similar to African cultures becoming African American culture, African traditional religions became African American Christianity. In fact, because African culture is inseparable from African religion, I interpret the emergence of African American Christianity to be an indigenous cultural expression of African American life.[2] African American Christianity is not a mere "black perspective" on European Christianity but a new expression of faith with its own theological underpinnings.

The interpretive frame that I am suggesting is a minor shift from what has been the norm for presenting Christianity among African Americans. Yet I believe this to be an important paradigm shift for the accurate articulation of our faith. Without this shift, dialogues with other faith communities of struggle will be fruitless and futile.

## A Resistance Culture

The dominant culture of the United States of America is balanced by a variety of countercultures. Each one, in many respects, stands in sharp contrast to and in defiance of the historical values espoused by what generically tends to be called American culture. Americans have an international description; and through an evaluation of the leading tenants of American life, the description is a fairly accurate one. The leading tenants, however, do not describe all quarters of American life. Even within our borders, there are many aspects of American life that are challenged and countered. There are a variety of ethnic groups, who are still American, that resist the central value system which established our international reputation.

Occasionally, ethnic group expressions are identified as popular culture, but many of those group expressions have emerged as countercultural expressions. As Jesus has spoken in the Gospel of Matthew, "But to what will I compare this generation? It is like children sitting in the marketplaces and calling to one another, 'We played the flute for you, and you did not dance; we wailed, and you did not mourn' " (Mt. 11.16–17). Refusing to be dominated by an opposing value system, a resistance culture clings to rituals, traditions, and relationships independent of the forces that compel people to conform or die. A resistance culture declares, "My experience is different from yours! We are who God has made us to be." For these groups, conformity would be death. The resistance culture understands its identity to be rooted in an historic self that transcends this present time and space. This historic self, guided by a spirituality to choose life, provides resources for the group's courage and commitment to live humanly, defying dehumanizing aggression and demoralizing expectations. Frequently seen as uninformed and immature, the critical voice that speaks against the resistance culture says, "once they grow, they will see and believe like me." A resistance culture, however, resists the need to be a replica of the opposing culture standing on its own historical sensibilities and encounters with the Divine.

For the purpose of this paper, I will not identify the cultural diversity of the U.S.A. as subcultures. Instead, I will use the term resistance culture. This will be done as an effort to avoid the trap of labeling all ethnic U.S. cultures as inferior to European American culture. By virtue of their existence, most ethnic cultures in the U.S.A. are resistance cultures. Through an identification with a national homeland, many groups cling to their ethnic heritage, celebrate their ethnic traditions, and pass on their ethnic rituals for the purpose of communal preservation. The maintenance of the culture is the living legacy passed on to future generations. While they identify with their nation of origin, they also proclaim their allegiance to their nation of citizenship. These ethnic cultures exert a countercultural force in order to resist the value system that is experienced as oppressive. Many of the values that define American life are as oppressive to some U.S. citizens as they are experienced by others in an international context.

African American culture fits the description of a resistance culture. Not only have we historically been deprived the opportunity of full participation, there are particular national attributes that are contrary to what we have believed as a people. Our survival in the U.S.A. has not been dependent upon how well we have fit in, but on how well we have been able to resist the dehumanizing forces that have sought to destroy our sense of God, family, and community. A significant part of our resistance activities have been organized and directed by the African American Christian church. I am of the opinion that the heart and soul of African American culture took root and grew out of the religious experience of Africans struggling to maintain their humanity in America. By integrating African culture with our American life circumstances, we resisted the chattel experience as the description of our souls and were inspired by the hope of human freedom and dignity. We believed God was for us and with us, so we resisted ultimate despair. Those early resistance activities fostered and nurtured African American church and culture.

## African American Christianity as a Resistance Culture

African American Christianity is grounded in our human struggle for freedom and justice. Although the majority of black believers have identified with the Protestant denominations, those of us who are

Baptist, Methodist, Presbyterian, and so on are Protestant only to the extent that we have faithfully resisted the oppression we have known in America. We did not participate in the Protestant Reformation and owe no debt to the culture or comments of the reformers. The founders of the mainstream denominational traditions did not fight to improve our standing in the world. Their message did not contribute to our efforts to maintain our full humanity. Nor did the message of the reformers positively influence the standard of life that we were forced to endure on these shores. The Protestant slavers of North America considered Africans to be soulless servants. For generations, we were thought to bear the mark of Cain or the curse of Ham. "Faithful" Protestant believers regarded Africans as chattel to be used for their personal pleasure and economic gain. A legacy such as this is hardly the foundation for the African American faith tradition that has nurtured generations of believers.

The Christian church in the Americas has rarely acted on behalf of Africans in our quest for freedom and justice. Racism and economic enterprises have frequently existed by a "hand-in-glove" relationship. At the beginning of the Atlantic Slave Trade, when there was an opportunity for the church to speak the words of peace and love on our behalf, the "missionary to the Indians," Bartolomé de Las Casas, made Africans the sacrificial lambs for the slaughter in order to end the Amerindian genocide.[3] Consequently, the foundations of African American Christianity are not found in Europe or in missionary evangelization. Its foundations are African religions, African spirituality, and our struggle to maintain our human dignity in the face of evil. The force of African American Christianity as a resistance culture is located in its maintenance of a heritage of unity and rituals of sacrifice for the greater good.

African American Christianity as a resistance culture refused to be dominated by the basic American religious value system. The system valued individual survival and "white only" privileges. Yet our survival system was based on communal and familial wholeness with privileges emanating from our human compassion and regard for one another. Our conversion experiences were so powerful and persuasive that turning away from the truths derived from those experiences would have meant death. We endured many brutalities in order to show the convictions of our beliefs. Guided by our spiritual heritage, we resisted becoming what the American religious context told us we were. Through resistance, we sustained our identity as the children of God and maintained the community relationships that supported our being.

## *The Faith History of African American Christianity*

To articulate the faith history of African Americans is to articulate the central component of African American culture. Faith history is the term I am employing to describe the worldview and survival skills that have sustained and stabilized dislocated Africans since 1441.[4] It has been our faith history that has insured our self-understanding as human beings when assaulted by de-humanizing forces; and it has maintained communal continuity when the environment was committed to destroying all familial relationships. Our humanity and dignity were established by our spirituality. Our world was given reason by our religion. And, rather than yielding to the forces of death, our commitment to life was nurtured by our faith.

Faith is a human act, and from an African perspective, faith is a communal act. Through faith, we accept our accountability to a Higher Being, and we express our responsibility for one another. Africans have understood the meaning of love, God, and neighbors well in advance of our contact with Europeans. Our cosmological sense of time and space located us in the world with our reverence for the past declaring our hopes for the future. We understood that without God (who is both above and in nature) and family, all life would come to an end. Through rituals, our faith has kept us actively engaged in community.

To better appreciate the faith history of African American Christianity, it is important to consider the foundations of this faithful tradition. An appropriate place to begin this exploration is to consider African traditional religions. African religion is the product of the thinking and experiences of former generations. A person is not evangelized by ministers of traditional religions, rather a person is born into that way of life. African religion is also more communal than individual in expression. It is pragmatic, realistic, and accommodative with no sacred scriptures or holy books. The tenets of African religion are communicated through oral tradition. The family and religious systems gave rise to political and social governance.

The essence of African religion is phenomenological and is very much tied to natural phenomena. Humanity is the center of the universe, as well as the priest of the universe, linking the universe with God. The obligatory work of humanity is to try to create a harmony with the universe. The faith that one espouses within African traditional religion is the outgrowth of one's lived experiences. Religion and faith provided the individual with his/her firm place in society, evidence of his/her own identity, and equipped him/her with survival skills. Because the human/Divine relationship is understood as incarnational (God sees, hears, smells, tastes, walks, speaks, thinks, remembers), many of the images for God are human and personal. God is spirit, good, merciful, omniscient, omnipotent, omnipresent, self-existent, never changing, and unknowable.

African faith has been far from a method of escaping the world. Our faith has given us the passion to love when we have been shown hate, the compassion to give when we have been denied gifts, and the courage to hope for tomorrow in the middle of the night. Our faith has helped us to remember where we have come from, to know that present problems are merely a temporary condition, and to see beauty in the world beyond the ugliness we have been shown. Faith cannot be expressed in isolation. From an African perspective, to be individually motivated is a faithless act. Faithfulness requires acts of the devotion toward God, family (both the living and the living-dead), and neighbors.

With a rich tradition of African religion and faith, African American Christianity took root. Floating on the watery grave of the Middle Passage, overcoming the shame of the auction block, and transcending the brutality of the chattel system, displaced Africans cradled their dignity and created African American Christianity. Their resource of traditional systems was more powerful than the evil oppressive forces that stood against them. The traditional components of African life combined with the conditions of American life developed the character and presentation of African American worship and community life. The theological concepts that undergird the formation of African American Christianity were God is with us, God is for us, and God will make free. Because these early believers believed that God was very present in the world, their faith was not intended to help them escape from the world, but it was their way of actually engaging and transforming the world. Therefore, the social and political activities of African American Christianity are expressions from the very heart and soul of this faithful tradition.

The life-giving work of the African American Christian Church has been countercultural. Due to the restrictions placed upon African Americans by a demoralizing social system, a liberating force had to emerge to positively direct resistance activities of the people. The African American Church was the first institution to address the human needs of African Americans. By transforming the rage into a creative force, African Americans were able to build healthy relationships. Church socials gathered us as a community. Church programs equipped us with life skills while building our self-esteem. And church worship encouraged us to celebrate life while giving us the resources for living. Inspiring us to interpret our present suffering as temporary, the African American church inspired our vision for freedom through the language of salvation, reflected our image as human through the language of family, and declared that we would one day "shout all over God's heaven."

## The Ministries of African American Christian Churches

The ministries of African American churches are the direct outgrowth of our African heritage and our African American experience. Each activity is intended to feed our spirits, reform our opinions, transform our griefs, and improve our quality of life and relationships. Although preaching is considered the centerpiece of the African American Christian church, it is best to think of it in the context of an oral culture. Through preaching, our history is kept alive, our pain is therapeutically addressed, our education is never ending, our knowledge of news events is kept current, our political climate is interpreted, and our hope for justice is made flesh. African American preaching is "nommo"at work. Nommo is the generative acts of word and sound. Situations are transformed by notes, tones, and the spoken word. Nommo is the power to make all things new. The various ministries of the church are introduced and given shape during the preaching moment. Although ministry is more than preaching, without preaching most ministries would remain uninitiated.

While there are a variety of ministries that could be identified, I would like to suggest five ministry themes that are of particular importance. They are the ministries of pastoral care, family, education, community revitalization, and social justice. Each theme supports our struggle for freedom and our fight for dignity as human beings. No single ministry is more important than another. In fact, each ministry theme supports the other themes.

The first, pastoral care, is the ministry of sharing responsibility for the well-being of another. Caregivers offer support and stability to persons in times when life seems to be shaken and without a stable foundation. Considering our traumatic history and our struggles of everyday life in America, community crisis has been the constant state of our being. We have been able to survive due to the quality of care we have given one another. During times of suffering or loss, the pastoral caregiver symbolizes the presence of God and declares the assurance that the person has not been abandoned by God in their time of uncertainty and need. When sufferers ask the questions, "why?" and "how long?," the pastoral caregiver must nurture the sufferer to speak their own answer using the resources of faith and spirituality.

African American pastoral care also has a social justice dimension that attends to the suffering which results from societal oppressions. This practice of pastoral care exercises the liberating aspects of the Gospel and seeks to restore people to human life. Because of the dehumanizing legacy of what it has meant to be African in America, African American pastoral care has high regard for the souls of black folks. It is an approach rooted in human beingness and "somebodiness." "Rooted" in human beingness means the approach is alive, dynamic, life-giving, and emphasizes communality. Consequently, African American pastoral theology seeks to restore our relationships and to launch a counter-attack on the evil that assaults our lives. The emphasis is upon healing. The method tends to be group work. The health concern is the restoration of dignity.

The second, family, is the ministry of helping people to survive through the promotion of relationships. The destruction of the African family by those who have desired to control our lives has been a prime objective since the beginning of the Atlantic slave trade. From the moment of our incarceration on the African continent, family groups, whether determined by blood, marriage, village, or tribe, were separated. After we were transported to North America, the family bond continued to be disrupted. The systematic attempt to prevent us from bonding as a social group was an effort to make us depend only upon our captors. Our survival, however, was not dependent upon those who enslaved us. We maintained the belief that family was essential for defining our humanity and sustaining our daily living. Our commitment to family was nurtured and encouraged by African American Christianity.

Through the creative reproduction of African family life, we enhanced an extended family system that functioned in opposition to the social setting. The context made it illegal for us to marry, but we still developed marriage rituals as a sign of our commitment to family. Family units were constantly disrupted by the auctioning of family members by the landholder, but that never deterred us from maintaining family as an important value. Love was identified as an important force in life, and family ties were not limited to blood ties. Adoption, therefore, played an important part in the establishment of family during the antebellum period.

After the reconstruction period, family disruption was wrought by terrorism and migration for employment. The lynching of African American men and the rape of African American women by European American men believing themselves to be defending their homes are prime examples of the terrorism we have known. Members of families or the nuclear family would leave the extended family with the hope of improving employment opportunities. During these dramatic experiences, the church remained a vital connecting point for family values and extended family unity. The church helped to maintain our esteem and dignity by a support system that encouraged relationality and human compassion.

The third, education, is the ministry of equipping people for life. Working to correct the atrocities of the U.S.A., the church set an educational agenda into action. Education was thought to be the primary vehicle for realizing power and hopes of freedom. To counter the inequities built into the American social system, the African American Christian church established schools and colleges to prepare people for equal participation in the wider society. Separate educational systems with unequal financial resources did not mean that the quality of our education was inferior. The church worked diligently to educate people, in counter-cultural fashion, against a system intent upon molding us into inferior beings.

The African American church continues to maintain its legacy of freedom through education. The church continues to equip young people with the skills for appropriate social engagement. Many of our most significant national leaders have been church men and women who received their primary education in the church. Through encouraging memory, building confidence through public speaking, mining the talents of the arts, promoting creative writing, and stimulating healthy debate, the church mentors future generations. Through college fairs, college tours, and college scholarships, the church invests future generations. Through retelling the stories of our past and inspiring a vision for our future, the church declares our liberation. There are two idioms that have to do with knowledge. One says "what you don't know won't hurt you," and the other says "knowledge is power." To these, the church says, "the things we have not known have hurt us" and "knowledge is the key to our future."

The fourth, community revitalization, is the ministry of loving neighbors. Because communality is a significant feature of the African American identity, most African American churches have ministries that seek to improve the quality of life for the neighborhood residents and members of the church. These ministries express its clear sense of responsibility to and for every person within and surrounding the church. As a principle, communality declares the welfare of humanity to be every person's responsibility. The principle emphasizes that when tragedy befalls people, the members of the community must fulfill their ritual responsibilities for everyone to be able to move beyond the tragedy. The interdependent nature of all things means that we must be attentive to everything and everyone in our surroundings. Churches have responded to this principle by developing housing and economic empowerment programs.

Many churches work to change the social centers of its surrounding area. A significant portion of African American church language centers around house and home. Although it may seem that this language is focused on the hereafter, there is an eschatological quality to house and home articulations. The safety and security of that place called home is fully acknowledged by the church. Consequently, many churches are engaged in housing development programs while seeking to make neighborhoods more secure and prosperous. The economic development components of these ministries include the development of business centers, job training programs, and employment services. The churches whose ministries include community revitalization are not only showing the love of neighbor, they are showing community responsibility as active agents of change.

The fifth, social justice, is the ministry of liberation. The church maintains African America's traditional theme of freedom through ministries that would seek justice and liberation for the people. And in this land where state and federal legislation was drafted against us, the church has been our judge advocate against the life denying forces of America. Although the nation espoused freedom and justice for all, the social and political agendas were designed for the benefit of others. As a people desiring to experience our human "inalienable rights," the church became our most significant vehicle for social change. Most every major movement for social justice in African America has been initiated by the African American church. During the times when the church was not in the lead, the church has been a participant reformer by inspiring the people to resist identifying with the negative images associated with our being.

With ministries based upon our interpretation of the life of Jesus, the church confronts the world. Although liberation is frequently presented through the language of salvation and justice described as the activities of God, the church engages or speaks plainly about political activities, responds to social crises, and develops relief services. Due to the admonishment to be "as wise as serpents and harmless as doves" (Matthew 10:16), sometimes the very subtle social justice resistance activities of the church are seen as escapist. We have never, however, thought ourselves to be anything other than social beings with social responsibility, nor have we ever been blind to the injustices of our condition. Furthermore, because African spirituality declares there is no separation between the spiritual and the physical worlds, striving for our spiritual freedom has simultaneously meant striving for our physical freedom.

## African American Survival in the Future

One of the critical resources for African American survival has been our oral tradition. The spirit of improvisation has allowed us to transform our lives creatively. Just as we make a song new by singing it in a different key, we have been able to remake our lives through always speaking what we believe our lives ought to be. We have always been able to integrate new circumstances into our being and present something new from our souls. Although we have not always known where we come from, we have always known who we are. The maintenance of our historical sense of self has not been accomplished through rigid adherence, but rather through a flexible accommodation of the new presenting issue. Sometimes this process has resulted in the development of new rituals. Without a doubt, the spirit of improvisation and accommodation has sustained us in our struggle to be free.

Continuing to live our lives as interactive relational beings, our future survival will undoubtedly include more coalitions and greater cooperation with Hispanic/Latino/a American ministries. A significant relationship, however, will not be easily developed. African American ministries defend as much as they uplift the people. We still long to be free from the bondage of oppression and from those who sin against us. Our shared history as Africans and Hispanics in the Americas has not always placed us on the same side of the oppression experience. Any coalitions we build will have to help us speak a new imagination into reality.

Perhaps the most significant barrier will be the one of language. As an oral culture, African American culture thrives by retelling its story, and by learning to tell its story more accurately. Our African tribal languages were reduced to one common language, American English. Now, I am not suggesting "English-only" for our common ground; but I am declaring, our cooperation will have to be based upon a shared dream. For our two communities to struggle together in a common cause, we will have to develop a new story with a common purpose. Pointing to a common adversary or a common past will not be enough. African American Christianity has retained its distinctiveness as a result of the structure of American life. While our experiences in America may not be unique, the forces that have shaped our experience have been particular. Inasmuch as our religious identity may never change, our methods of survival must change with the times. The spirit of improvisation and accommodation will be the key.

# Response

## by Luis Pedraja

According to Paul Tillich, God's revelation occurs, not apart from culture, but through culture, as a part of it.[1] In reading Butler's paper, it strikes me that to some extent he is making a similar point in respect to African American Christianity. Granted, his argument focuses more on the manner in which American Christianity and African religions came together to form the new reality of African American religion. Yet, I believe this is the point of Tillich's argument, that religion cannot be separated from culture. Hence, each particular culture provides a new expression and vehicle of revelation within that culture. These unique expressions of Christianity are not a mere perspective or slant on a universal expression of the Christian faith, as Butler argues, but a new and unique expression of Christianity that can ultimately enrich the church as a whole through its own particularity.

Unfortunately, many, including the Baptist pastor encountered by Butler and Tillich in some of his other works, often forget that all expressions of Christianity are indeed culturally bound. Thus, European and American expressions of Christianity become accepted as the norm, easily identified with a purer or more universal expression of a "heaven given" Christianity that is not influenced by culture. Like Butler, I argue against this notion of a non-contextual or acultural form of Christianity, not only because I believe it to be impossible, but also because claims to the contrary often culminate in the establishment of one expression of Christianity as normative over all others.

By privileging Euro-American expressions of Christianity over all others, the church and the academy relegate other expressions to a marginal status, minimizing their value and diminishing their impact upon those expressions that see themselves as central to the faith—expressions that are generally associated with a dominant culture. The resulting marginalization creates a biased and culturally bound "center" that incorrectly believes itself to be both unbiased and normative, inevitably weakening and impoverishing Christianity as a whole by excluding other voices and expressions of the Christian faith from which we might learn.

Butler's rejection of the adjective "perspective" for describing African American religion makes a significant point that many of us, including myself, often forget—that in referring to marginalized theologies as coming from a given perspective, we are assuming that there is a given universal Christianity that is unaffected by culture. For many years, and even in my essay for this book, I have referred to my theology as being from a Hispanic perspective, unwittingly acknowledging a given universal. Thus, Butler makes an excellent point in this regard.

Yet, it may still be possible to use the term "perspective" as long as we understand that Christianity, as encountered in our world, is always from a human perspective—a perspective that is inevitably bound by culture, biases, linguistic limitations, and social location. But then, maybe, that is the point of the incarnation. God is present there, in the midst of history and humanity, with all its frailties and uniqueness. Maybe the point of the incarnation is the intentional shifting of God's locus to the concrete, the particular, the historical, and away from the abstract, universal, and ahistorical. If this is the case, then, Christianity is meant to be encountered through culture.

Hence, we can say that it is not a matter of Christ and culture, or Christ against culture, or any of the other paradigms offered to us by Niebuhr. But rather, that the paradigm is actually Christ through culture—uniquely, particularly, and incarnationally expressed through a given culture as it instantiates Christ for us. Christologically speaking, the hypostatic union would be extended to include not only God and humanity, but also culture as an essential aspect of our humanity in its particularity. I believe Butler offers a tantalizing glimpse into one such incarnate expression of Christianity—an expression rich with life in its struggle against death and oppression. In many ways, this is a struggle that the Latino/a people can understand, for we too live in the midst of the struggle of life opposing death.[2] And it is a struggle that is fully embodied in our lives, cultures, and communities.

Butler's preference for the term "resistance cultures" is also significant in two respects. First, it provides an active paradigm for the struggle in which marginalized cultures are engaged as they seek to retain their identity and humanity. Second, it also provides a link between different cultures that face similar struggles. Yet, I appreciate that Butler feels that this link through struggle is insufficient in itself to bring our respective communities together. Nevertheless, in defining the struggle as a struggle for justice and for retaining one's humanity, I think Butler has provided an additional connection for our common *telos* toward human dignity and empowerment. Again, in an incarnational understanding of our faith, an odd statement for a Baptist like me to make, God is ultimately encountered in humanity, forcing us to recognize in all human beings value and worth as bearers of the *imago dei*. Hence, it should be the struggle of all Christians, not just those who are marginalized and oppressed, to work toward an understanding of justice and dignity for all human beings.

Although Butler did not elaborate the connections between Latino/a religion and African American religion through his article, I was impressed at the number of similarities that exist between the two. It is clear that we share a struggle for justice and human dignity. We also value our communal and family identities, from which we draw strength. Butler makes a strong point that I also echo in my contribution, something that I think points to a common realization in both our cultures that can benefit Christianity as a whole to rediscover, that is, that "faith cannot be expressed in isolation." In both our communities, and even in our methodologies as I shared in my essay, the communal value of our faith and theological reflection is essential to who we are and how we express our faith.

In many respects, Butler's description of African American religious expressions and their role in the forging of identity and resistance are almost identical to the significance and role of "popular religion" (the religion of the people) in Latino/a religion. The "faithful tradition" of African American religion as described by Butler could easily be compared to the "faithful intuition" of Latinos/as in the work of Orlando Espín.[3] The same can be said for Butler's emphasis on lived experience and the work of many of the *mujerista* theologians, like Ada María Isasi-Díaz. Even the role of African religions in African American expressions of Christianity can be paralleled to the influence of indigenous religions and African Yoruba religion found in Latino/a religious expressions.

In his conclusion, Butler points us toward some of the challenges that must be overcome if we are to come together in our shared struggles. It is true that Latinos/as have been both oppressed and oppressors just as it is true that some of us share African heritages, while others do not. Latinos/as have to come to terms with the racism that exists in many of our communities and work in solidarity with our African American and African Hispanic brothers to overcome all forms of oppression, both external and internal to our communities. As I state in my essay, it is imperative that Latinos/as examine their understanding of race. It is also imperative that they recognize the role that skin color and "blackness" play in the embodied reality of people of African descent—not only in African American culture, but in our own Hispanic brothers and sisters of African descent. In our struggle for liberation and justice, we must acknowledge our own prejudices and move toward healing within our own communities that have often been marred by racial discrimination and biases. But African Americans must also realize that today some African Americans are also in similar positions as those of some Latinos/as, positions that make them not only oppressed, but also oppressors. And we must all realize that even oppressed groups can be biased against other minority groups and against others within their own group who are different from them.

As Butler points out in his essay, language might also be a challenge, although not an insurmountable one. Many Hispanics, born in the U.S., speak better English than Spanish. With English being the lingua franca, most strive to a working knowledge of English. African Americans can even help Hispanics learn English, a collaborative undertaking that many churches in transitional neighborhoods might undertake. However, I think that the greatest challenge we must overcome is our very human distrust of others who are different from us, as well as our sense of competitiveness. Empowerment is not about competing for a limited amount of power, as we often do, but about the recognition, as people of faith, that God's power is sufficient for all and that our struggle for justice is the struggle of the whole church.

# Concluding Observations

The academic exploration of African American and U.S. Hispanic American/Latino/a theology has been largely conducted without substantive internal dialogue occurring between these two discursive modes. That is to say, although African American and U.S. Hispanic American scholars have worked under the assumption that theology is best understood as a dialogical practice, the development and analysis of theologies within these two groups have occurred independently. This volume was conceived as an opportunity to make introductions and arrange an important circle of conversation partners that we hope will expand with time. In this way, we have taken an important step, a prolegomenon, in the creation of a comparative dialogue. However, we also recognize the shortcomings found here as a way of refining our challenge to dialogue posed in the introduction to this volume. Within the last several pages of this volume, we would like to reflect on the nature and content of subsequent work.

This project sought to provide a dialogical take on important issues as opposed to a simple outlining of perspectives devoid of exchange, with the readers having to imagine an exchange between the various contributors. We saw the inclusion of a "response" to each paper as a way to accomplish this feat. And, whereas we thought it useful at the time, we recognize that it is a rather limited form of dialogical exchange. In the future, within our own work and the other projects we hope this volume encourages, effort should be made to engage in a more direct exchange. One way of accomplishing this is through transcribed conversations between the two communities.

By arranging transcribed face-to-face exchanges, either through personal meetings or Internet gatherings (for example, e-mail exchange or a scheduled "chat-room" type exchange), the nuance and "flow" associated with conversation is better maintained. Furthermore, we believed it was important in this initial volume to limit the "response" sections to reflections on similarities and differences without a great concern for critical, analytical engagement. We believed this important because the ability to describe the realities and concerns, method and theoretical framework, as well as praxis of others, is the first step in a long term dialogue. After this, however, we understand that critical, analytical engagement is necessary. The working out of differences and similarities in a more critical fashion must follow. Such an exchange should help develop strategies for a theological engagement of social transformation that is comparative and far-reaching.

It is obvious that the voices of women must be better represented in the next wave of dialogical exchange. Connected to this, the format must include but also extend beyond the "women talking to women" and "men talking to men" model. Maintenance of this gendered approach can easily lend itself to narrow, parochial understandings of oppression and liberation. Also related to the selection of participants, we understand now more fully than at the outset that more attention must be given to a greater representation from the various "generations" or "waves" of theological thought within each community. Tied to this should be a greater commitment to intergenerational conversation. Through such an approach readers and participants will gain a better sense of how theological issues and agendas change over time and in light of the social realities into which theologians develop. Subsequent work must be more sensitive to the changing context and meaning of social transformation and liberation encountered by the various "generations" or "waves" of theologians.

Continuation of this dialogue should include an expanded corpus of issues. For example, it would be useful to explore the theological significance of the human body. This is particularly important for these two communities in that much of the discrimination and exoticism experienced is undeniably tied to the way in which non-Hispanic/Latino/a and non-African Americans have historically "constructed" the lived body (male and female) and the social body. Both communities understand the meaning of marginal status in a country that often expresses a strong aversion to "brown" bodies. Within both communities a sense of self-consciousness and subjectivity have been forged in part through expressive culture. It is true that non-European bodies were "contested terrain" upon which the struggle for power was waged. The desire to dominate and control these bodies was not passively accepted by those from whom twenty-first century African Americans and Hispanic/Latino/as descend. Rather, gestures, styles of walking, and other bodily movements speak to a level of rebellion or the forging of self that has religious and theological significance.[1] In this way, expressive culture within both communities is theological ground upon which work beyond *Ties That Bind* might take place.

A discussion of the lived body could be extended to include sensitive, "in the community," issues such as colorism. That is to say, in both communities the marked movement of modernity and the colonization of the Americas has resulted in an internal struggle for subjectivity and self-worth. And, this is often manifest through color bias—dark skin is "bad" and light skin is "good." Both communities suffer from this internalized racism, and theological reflection on this in dialogical manner should prove useful. Such a conversation, however, must be conducted with sensitivity and with an eye toward the mutual, theological growth and increased understanding such an exchange can entail.

In addressing constructions of the body and the politics of pleasure, dialogue between Hispanic/Latino/a and African American theologians should underscore and correct for the relative lack of attention to heterosexism and homophobia operating in both communities. Particularly with respect to Christian identity within both communities, there has been a tendency to ignore these forms of oppression or to give them only a passing reproach. More needs to be done. We have done a tremendous job of pointing out the oppressive nature of racial and gender discrimination and we have, in both communities, provided a pointed reproach of classism. Yet, we often fail to recognize or at least speak out against the oppression of members of our communities based on sexual orientation. In a very real way, our ability to address forcefully numerous other issues such as health care requires attention to homophobia and heterosexism.

Furthermore, theologians in both communities share concerns and strategies related to the economic plight facing people of color in the United States. More than one child is born into poverty every minute and, although most of these children are white Americans, distortions haunt U.S. thinking on poverty and foster an assumption that the majority of the poor are people of color who are lazy and dangerous.[2] Of course this is far from the truth. In other words,

> people of color, specifically African Americans, Native Americans and Latinos/as, are disproportionately represented among the poor. But truth is gravely distorted when images of people of color are offered as standard fare in news broadcasts whenever stories pertain to poverty or hunger, homelessness or unemployment, welfare or food stamps, and teenage parents or fathers ignoring child support orders.[3]

Poverty is an issue Hispanic/Latino/a and African American theologians should discuss together because of the ways in which real poverty and perceived poverty (e.g., the assumed economic failure of people of color) impact both communities. We began to recognize this connection during the late years of the Civil Rights movement and continued exchange might result in useful strategies. The shared commitment to liberation as a basic principle of religious faith easily serves as an impetus for this dialogue. And, a comparative theological discussion of poverty would enhance our understanding of the factors affecting the development of communities of color, and this might lead, in the long run, to a richer and more textured vision of economic justice.

The ramifications of poverty should also be addressed. That is to say, a dialogue on economics cannot avoid health care issues that impact communities of color in large part due to insurance and available care differentials connected to issues of race and class. With regards to insurance, for example, as of 1990 thirty-three percent of the uninsured in the United States were Hispanic/Latino/as and twenty percent were African Americans.[4] As Emilie Townes notes, "regardless of racial-ethnic identity or geographic location, working-class and poor folks face an almost insurmountable challenge in finding appropriate, affordable care. The urban and rural poor suffer from a dearth of health services in their respective communities."[5]

Finally, we would like to conclude by pointing back to where we started—an invitation to theological dialogue. African Americans and Hispanic/Latino/as have an overlapping history which has given rise to overlapping theological concerns. We share geographic, intellectual, and cultural spaces, areas of connection and contact that hold great theological promise or peril. Which one we encounter—promise or peril—is dependent on us and our ability to talk honestly and often.

# Notes

## Introduction

1. Otto Maduro, "Liberation Theology," in *A New Handbook of Christian Theology*, ed. Donald W. Musser and Joseph L. Price (Nashville: Abingdon Press, 1992), 288.

2. See, for instance, George Cummings, *A Common Journey: Black Theology and Latin American Liberation Theology* (Maryknoll, N.Y.: Orbis Books, 1993), and Dwight Hopkins, *Introducing Black Theology of Liberation* (Maryknoll, N.Y.: Orbis Books, 1999), esp. 157–180.

3. See Ana Maria Pineda, "Pastoral de Conjunto," in *New Theology Review* 3, no. 4 (1990): 28–34; Jose David Rodriguez and Loida I. Martell-Otero, "Introduction," in *Teologia en Conjunto: A Collaborative Hispanic Protestant Theology*, ed. Jose David Rodriguez and Loida I. Martell-Otero (Louisville: Westminster John Knox Press, 1997), 1–10; and Luis Pedraja, "Guideposts along the Journey: Mapping North American Hispanic Theology," in *Protestantes/Protestants: Hispanic Christianity within Mainline Traditions*, ed. David Maldonado Jr. (Nashville: Abingdon Press, 1999), esp. 136–137.

4. This conversation must gain another level of complexity through the eventual expansion to include additional communities of scholars such as American Indians.

5. A full discussion of the development of Hispanic/Latino/a and African American identities in the Americas is beyond the scope of this introduction and this volume. However, readers interested in additional information related to this topic should see, for example: Alex Garcia-Rivera, *St. Martin de Porres: The "Little Stories" and the Semiotics of Culture* (Maryknoll, N.Y.: Orbis Books, 1995); Jorge Gracia, *Hispanic-Latino/a Identities: A Philosophical Perspective* (Malden, M.A.: Blackwell Publishers, 2000); Charles Gibson, *Spain in America* (N.Y.: Harper & Row, 1966); Winthrop D. Jordan, *White Over Black: American Attitudes Toward the Negro, 1550–1812* (Chapel Hill: The University of North Carolina Press, 1968); Michael Angelo Gomez, *Exchanging Our Country Marks: The Transformation of African Identities in the Colonial and Antebellum South* (Chapel Hill: The University of North Carolina Press, 1998); Eddie S.

Glaude, Jr. *Exodus! Religion, Race, and Nation in Early Nineteenth-Century Black America* (Chicago: University of Chicago Press, 2000).

6. Charles Long, "Freedom, Otherness, and Religion: Theologies Opaque." In *Significations: Signs, Symbols, and Images in the Interpretation of Religion* (Philadelphia: Fortress Press, 1986), 190.

7. William Julius Wilson, *The Bridge Over the Racial Divide: Rising Inequality and Coalition Politics* (Berkeley, Calif.: University of California Press, 1999), 11.

8. For more on this topic, see William Julius Wilson, *The Bridge Over the Racial Divide*, esp. 23–33.

## 1. Black Theology in Historical Perspective

1. Charles Long, "The Oppressive Elements in Religion and the Religions of the Oppressed," in *Significations: Signs, Symbols, and Images in the Interpretation of Religion* (Philadelphia: Fortress Press, 1986; reissued in 1999 by The Davies Group), 170.

2. Ibid.

3. I discuss this idea with respect to humanism as a religious orientation in the currently unpublished paper titled "Earth Bound: Toward a Black Theology of Immanence." This paper contains the basic assertions that will be more fully developed in *Earth Bound: Toward a Theology of Fragile Cultural Memory and Religious Diversity* (working title) to be published by Fortress Press. It is also present in an essay titled "Some Praise Jesus and Some Don't: Thoughts on the Nature of African American Religious Identity and Those Who Interpret It," "Becoming American" conference, Georgetown University (Center for Christian-Muslim Understanding), May 11–12, 2000.

4. The academic treatment of African American religious experience, particularly with respect to the black churches, does not begin with late twentieth century, academic black theology. To suggest this is to dismiss the work of figures such as W. E. B. DuBois, Carter Woodson, E. Franklin Frazier, and Benjamin E. Mays who provided treatments of black churches with respect to their development and activities.

A discussion of these two movements is beyond the scope of this essay. For readers interested in this information, the following provide important insights: Stokely Carmichael and Charles V. Hamilton, *Black Power: The Politics of Liberation in America* (New York: Vintage Books, 1967); Floyd B. Barbour, compiler, *The Black Power Revolt: A Collection of Essays* (Boston, P. Sargent [1968]); Clayborne Carson, *In Struggle: SNCC and the Black Awakening of the 1960s* (Cambridge, Mass.: Harvard University Press, 1981); Martin L. King, *Where Do We Go from Here: Chaos or Community?* (New York: Harper & Row, 1967); Malcolm X, *The Last Speeches*. Edited by Steve Clark (New York: Pathfinder Press, 1992); Taylor Branch, *Parting the Waters: America in the King Years, 1954–63* (New York: Simon & Schuster, 1988); Taylor Branch, *Pillar of Fire: America in the King Years, 1963–65* (New York: Simon & Schuster, 1998).

5. "The Black Manifesto," in Gayraud S. Wilmore and James H. Cone, editors, *Black Theology: A Documentary History, 1966–1979* (Maryknoll, N.Y.: Orbis Books, 1979), 83–84.

6. "The National Committee of Black Churchmen's Response to the Black Manifesto," in Wilmore and Cone, *Black Theology*, 90–92.

7. "Statement by the National Committee of Black Churchmen, June 13, 1969," in Wilmore and Cone, *Black Theology*, 100–101 and "General Introduction," in Wilmore and Cone, *Black Theology*, 1. The NCBC was not alone in rethinking scripture in light of African American communities. Figures such as the late Albert Cleage, founder and pastor of the Shrine of the Black Madonna, embraced a black-centered interpretation of scripture. And because of this reading, Reverend Cleage argued that Jesus was, physiologically, the black Messiah and, in this role, would bring about the total liberation of African peoples. What distinguished Cleage's argument from that being put forth by NCBC was his strong cultural nationalism and his complete rejection of King's methods. See: Albert B. Cleage, *The Black Messiah* (New York: Sheed and Ward, 1968) and Cleage, *Black Christian Nationalism: New Directions for the Black Church* (New York: W. Morrow, 1972).

For a concise discussion of several of the major developments during this period, on the institutional level (NCBC and the black theology Project) see: Mary R. Sawyer, *Black Ecumenism: Implementing the Demands of Justice* (Valley Forge, Penn.: Trinity Press International, 1994), chapters 3, 5, and 7.

8. This assertion countered Joseph Washington's argument that the black church was irrelevant. He would later soften his position. See: Washington, *Black Religion: The Negro and Christianity in the United States* (Boston: Beacon Press, 1964) and Washington, *The Politics of God* (Boston: Beacon Press, 1967).

9. Luke 4:18–19 (KJV); also see Isaiah 61:1–2.

10. James Cone, *My Soul Looks Back* (Nashville: Abingdon Press, 1982); James Cone, *Black Theology and Black Power* (New York: Seabury Press, 1969). The quotation is from the "Preface to the 1989 Edition" of *Black Theology and Black Power*, 20th anniversary edition (San Francisco: Harper & Row, [1989], c1969), vii. For an important exploration of the "public" dimensions of Cone's first books see: Dwight Hopkins, editor, *Black Faith and Public Talk: Critical Essays on James H. Cone's Black Theology & Black Power* (Maryknoll, N.Y.: Orbis Books, 1999). Also see the companion essays by Delores Williams, Gayraud Wilmore, and others in the anniversary edition of Cone's *A Black Theology of Liberation*, 2nd ed. (Maryknoll, N.Y.: Orbis Books, 1986).

11. See for example: James Cone, *The Spirituals and the Blues* (New York: Seabury Press, 1972); *God of the Oppressed* (New York: Seabury Press, 1975); James Cone, *For My People: Black Theology and the Black Church* (Maryknoll, N.Y.: Orbis Books, 1984); James Cone, *Martin & Malcolm & America: A Dream or a Nightmare* (Maryknoll, N.Y.: Orbis Books, 1991). For reactions to black theology at this stage see: Wilmore and Cone, *Black Theology*, 1979, Part III. A major critique of Cone's theological sources such as Barth and Tillich is provided by his brother Cecil Cone in *The Identity Crisis in Black Theology* (Nashville, Tenn.: AMEC, 1975). An interesting embrace of black theology by someone external to the conversation is found in Theo Witvliet's *The Way of the Black Messiah* (Oak Park, Ill: Meyer-Stone Books, 1985; translated in 1987).

Cone has recently provided an overview of black theology's development titled *Risks of Faith: The Emergence of a Black Theology of Liberation, 1968–1998*

(Boston: Beacon Press, 1999). Readers interested in overviews of black theology should also see Dwight Hopkins's *Introducing Black Theology of Liberation* (Maryknoll, N.Y.: Orbis Books, 1999).

12. For examples of J. Deotis Roberts's work see: J. Deotis Roberts, *Liberation and Reconciliation: A Black Theology* (Philadelphia: Westminster Press, 1971); J. Deotis Roberts, *A Black Political Theology* (Philadelphia: Westminster Press, 1974); J. Deotis Roberts, *Black Theology in Dialogue* (Philadelphia: Westminster Press, 1987); Major Jones, *Black Awareness: A Theology of Hope* (Nashville: Abingdon Press, 1971); Major Jones, *Christian Ethics for Black Theology* (Nashville: Abingdon Press, 1974); Preston Williams, "The Black Experience and Black Religion," *Theology Today*, Vol. 26 (October 1969), 246–61; Preston Williams, "James Cone and the Problem of a Black Ethic," *Harvard Theological Review*, Vol. 65 (October 1972); Henry Mitchell, *Black Preaching* (Philadelphia: Lippincott, 1970); Henry Mitchell, *Black Belief: Folk Beliefs of Blacks in America and West Africa* (New York: Harper & Row, 1975); Gayraud Wilmore, *Black Religion and Black Radicalism* (Garden City, N.Y.: Anchor Press/Doubleday, 1973); William Jones, *Is God a White Racist?: A Preamble to Black Theology* (Garden City, N.Y.: Anchor Press/Doubleday, 1973). The figures referenced above were also responsible for developing an institutional means by which to explore African American religion and theology called the Society for the Study of Black Religion (SSBR). See Shelby Rooks, *Revolution in Zion: Reshaping African American Ministry, 1960–1974* (New York: Pilgrim Press, 1990). They also participated in the Black Theology Project sponsored by the "Theology in the Americas" initiative.

13. A prime example of this is Cornel West, *Prophesy Deliverance!: An Afro-American Revolutionary Christianity* (Philadelphia: Westminster Press, 1982). Also of interest is the personal narrative contained in Cornel West, *The Cornel West Reader* (New York: Basic Civitas Books, 1999), "Autobiographical Prelude" section. I have in mind volumes such as: Michael Eric Dyson, *Reflecting Black: African American Cultural Criticism* (Minneapolis: University of Minnesota Press, 1993) and Michael Dyson, *Race Rules: Navigating the Color Line* (New York: Addison-Wesley Publishing Company, 1996).

14. Cornel West, *Keeping Faith: Philosophy and Race in America* (New York: Routledge, 1993), 129.

15. Cornel West, "The Crisis in Contemporary American Religion," in *The Cornel West Reader*, 358.

16. In this essay second generation connotes a recognition of theologians who entered the Academy after the radical break with notions of the University held until the massive influx of students of color in the 1960s and early 1970s. In terms of disciplinary opportunities, second generation theologians benefit from the establishment, for example, of black studies programs in major universities, and also the "acceptance" of black theology as a viable discipline.

17. In rare cases, this theologizing has stepped outside the traditional boundaries of "church-talk." An early example of this is the process theology of blackness offered by Eulalio Baltazar and more recently the process leanings of Henry Young and Theodore Walker. In addition, there has been a humanist turn in theology offered by William R. Jones and Anthony Pinn. See: Henry Young, *Hope in Process: A Theology of Social Pluralism* (Minneapolis: Fortress Press, 1990); Theodore Walker, *Empower the People: Social Ethics for the African-*

*American Church* (Maryknoll, N.Y.: Orbis Books, 1991); Eulalio R. Baltazar, *The Dark Center: A Process Theology of Blackness* (New York: Paulist Press, 1973); William R. Jones, *Is God a White Racist?*; Anthony Pinn, *Why, Lord?: Suffering and Evil in Black Theology* (New York: Continuum, 1995).

18. Representative works include: Josiah Young, *Black and African Theologies: Siblings or Distant Cousins?* (Maryknoll, N.Y.: Orbis Books, 1986); Josiah Young, *A Pan-African Theology: Providence and the Legacies of the Ancestors* (Trenton, N.J.: Africa World Press, 1992); Dwight Hopkins, *Black Theology U.S.A. and South Africa: Politics, Culture, and Liberation* (Maryknoll, N.Y.: Orbis Books, 1989); Dwight Hopkins and George Cummings, editors, *Cut Loose Your Stammering Tongue: Black Theology in the Slave Narratives* (Maryknoll, N.Y.: Orbis Books, 1991); Dwight Hopkins, *Shoes That Fit Our Feet: Sources for a Constructive Black Theology* (Maryknoll, N.Y.: Orbis Books, 1993); James Evans, *We Have Been Believers: An African American Systematic Theology* (Minneapolis: Fortress Press, 1992).

19. See for example: Jon Michael Spencer, editor, *The Theology of American Popular Music*. A special issue of *Black Sacred Music: A Journal of Theomusicology* 3/2 (Fall 1989); Spencer, editor, *Sacred Music of the Secular City: From Blues to Rap*. A special issue of *Black Sacred Music: A Journal of Theomusicology* 6/1 (Spring 1992).

20. Garth Kasimu Baker-Fletcher, *Xodus: An African American Male Journey* (Minneapolis: Fortress Press, 1996); Garth Kasimu Baker-Fletcher and Karen Baker-Fletcher, *My Sister, My Brother: Womanist and Xodus God-Talk* (Maryknoll, N.Y.: Orbis Books, 1997). Readers may also be interested in the conversation between bell hooks and Cornel West: bell hooks and Cornel West, *Breaking Bread: Insurgent Black Intellectual Life* (Boston: South End Press, 1991).

21. Jacquelyn Grant, "Black Theology and the Black Woman," in Wilmore and Cone, *Black Theology*, 1979, 418–33; Frances Beale, "Double Jeopardy: To Be Black and Female," in Wilmore and Cone, *Black Theology*, 1979, 368–76; Theressa Hoover, "Black Women and the Churches: Triple Jeopardy," in Wilmore and Cone, *Black Theology*, 1979, 377–88.

22. See Maria Stewart, *America's First Black Woman Political Writer: Essays and Speeches*, edited by Marilyn Richardson (Bloomington: Indiana University Press, 1987); *Anna Julia Cooper: A Voice From the South* (1892: New York: Oxford University Press, 1988). Relevant essays by Murray include "Black, Feminist Theologies: Links, Parallels and Tension," Pauli Murray papers, Box 84, folder 1464, 86–95; "Black Theology and Feminist Theology: A Comparative Study," Pauli Murray papers, Box 23, folder 475. The Murray papers are held at the Schlesinger Library, Radcliffe College, Harvard University. Alice Walker, *In Search of Our Mothers' Gardens: Womanist Prose* (San Diego: Harcourt Brace Jovanovich, 1983).

23. Katie Cannon, "The Emergence of Black Feminist Consciousness," in Letty M. Russell, editor, *Feminist Interpretation of the Bible* (Louisville: Westminster Press, 1985) and Delores Williams, "Womanist Theology: Black Women's Voices," in *Christianity and Crisis* 47 (March 2, 1987).

24. Cheryl Kirk-Duggan, *Exorcising Evil: A Womanist Perspective on the Spirituals* (Maryknoll, N.Y.: Orbis Books, 1997); Traci C. West, *Wounds of the Spirit: Black Women, Violence, and Resistance Ethics* (New York: New York University Press, 1999); Diana L. Hayes, *And Still We Rise: An Introduction to Black Liberation Theology* (New York: Paulist Press, 1996); M. Shawn Copeland, " 'Wad-

ing through Many Sorrows: Toward a Theology of Suffering in Womanist Perspective," in Emilie M. Townes, editor, *A Troubling in My Soul: Womanist Perspectives on Evil and Suffering* (Maryknoll, N.Y.: Orbis Books, 1993); Cheryl Townsend Gilkes, "The Politics of 'Silence': Dual-Sex Political Systems and Women's Traditions of Conflict in African American Religion," in Paul E. Johnson, editor, *African American Christianity: Essays in History* (Berkeley: University of California Press, 1994); Cheryl Townsend Gilkes, "The 'Loves' and 'Troubles' of African American Women's Bodies," in Emilie M. Townes, editor, *A Troubling in My Soul.*

Also of importance here is the work of Marcia Y. Riggs. In addition to her work in Womanist ethics, Riggs has undertaken theological archaeological work by collecting important materials by African American women who shed light on the liberative nature of black religion. See: Marcia Riggs, editor, *Can I Get A Witness: Prophetic Religious Voices of African American Women, An Anthology* (Maryknoll, N.Y.: Orbis Books, 1997).

25. Katie Cannon, "Moral Wisdom in the Black Woman's Literary Tradition," in *Katie's Canon: Womanism and the Soul of the Black Community* (New York: Continuum, 1995), 59–60.

26. Cheryl Sanders, "Christian Ethics and Theology in Womanist Perspective," *Journal of Feminist Studies in Religion* 5, no. 2 (Fall 1989).

27. Renee L. Hill, "Who Are We for Each Other?: Sexism, Sexuality and Womanist Theology," in Gayraud S. Wilmore and James H. Cone, editors, *Black Theology: A Documentary History, Volume II, 1980–1992* (Maryknoll, N.Y.: Orbis Books, 1993); Kelly Brown Douglas, *Sexuality and the Black Church: A Womanist Perspective* (Maryknoll, N.Y.: Orbis Books, 1999); Emilie Townes, *In A Blaze of Glory: Womanist Spirituality as Social Witness* (Nashville: Abingdon Press, 1995); Michael Dyson, "When You Divide Body and Soul, Problems Multiply: The Black Church and Sex," in Dyson's *Race Rules: Navigating the Color Line* (New York: Addison-Wesley Publishing Company, Inc., 1996), 77–108; Cornel West, "Christian Love and Heterosexism," in West's *The Cornel West Reader*, 401–14.

28. Delores Williams, "Black Women's Surrogacy Experience and the Christian Notion of Redemption," in Paula Cooey, William R. Eakin, and Jay B. McDaniel, editors, *After Patriarchy: Feminist Transformations of the World Religions* (Maryknoll, N.Y.: Orbis Books, 1991), 1–14. Williams further develops this argument in *Sisters in the Wilderness: The Challenge of Womanist God-Talk* (Maryknoll, N.Y.: Orbis Books, 1993).

29. JoAnne Terrell, *Power in the Blood? The Cross in the African American Experience* (Maryknoll, N.Y.: Orbis Books, 1998); Jacquelyn Grant, *White Women's Christ and Black Women's Jesus: Feminist Christology and Womanist Response* (Atlanta: Scholars Press, 1989); Karen Baker-Fletcher, *Sisters of Dust, Sisters of Spirit: Womanist Wordings on God and Creation* (Minneapolis: Fortress Press, 1998); Alice Walker, *Living By the Word: Selected Writings, 1973–1987* (New York: Harcourt Brace Jovanovich, Publishers, 1988).

30. Victor Anderson, *Beyond Ontological Blackness* (New York: Continuum, 1995).

31. Diana L. Hayes and Cyprian Davis, O.S.B., editors, *Taking Down Our Harps: Black Catholics in the United States* (Maryknoll, N.Y.: Orbis Books, 1998), 3.

32. See: Charles Long, "Perspectives for a Study of Afro-American Religion

in the United States" and "Freedom, Otherness, and Religion: Theologies Opaque," in *Significations*, 1986.

33. Howard Thurman's religious mysticism may prove helpful with the development of religious sensitivity and appreciation for religious diversity sought here. See for example: Howard Thurman, *A Strange Freedom: The Best of Howard Thurman on Religious Experience and Public Life*, Walter E. Fluker and Catherine Tumber, editors (Boston: Beacon Press, 1998).

34. Movements in this direction include the theologically informed anthropology currently being done by Linda Thomas of Garrett Evangelical Theological Seminary. See: Linda Elaine Thomas, *Under the Canopy: Ritual Process and Spiritual Resilience in South Africa* (Columbia: University of South Carolina, 1999). Donald H. Matthews's *Honoring the Ancestors: An African Cultural Interpretation of Black Religion and Literature* (New York: Oxford University Press, 1999) is also concerned with developing methodological alternatives in black theology.

35. Katie Cannon, for example, has noted the importance of the physical body in essays such as "Womanist Perspectival Discourse and Canon Formation," in *Katie's Canon* (New York: Continuum, 1995), 69–76. This is also the case with Emilie Townes, *In a Blaze of Glory: Womanist Spirituality As Social Witness* (Nashville: Abingdon Press, 1995). Charles Long's work in the History of Religion also points to the importance of the body ("Freedom, Otherness, and Religion: Theologies Opaque," in *Significations*).

## 2. Strangers No More

1. The focus of my overview is on the theologies of Latinos and Latinas living in the United States. Hence, I will not be considering here the development of Puerto Rican theology in Puerto Rico, although the island is a territory of the United States by reason of its commonwealth (i.e., colonial) status. It is important to note, however, first that there in fact exists a theology which is articulated from a Puerto Rican context, and second that dialogue and the exchange of ideas does exist between Puerto Rican theologians in Puerto Rico, such as Luis Rivera Pagan, Yamina Apolinaris, and Sandra Mangual-Rodriguez, and Latino/a theologians in the United States.

2. It is possible to find a few rare examples of theological writings written by Hispanic/Latino/a theologians prior to this date. Nevertheless, these tended to be very brief articles that did not offer examples of thorough or systematic theological reflections, nor of a self-conscious and intentioned Latino/a theological perspective. I suggest that the move toward a more thorough, systematic, and book-length theological articulation of Latino/a life and culture, written from a fully intentional and uniquely Hispanic theological perspective, begins with the 1975 publication of Virgilio Elizondo's *Christianity and Culture: An Introduction to Pastoral Theology and Ministry for the Bicultural Community* (Huntington, Indiana: Our Sunday Visitor, Inc., 1975).

3. I have found an article by M. Shawn Copeland to be helpful in deciphering these historical stages of development within U.S. Hispanic/Latino/a theology: see Copeland, "Black, Hispanic/Latino, and Native American Theologies," in *The Modern Theologians: An Introduction to Christian Theology in The Twentieth Century*, 2d ed., ed. David Ford (Cambridge, Mass.: Blackwell

Publishers, 1997), especially 367–75. It is important to note, however, that I do not agree with the historical markers that M. Shawn Copeland provides in this article. Hence, I have here suggested my own stages, phases, time frames, and interpretive designations.

4. Although the popular perception is that Hispanics are foreign newcomers to the United States, the fact is that Hispanic history in North America actually precedes the history of the United States by more than two centuries. In point of fact, the Hispanic legacy, in what is now known as the United States, begins with the Spanish exploration and colonization of the North and South American continents commencing with Christopher Columbus's arrival in the Americas in 1492. This legacy has since evolved to incorporate the histories, cultures, pecularities, and contributions of a host of other different, yet historically, culturally, racially, and culturally linked, persons. Indeed, it is important to keep in mind that the term "Hispanic," or the term "Latino," is actually an ethnic label that lumps together the histories and the racial and cultural idiosyncracies of different peoples of Spanish-speaking or Latin ancestry who at present collectively number more than 30 million U.S. citizens and comprise approximately 11 percent of the total U.S. population. It is important, then, that the use of such umbrella terms as Latino/a or Hispanic not obscure the different historical trajectories of the groups that they call to mind—the Mexican American and/or Chicano, Puerto Rican, Cuban, Dominican, Central American, South American, and Spanish peoples living in the United States. For data on the general Latino/a population in the United States consult the U.S. Census Bureau, *Middle Series* (January 1, 1998) and *Current Population Reports* (Washington, D.C.: U.S. Bureau of the Census, 1996). See also the study put out by The Strategy Research Corporation entitled *1998 U.S. Hispanic Market* (Miami, Fla.: Strategy Research Corporation, 1997). For a sophisticated and critical study on the history and current use of the "Hispanic" and/or "Latino" label, see Juan Flores, "Pan-Latino/Trans-Latino: Puerto Ricans in the New Nueva York," *Centro: The Journal of the Center for Puerto Rican Studies* 8, no. 1&2 (1996): 171–86, and Suzanne Oboler, *Ethnic Labels, Latino Lives: Identity and the Politics of (Re)Presentation in the United States* (Minneapolis: University of Minnesota Press, 1995).

5. For more information on these occurrences and recent Latino/a history more generally, consult the following works: (1) Geoffrey Fox, *Hispanic Nation: Culture, Politics, and The Construction of Identity* (Tucson: University of Arizona Press, 1996); (2) Anthony Stevens-Arroyo, "The Emergence of a Social Identity among Latino Catholics: An Appraisal," in *Hispanic Catholic Culture in the U.S.: Issues and Concerns*, ed. Jay Dolan and Allan Figueroa Deck (Notre Dame, Ind.: University of Notre Dame Press, 1994), 77–130; (3) *Handbook of Hispanic Cultures in the United States: History*, vol. 2, ed. Alfredo Jimenez (Houston: Arte Publico Press/University of Houston, 1994); and (4) *The Hispanic Experience in the United States: Contemporary Issues and Perspectives*, ed. Edna Acosta-Belen and Barbara R. Sjostrom (New York: Praeger Publishers, 1988).

6. I am restricting my overview here to those theologians who most perceptibly influenced the direction of Latino/a theology in the United States through their multiple publications and organizational activities. But it is important to note that there were others who articulated theologies during

this time and who contributed to the annals of U.S. Hispanic/Latino theology, such as Andres Guerrero, Allan Figueroa Deck, Marina Herrera, and Ana Maria Pineda. These thinkers were also part of the first wave of Latino/a theological articulation in the United States.

7. Allan Figueroa Deck, *Frontiers of Hispanic Theology in the United States* (Maryknoll, N.Y.: Orbis Books, 1992), xii.

8. See Elizondo, "Educacion religiosa para el Mexico-Norte Americano/ Religious Education for the North-American Mexico," 83–86.

9. Elizondo, *Galilean Journey: The Mexican-American Promise* (Maryknoll, N.Y.: Orbis Books, 1983).

10. Elizondo, *The Future is Mestizo: Life Where Cultures Meet* (Bloomington, Ind.: Meyer Stone Books, 1988).

11. See especially Elizondo's *Christianity and Culture; La Morenita: Evangelizer of the Americas* (San Antonio: Mexican American Cultural Center, 1980); "Popular Religion as the Core of Cultural Identity in the Mexican American Experience," in *An Enduring Flame: Studies On Latino/a Popular Religiosity*, ed. Anthony Stevens-Arroyo and Ana Maria Diaz-Stevens (New York: PARAL, 1994); and *Guadalupe: Mother of the New Creation* (Maryknoll, N.Y.: Orbis Books, 1997).

12. For an informative biographical sketch of Elizondo's life and work, see David Nichols, "Virgil Elizondo: A Particular Man," in *Sources of Inspiration: Fifteen Modern Religious Leaders*, ed. Gene I. Maeroff (Kansas City: Sheed & Ward, 1992), 86–107. See also *Beyond Borders: Writings of Virgilio Elizondo and Friends*, ed. Timothy Matovina (Maryknoll, N.Y.: Orbis Books, 1999).

13. See Orlando Costas, *Christ outside the Gate: Mission beyond Christendom* (Maryknoll, N.Y.: Orbis Books, 1982). Many of the themes presented in this book are also displayed in his posthumously published book *Liberating News: A Theology of Contextual Evangelization* (Grand Rapids, Mich.: Eerdmans Publishing Co., 1989).

14. David Traverzo, "A Paradigm for Contemporary Latino Thought and Praxis: Orlando Costas' Latino Radical Evangelical Approach," in *Latino Studies Journal* 5, no. 3 (1994): 113.

15. See González, *History of Christian Thought*, 3 vols. (Nashville: Abingdon Press, 1970).

16. González, *Out of Every Tribe and Nation: Christian Theology at the Ethnic Roundtable* (Nashville: Abingdon Press, 1992); *Voces: Voices from the Hispanic Church* (Nashville: Abingdon Press, 1992); and *Santa Biblia: The Bible through Hispanic Eyes* (Nashville: Abingdon Press, 1996). It is important to note that, besides the academically oriented books written in English which I have here mentioned, Justo González has also published many popular books in Spanish that have sought to contribute to the theological and overall biblical preparation of ministers and lay persons in the Latino/a churches.

17. The Hispanic Summer Program was initiated in 1988 by the Fund for Theological Education, and is now under the direction of AETH. The program offers Latino/a theological students and religious leaders the opportunity to take courses on Hispanic theology and religiosity during the summer. AETH was established in 1991. Its focus is generally the theological education of Latinos/as in the United States, and it seeks to help the quality of such an education by offering programs pertaining to theological training and also

becoming involved with U.S. seminaries with the hopes of improving the quality of education and Latino/a enrollment. The Hispanic Theological Initiative, a program sponsored by The Pew Charitable Trusts, was launched in 1996. Its focus is not only the provision of scholarships to distinguished Latino/a Master's level seminarians, doctoral students, and postdoctoral fellows, but also the building of networks, mentorship programs, and community-building projects among Latino/a religious scholars and students. Justo González has been instrumental in the founding, organization, and running of all of these institutions.

18. For other writings by Yolanda Tarango, see "The Hispanic Woman and Her Role in the Church," *New Theology Review* 3, no. 4 (November 1990): 56–61, and "National Pastoral Plan for Hispanic Ministry," *Origins* 17, no. 26 (December 1987): 10–19.

19. Isasi-Díaz, "Mujeristas: A Name of Our Own," *The Christian Century* (May 24–31, 1989): 560–62.

20. Isasi-Díaz, *En la Lucha/In the Struggle: Elaborating a Mujerista Theology* (Minneapolis: Fortress Press, 1993), 4.

21. Isasi-Díaz, *Mujerista Theology: A Theology for the Twenty-First Century* (Maryknoll, N.Y.: Orbis Books, 1996), 192.

22. See Isasi-Díaz, "Round Table Discussion: Mujeristas, Who We Are and What We Are About," *Journal of Feminist Studies in Religion* 8, no.1 (Spring 1992): 105–25.

23. I am referring here to the following seven anthologies: (1) *We Are A People: Initiatives in Hispanic American Theology*, ed. Roberto S. Goizueta (Minneapolis: Fortress Press, 1992); (2) *Voces: Voices from the Hispanic Church* (1992); (3) *Frontiers of Hispanic Theology in the United States* (1992); (4) *Mestizo Christianity: Theology from the Latino Perspective*, ed. Arturo Banuelas (Maryknoll, N.Y.: Orbis Books, 1995); (5) *Hispanic/Latino Theology: Challenge and Promise* (1996); (6) *Teologia en Conjunto: A Collaborative Hispanic Protestant Theology*, eds. Jose David Rodriguez and Loida I. Martell-Otero (Louisville: Westminster John Knox Press, 1997); and (7) *From the Heart of Our People: Latino/a Explorations in Catholic Systematic Theology*, eds. Orlando O. Espín and Miguel H. Díaz (Maryknoll, N.Y.: Orbis Books, 1999). On the study of Latino/a religion, more generally, see the four volume titles in the PARAL Studies Series (The Program for the Analysis of Religion Among Latinos): (1) *An Enduring Flame: Studies on Latino Popular Religiosity*, vol. 1, eds. Anthony Stevens-Arroyo and Ana Maria Diaz-Stevens (1994); (2) *Old Masks, New Faces: Religion and Latino Identities*, vol. 2, eds. Anthony Stevens-Arroyo and Gilbert Cadena (1995); (3) *Enigmatic Powers: Syncretism with African and Indigenous Peoples' Religions among Latinos*, vol. 3, eds. Anthony Stevens-Arroyo and Andres I. Perez (1995); and (4) *Discovering Latino Religion: A Comprehensive Social Science Bibliography*, eds. Anthony Stevens-Arroyo and Segundo Pantoja (1995). For overviews on the history of the U.S. Latino/a Christian Churches, see these works: (1) Moises Sandoval, *On the Move: A History of the Hispanic Church in the United States* (1990); (2) *The Notre Dame History of Hispanic Catholics in the U.S.* (1994); (3) *Hidden Stories: Unveiling the History of the Latino Church* (1994); and (4) *Protestantes/Protestants: Hispanic Christianity within Mainline Traditions*, ed. David Maldonado, Jr. (Nashville: Abingdon Press, 1999).

24. I actually believe that at present we are beginning to witness a third

wave in the articulation of Latino/a theological thought, and more generally in the theoretical interpretation of the varieties of Latino/a religious experience, with the initial and distinctive writings of thinkers such as Edwin Aponte, Rudy Busto, Miguel de la Torre, Gaston Espinoza, Francisco Lozada, Jr., Lara Medina, Manuel Mejido, Loida Martell-Otero, Luis Pedraja, Nancy Pineda, and myself, Benjamin Valentin. The works of some of these authors has begun to promote a critical expansion of the horizons of Latino/a theology.

25. Fernando Segovia, *Hispanic/Latino Theology: Challenge and Promise*, 21.

26. Alex Garcia-Rivera, *St. Martin de Porres: The "Little Stories" and the Semiotics of Culture* (Maryknoll, N.Y.: Orbis Books, 1995), 40. It is important to note that the term *mestizaje*, or *mestizo/a*, technically refers to someone who is an offspring of Iberian and Amerindian/indigenous race and culture. Hence, it is in every way an appropriate signifier for Mexican Americans and other Latinos/as who directly trace their ancestry to Iberian and Amerindian heritage. But Caribbean Latinos/as and others, who are *especially* or *more directly* marked by African roots, may find more resonant the term *mulatez* in emphasizing the African element in their racial and cultural descent. Thus, the universalistic use of the term "mestizaje" as a catch-all phrase to signify racial and cultural hybridity may be problematic. Being sensitive to this fact, and in an attempt to balance the usage of the terms *mestizaje* and *mulatez*, Latina theologian Ada María Isasi-Díaz and Latino/a theologian Fernando Segovia have recently taken to the use of both terms side by side (i.e., *mestizaje/mulatez*). This bi-fold signifier appears for the first time in Ada María Isasi-Díaz's book *Mujerista Theology: A Theology for the Twenty-First Century* (Maryknoll, N.Y.: Orbis Books, 1996). To my knowledge, Fernando Segovia was the first theologian to make use of this more nuanced signifying designation. See his article, "Two Places and No Place on Which to Stand: Mixture and Otherness in Hispanic American Theology," *Listening: Journal of Religion and Culture* 27, no. 1 (Winter 1992): 26–40. The predominant inclination, not only in Latino/a theology but in Latino/a scholarship overall, however, continues to be that of using the term *mestizaje* in an all-encompassing manner in order to represent hybridity.

27. Homi Bhaba, "The Third Space," in *Identity, Community, Culture Difference*, ed. J. Rutherford (London: Lawrence and Wishart, 1990), 211.

28. See Jose Vasconcelos's influential 1925 essay *La Raza Cosmica*, republished in a bilingual edition as *The Cosmic Race/La Raza Cosmica* (Baltimore: Johns Hopkins University Press, 1997).

29. See especially Daniel Cooper Alarcon, *The Aztec Palimpsest: Mexico in the Modern Imagination* (Tucson: University of Arizona Press, 1997); Guillermo Gomez-Pena, *Warrior for Gringostroika* (Saint Paul: Graywolf Press, 1993); Cherrie Moraga, *The Last Generation* (Boston: Southend Press, 1993); and Gloria Anzaldua, *Borderlands/La Frontera: The New Mestiza* (San Francisco: Aunt Lute, 1987).

30. I borrow this line from Charles Lippy, who uses it in *Being Religious, American Style: A History of Popular Religiosity in the United States* (Westport, Conn.: Greenwood Press, 1994), 2.

31. Luis Pedraja, "Guideposts along the Journey: Mapping North American Hispanic Theology," in *Protestantes/Protestants: Hispanic Christianity within Mainline Traditions*, 136.

32. See Isasi-Díaz and Tarango, *Hispanic Women: Prophetic Voice in the Church*, esp. ix–xvii and 12–59.

33. See Justo González, *Mañana: Christian Theology from a Hispanic Perspective*, esp. 28–30.

34. See Roberto Goizueta Jr., *Caminemos con Jesús: Toward a Hispanic/Latino Theology of Accompaniment* (Maryknoll, N.Y.: Orbis Books, 1995).

35. M. Shawn Copeland, "Black, Hispanic/Latino, and Native American Theologies," 374.

36. For examples of these themes, see especially the following authors and works: (1) on the use of autochthonous cultural memory and production in theology, Jeanette Rodriguez-Holguin, "Sangre llama a Sangre: Cultural Memory as a Source," in *Hispanic/Latino Theology: Challenge and Promise*, 117–133; (2) on the theorizing of *mestizaje*, Virgilio P. Elizondo, *The Future is Mestizo* and Andres G. Guerrero, *A Chicano Theology* (Maryknoll, N.Y.: Orbis Books, 1987); (3) on the theorizing of Latino/a popular religion, Orlando Espín, *The Faith of the People* (Maryknoll, N.Y.: Orbis Books, 1997), Alex Garcia-Rivera, *St. Martin de Porres*, Virgilio Elizondo, "Popular Religion as the Core of Cultural Identity in the Mexican American Experience," in *An Enduring Flame*, 113–32, and Jeannette Rodriguez, *Our Lady of Guadalupe: Faith and Empowerment Among Mexican-American Women* (Austin: University of Texas Press, 1994); (4) on the elaboration of a *mujerista theology*, Ada María Isasi-Díaz, *En La Lucha* and *Mujerista Theology*; (5) on the historical Jesus as a *mestizo*, Virgilio Elizondo, *Galilean Journey*; (6) on an urban ecclesiology, Harold J. Recinos, *Hear the Cry: A Latino Pastor Challenges the Church* (Louisville: Westminster/John Knox Press, 1989), "The Barrio as the Locus of a New Church," in *Hispanic/Latino Theology*, 183–194, and *Who Comes in the Name of the Lord?: Jesus at the Margins* (Nashville: Abingdon Press, 1997); (7) on the reading of the Bible through Hispanic eyes, Justo L. González, *Santa Biblia*; (8) on the use of postcolonial studies within biblical hermeneutics, Fernando F. Segovia, "Two Places and No Place on Which to Stand," 26–40 and "In the World but Not of It: Exile as Locus for a Theology of the Diaspora," in *Hispanic/Latino Theology*, 195–217; and (9) on Christian ethics from a Hispanic/Latino/a perspective, Ismael Garcia, *Dignidad: Ethics through Hispanic Eyes* (Nashville: Abingdon Press, 1997).

37. Fernando Segovia, *Hispanic/Latino Theology: Challenge and Promise*, 42.

38. For a fuller treatment of this particular theme and argument see my article "Nuevos Odres para el Vino: A Critical Contribution to Latino/a Theological Construction," in *Journal of Hispanic/Latino Theology* 5, no. 4 (1998): 30–47.

39. For more on these intimations, see my study entitled "Going Public: Negotiating the Intersections of a Hispanic/Latino and U.S. Public Theology" (Ph.D. diss., Drew University, 2000), esp. 53–104. See also my article "Nuevos Odres para el Vino," esp. 43–47.

### 3. Scripture, Tradition, Experience, and Imagination

1. Fernando Segovia, "Reading the Bible as Hispanic Americans," *The New Interpreter's Bible*, vol. 1 (Nashville: Abingdon, 1994), 167–73. See some further reflections on Segovia's typology, and on Hispanic hermeneutics in general,

in Luis R. Rivera-Rodríguez, "Reading in Spanish from the Diaspora through Hispanic Eyes," *Theology Today*, 54/4 (January, 1998): 480–90.

2. Maryknoll: Orbis, 1983. Revised and expanded edition: 2000.

3. Segovia builds his argument on an article by Isasi-Díaz, "The Bible and Mujerista Theology," in Susan B. Thistlethwaite and Mary Potter Engel, *Lift Every Voice: Constructing Theologies from the Underside* (San Francisco: Harper & Row, 1990), 1–15.

4. Ibid., 170.

5. Ada María Isasi-Díaz and Yolanda Tarango, *Hispanic Women: Prophetic Voice in the Church* (San Francisco: Harper & Row, 1988), 66.

6. See specifically Harold J. Recinos, *Hear the Cry! A Latino Pastor Challenges the Church* (Louisville: Westminster/John Knox, 1989), 65–74.

7. Ibid., 170. For a fuller example of my own approach, the reader may wish to look at a book that was not available to Segovia as he wrote these lines: *Santa Biblia: The Bible through Hispanic Eyes* (Nashville: Abingdon, 1996).

8. Justo L. González, *Hechos* (Miami: Caribe, 1992), 61–68.

9. Justo L. González, "View from the Crossroads," *Perspectives*, McCormick Theological Seminary (Fall 1993): 1–3. Also *Hechos*, 203–5.

10. In David Maldonado, Jr., ed., *Protestantes/Protestants: Hispanic Christianity within Mainline Traditions* (Nashville: Abingdon: 1999), 297.

11. Gary Riebe-Estrella, "Latino Religiosity or Latino Catholicism?," *Theology Today*, 54/4 (January, 1998): 512.

12. Ibid., 513.

13. Ibid.

14. *The Faith of the People: Theological Reflections on Popular Catholicism* (Maryknoll: Orbis, 1997), 65.

15. "Pueblo and Church," in Orlando O. Espín and Miguel H. Díaz, eds., *From the Heart of Our People: Latino/a Explorations in Catholic Systematic Theology* (Maryknoll: Orbis, 1999), 172–88.

16. Basing his work on that of Richard A. Shweder and Edmund J. Bourne, "Does the Concept of Person Vary Cross-Culturally?" in Richard Shweder and Edmund J. Bourne, eds., *Culture Theory: Essays on Mind, Self, and Emotion* (Cambridge: Cambridge University Press, 1984), 188–95.

17. María Pilar Aquino, "Theological Method in U.S. Latino/a Theology," in *From the Heart . . .* , 39.

18. Alejandro García-Rivera, *The Community of the Beautiful: A Theological Aesthetics* (Collegeville: The Liturgical Press, 1999).

19. I have discussed how this relates to our view of the world in *Mañana: Christian Theology from a Hispanic Perspective* (Nashville: Abingdon, 1990), 120–22. On the relation between this and the debate regarding modernity and postmodernity, see "Metamodern Aliens in Postmodern Jerusalem," in Ada María Isasi-Díaz and Fernando Segovia, eds., *Hispanic/Latino Theology: Challenge and Promise* (Minneapolis: Fortress, 1996), 340–50.

20. *For the Healing of the Nations: The Book of Revelation in an Age of Cultural Conflict* (Maryknoll: Orbis, 1999), 99.

## 4. "We See Through a Glass Darkly"

1. James H. Cone, *God of the Oppressed* (New York: Seabury Press, 1975), 5, 14.

2. Dwight N. Hopkins and George Cummings, eds. *Cut Loose Your Stammering Tongue: Black Theology in the Slave Narratives* (Maryknoll, N.Y.: Orbis, 1991).

3. Hopkins, "Introduction," *CLST*, xx.

4. Mark L. Chapman has given a great deal of attention to this third line of criticism in *Christianity on Trial: African American Religious Thought before and after Black Power* (Maryknoll, N.Y.: Orbis, 1996).

5. *Spirituals and the Blues* (New York: Seabury, 1972), *God of the Oppressed* (New York: Seabury Press, 1975), and "Christian Theology and Scripture as the Expression of God's Liberating Activity for the Poor" and "Sanctification and Liberation in the Black Religious Tradition, with Special Reference to Black Worship" in *Speaking the Truth* (Grand Rapids: Eerdmans, 1986), 4–34.

6. Anthony B. Pinn, *Why Lord? Suffering and Evil in Black Theology* (New York, N.Y.: Continuum, 1995), 21–38.

7. James H. Cone, "Black Theology and the Black Church," in *What Does it Mean to be Black and Christian?*, edited by Forrest Harris et al. (Nashville: Townsend Press, 1995), 57.

8. James H. Evans, *We Have Been Believers* (Minneapolis: Fortress, 1992), 1.

9. Ibid., 5–6.

10. Dwight N. Hopkins, *Shoes That Fit Our Feet: Sources of a Constructive Black Theology* (Maryknoll, N.Y.: Orbis, 1993); also see Hopkins's *Down, Up and Over: Slave Religion and Black Theology* (Minneapolis: Fortress Press, 2000).

11. The materials were collected between 1936–38 under the auspices of the Folklore Division of the Federal Writers' Project and inaugurated by President Roosevelt as a division of the Federal Works Administration. The project was one means of keeping mostly white, white-collar workers employed during the depression years. The collection contains interviews depicting the experience of former slaves in the United States. Although the collection was mostly a federal project, some individual states, including Virginia and Louisiana, and the American Freedmen Inquiry Commission had already begun collecting slave narratives as early as 1863. However, these were a very small number of cases. A number of personal journals and autobiographies that trace the rise of many free men and women from slavery to freedom are also regarded by Hopkins and his colleagues as sources for constructive black theology.

12. George Cummings, "Slave Narratives, Black Theology of Liberation (U.S.A.), and The Future," in *CLST*, 137–38.

13. Hopkins, "Slave Theology," *CLST*, 44.

14. Will Coleman, "Coming Through Legion: Metaphor in Non-Christian and Christian Experiences with the Spirit(s) in African American Slave Narratives," *CLST*, 68; also see Coleman's recently published *Tribal Talk*.

15. Ibid.

16. Hopkins, *Shoes That Fit Our Feet*, 47.

17. Ibid., 48.

18. Coleman, *CLST*, 96–97.

19. Cheryl J. Sanders, "Liberation Ethics in the Ex-Slave Interviews," in *CLST*, 103.

20. Ibid., 104.

21. Ibid., 114.

22. Ibid., 122–24.

23. Ibid., 124–27.

24. Ibid., 132.

25. Sanders, *Empowerment Ethics for a Liberated People* (Minneapolis: Fortress Press, 1995).

26. Ibid., 25.

27. Hopkins, "Slave Theology," *CLST*, 2.

28. Ibid., 2–3.

29. Hopkins, "Introduction," *CLST*, ix.

30. Ibid., x.

31. Hopkins, *Down, Up, and Over: Slave Religion and Black Theology*, 6–10.

32. Hopkins, *Shoes That Fit Our Feet*, 22.

33. Charles H. Long, *Significations: Signs, Symbols, and Images in the Interpretation of Religion* (Philadelphia: Fortress Press, 1986), 9; hereafter page references to Professor Long's work are given in the text.

34. Victor Anderson, *Beyond Ontological Blackness: An Essay in African American Religious and Cultural Criticism* (New York: Continuum, 1995), 120–32.

35. Ibid., 161.

## 5. Black Theology on God

1. For definitional options and nuances in both concepts of the popular and culture, see Kathryn Tanner, *Theories of Culture: A New Agenda for Theology* (Minneapolis: Fortress Press, 1997); John Storey, *An Introductory Guide to Cultural Theory and Popular Culture* (Athens: University of Georgia Press, 1993); Chris Jenks, *Culture* (New York: Routledge, 1993); and Chandra Mukerji and Michael Schudson, eds., *Rethinking Popular Culture: Contemporary Perspectives in Cultural Studies* (Berkeley: University of California Press, 1991).

2. "Narrative of Lunsford Lane" in *Five Slave Narratives* (New York: Arno Press, 1968 reprint), 20.

3. William Still, *The Underground Railroad, A Record of Facts, Authentic Narratives, Letters, etc., Narrating the Hardships, Hair-breadth Escapes and Death Struggles of the Slaves in their Efforts for Freedom As Related by Themselves and Others, Or Witnessed by the Author* (Chicago: Johnson Publications, 1970 reprint of 1870 original), 458.

4. Amy Griffith, *Autobiography of a Female Slave* (New York: Negro University Press, 1969 reprint of 1857 original), 242.

5. George P. Rawick, *The American Slave: A Composite Autobiography*, vol. 12, *Georgia* (Westport, Conn.: Greenwood, 1972), part 1, p. 13. For the connection of God's act of using the Yankees in the Civil War to other divine acts, see Sarah Bradford, *Harriet Tubman* (Secaucus, N.J.: The Citadel Press, 1961), 106.

6. Henry Bibb, *Narrative of the Life and Adventure of Henry Bibb An American Slave, Written By Himself* (Philadelphia: Rhistoric Publications, 1969 reprint of 1849 original), 48.

7. Kate Drumgoold, "A Slave Girl's Story: Being an Autobiography of Kate Drumgoold" in *Six Women's Slave Narratives*, The Schomburg Library of Nineteenth-Century Black Women Writers (New York: Oxford University Press, 1988 reprint), 30. Kate Drumgoold was born a slave in Virginia.

8. David Walker, *David Walker's Appeal To the Coloured Citizens of the World, but in particular and very expressly, to those of The United States of America* (New York: Hill and Wang, 1965 reprint of 1829 original), 3.

9. John W. Blassingame, ed., *Slave Testimony: Two Centuries of Letters, Speeches, Interviews, and Autobiographies* (Baton Rouge: Louisiana State University Press, 1977), 131.

10. Kate Drumgoold, *Six Women's Slave Narratives*, 3.

11. Kate Drumgoold, *Six Women's Slave Narratives*, 23–24.

12. Old Elizabeth, "Memoir of Old Elizabeth, A Coloured Woman," in *Six Women's Slave Narratives*, 17.

13. Nancy Williams, in *Weevils in the Wheat: Interviews with Virginia Ex-Slaves*, ed. Charles L. Perdue, Jr. (Bloomington: Indiana University Press, 1980) 319–20.

## 6. Popular Religion, Political Identity, and Life-Story Testimony in an Hispanic Community

2. Stephen, Lyn and James Dow, eds., *Class, Politics, and Popular Religion in Mexico and Central America* (Washington, D.C.: American Anthropological Association, 1990) 1–8.

3. Ibid., 8–9.

4. See Roger N. Lancaster, *Thanks to God and the Revolution: Popular Religion and Class Consciousness in the New Nicaragua* (New York: Columbia University, 1988).

5. See Robert Redfield, *Tepoztlan, A Mexican Village: A Study in Folk Life* (Chicago: University of Chicago, 1930), *The Folk Culture of Yucatan* (Chicago: University of Chicago Press, 1941), and *The Little Community, and Peasant Society and Culture* (Chicago: University of Chicago Press, 1960).

6. Lancaster, *Thanks to God and the Revolution*, 32–33.

7. Ibid., 44.

8. Ibid., 44–45.

9. June Nash, *We Eat The Mines and the Mines Eat Us: Dependency and Exploitation in Bolivian Tin Mines* (New York: Columbia University Press, 1979).

10. Ibid., 320.

11. Gustavo Gutiérrez, *The Power of the Poor in History* (Maryknoll N.Y.: Orbis, 1984), 193.

12. Phillip Berryman, *The Religious Roots of Rebellion: Christians in Central American Revolutions* (Maryknoll, N.Y.: Orbis, 1987), 6.

13. Jon Sobrino and Ignacio Martin-Baro, eds., *The Political Dimension of Faith* (Maryknoll, N.Y. Orbis Books, 1990 [orig. 1980]), 133–34.

14. Victor Turner, *Dramas, Fields and Metaphors* (Ithaca: Cornell University, 1974), 64.

15. Ibid., 68.

## 7. Preoccupations, Themes, and Proposals of Mujerista *Theology*

1. Iris Marion Young, *Justice and the Politics of Difference* (Princeton: Princeton University Press, 1990), 39–65.

2. Ignacio Ellacuría, "Hacia una fundamentación del método teológico

latinoamericano," *Estudios centroamericanos* 30, No. 322– 323 (Agosto–Septiembre, 1975): 419.

3. Ruth Ginzberg, "Philosophy is Not a Luxury," in *Feminist Ethics*, ed. Claudia Card (Lawrence: University Press of Kansas, 1991), 126–145.

4. Ada María Isasi-Díaz, *Mujerista Theology: A Theology for the Twenty-First Century* (Maryknoll, N.Y.: Orbis Books, 1996), 86–104.

5. I am grateful to Manuel Mejido, a doctoral student at Emory University, for discussions regarding the need for new sociological perspectives.

6. I am grateful to Franz Hinkelammert for making clear the need to differentiate between globality and globalization.

7. Ivone Gebara, *Longing for Running Water* (Minneapolis: Fortress Press, 1999) 67–99.

## Response by Chandra Taylor Smith

1. See note 4 in chap. 8 below.

2. Delores S. Williams, "Women's Oppression and Life-Line Politics in Black Women's Narratives," in *Journal of Feminist Studies in Religion*, Vol. 1, no. 2 (Fall 1985): 62.

3. An emphasis should be placed on predominate in this point, because indeed there are Roman Catholic Womanist theologians as well as Latinas who are Protestant.

4. Ada María Isasi-Díaz, "Mujerista Theology: A Challenge to Traditional Theology," in *Mujerista Theology: A Theology for the Twenty-First Century* (Maryknoll, N.Y.: Orbis Books, 1996), 65.

## 8. Womanist Theology

1. Alice Walker, *In Search of Our Mothers' Gardens* (San Diego: Harcourt Brace Jovanovich, 1983). Walker's example of being "universalist" is portrayed in the question: "Mama, why are we brown, pink, and yellow, and our cousins are white, beige, and black?" Ans.: "Well, you know the colored race is just like a flower garden, with every color flower represented." So, being universalist explicitly pertains to embracing the rich diversity of African Americans, literally in skin tone. But there is an implicit sense of the affirmation of the myriad of other expressions of being African American, as well.

2. For a thorough systematic, historical overview of Womanist theology see the fourth chapter, entitled "Womanist Theology" in Dwight N. Hopkins, *Introducing Black Theology of Liberation* (New York: Orbis Books, 1999), 125–56. He appropriately locates the historical origins of Womanist theology in black civil rights and black power movements in the 1960s and 1970s, as well as in the white feminist movement in the 1970s. Hopkins identifies Jacquelyn Grant's 1979 article entitled "Black Theology and the Black Woman" as the first place that a black feminist theology was discussed. In 1985, Katie G. Cannon's essay entitled "The Emergence of Black Feminist Consciousness" was the first written text to use the term "Womanist."

3. Walker, "Gifts of Power: The Writings of Rebecca Jackson," *In Search of Our Mothers' Gardens*, 82.

4. See, "Roundtable Discussion: Christian Ethics and Theology in Womanist Perspectives," in *Journal of Feminist Studies in Religion* 5 (Fall 1989): 105.

5. Jacquelyn Grant argues in her essay, "Womanist Theology: Black Women's Experience," in *Black Theology: A Documentary History Vol. II, 1980–1992*, ed. James Cone and Gayraud S. Wilmore (Maryknoll, N.Y.: Orbis Books, 1993), that Womanist theology is potentially holistic precisely because "the experience out of which it emerges is totally interconnected with other experiences" (287).

6. See Frances Beale, "Double Jeopardy: To Be Black and Female," in Cone and Wilmore, *Black Theology*, 369–76; Theressa Hoover, "Black Women and the Churches: Triple Jeopardy," in Cone and Wilmore, *Black Theology*, 377–88; Beverly Lindsay, "Minority Women in America: Black American, Native American, Chicana, and Asian American Women," in *The Study of Women: Enlarging Perspectives of Social Reality*, ed. Eloise C. Snyder (New York: Harper & Row, 1979), 318–63; and Deborah K. King, "Multiple Jeopardy, Multiple Consciousness: The Context of a Black Feminist Ideology," in *Signs: Journal of Women in Culture and Society* 14 (1988): 42–72.

7. Karen Baker-Fletcher, *A Singing Something: Womanist Reflections on Anna Julia Cooper* (New York: Crossroads, 1994), 156.

8. Ibid.

9. Clarice J. Martin, "Womanist Interpretations of the New Testament: The Quest for Holistic and Inclusive Translation and Interpretation," in Cone and Wilmore, *Black Theology*, 232–36.

10. Walker, *In Search*, xi.

11. See also Kelly Brown Douglas, *The Black Christ* (Maryknoll, N.Y.: Orbis Books, 1994).

12. These stereotypical images have been examined by many Womanist scholars. Patricia Hill Collins offers a critical socio/historical-based constructive analysis of these and other stereotypical images in her text, *Black Feminist Thought: Knowledge, Consciousness, and the Politics of Empowerment* (New York: Routledge, 1990).

13. Walker, *In Search*, xi.

14. Central to Walker's reasoning is the problem of a non–African American imposing the term lesbian on an African American woman's relationship when culturally she as an African American woman has not been defined as so. The word "lesbian," suggests Walker, "may not, in any case, be suitable (or comfortable) for black women, who surely would not have begun their women-bonding earlier than Sappho's residency on the Isle of Lesbos" (81). Walker asserts that the word that African American women would use would have to be "organic, characteristic, not simply applied." For Walker, the word Womanist fits this bill.

15. "Roundtable Discussion," 86.

16. Ibid., 90.

17. Ibid., 100.

18. Ibid., 93.

19. Paul Tillich, *Dynamics of Faith* (New York: Harper Torchbooks, 1957), 17.

20. Ibid., 10.

21. "Roundtable Discussion," 97.

22. Ibid., 94.

23. Shipley, Joseph T., *Dictionary of Word Origins*, 239.

24. Walker, *In Search*, 238–39.

25. Delores S. Williams, *Sisters in the Wilderness: The Challenge of Womanist God-Talk* (Maryknoll, N.Y.: Orbis Books, 1993), 1.

26. Walker, *In Search*, 231–31.

27. Jacquelyn Grant, "Womanist Theology: Black Women's Experience," in Cone and Wilmore, *Black Theology*, 279.

28. Katie G. Cannon, *Black Womanist Ethics* (Atlanta, Ga.: Scholars Press, 1988), 2.

29. Renita Weems, "Reading Her Way Through the Struggle: African American Women and the Bible," in *Stony the Road We Trod*, ed. Cain Hope Felder (Minneapolis: Fortress Press, 1991), 61–63.

30. Weems cites this passage from Howard Thurman, *Jesus and the Disinherited* (Nashville: Abingdon Press, 1949), 30–31.

31. Cannon, *Black Womanist Ethics*, 4.

32. Delores Williams, "Womanist Theology: Black Women's Voices," in Cone and Wilmore, *Black Theology*, 271.

33. Ibid. Note, that in the paraphrase of Williams, I added the italicized words and emphasis.

34. Clarice J. Martin, "Womanist Interpretation of the New Testament: The Quest for Holistic and Inclusive Translation and Interpretation," in *Journal of Feminist Studies in Religion* 6, no. 2 (Fall 1990): 42.

35. Williams, "A Womanist Perspective on Sin," in *A Troubling in My Soul: Womanist Perspectives on Evil and Suffering*, ed. Emilie M. Townes (Maryknoll, N.Y.: Orbis Books, 1993), 146.

36. Ibid., 145–46.

37. Ibid.

38. Kelly Brown Douglas, "God Is as Christ Does: Toward a Womanist Theology," in *The Journal of Religious Thought* 46, no. 1 (Summer–Fall 1989): 12.

39. Ibid. Douglas refer her readers to the following works which represent some of the earlier articles and essays written that challenged feminist and black theologians: Jacquelyn Grant, "The Development and Limitations of Feminist Christology: Toward an Engagement of White Women's and Black Women's Religious Experiences," Ph.D. dissertation, Union Theological Seminary, 1985; Audre Lorde, "An Open Letter to Mary Daly," in *This Bridge Called My Back*, eds. Cherríe Moraga and Gloria Anzaldua (New York: Kitchen Table Press, 1983); Angelique Walker-Smith, "Exclusive Language Reflects Inner Beliefs," in *Christianity and Crisis* 45, no. 7 (April 29, 1985): 146; Delores S. Williams, "The Color of Feminism," in *Christianity and Crisis* 45, no. 7 (April 29, 1985): 146–65.

40. Cannon, *Black Womanist Ethics*, 137.

41. Frances E. Wood, " 'Take My Yoke Upon You': The Role of the Church in the Oppression of African American Women," in *A Troubling in My Soul*, 39.

42. Delores S. Williams, "The Color of Feminism: Or Speaking the Black Woman's Tongue," in *The Journal of Religious Thought* 43, no. 1 (Spring–Summer 1986): 52. Williams explains that "demonarchy can be understood as the

demonic governance of black women's lives by white male and white female ruled systems using racism, violence, violation, retardation, and death as instruments of social control. . . . It is informed by a state of consciousness that believes white women are superior to and more valuable than any woman of color and that white men are superior to and the most valuable and superior forms of life on earth."

43. Ibid., 55.

44. "A Black Feminist Statement: The Combahee River Collective," in *All the Women are White, All the Blacks are Men, But Some of Us are Brave: Black Women's Studies*, eds. Gloria T. Hull, Patricia Bell Scott, and Barbara Smith (New York: The Feminist Press, 1982), 16.

45. Teresa L. Brown, "Avoiding Asphyxiation: A Womanist Perspective on Intrapersonal and Interpersonal Transformation," in *Embracing the Spirit: Womanist Perspectives on Hope, Salvation and Transformation* (Maryknoll, N.Y.: Orbis Books, 1997), 75.

46. Ibid. See in Brown's essay her discussion about the organization that she helped to found among the African Methodist Episcopal Church community in Denver Colorado. The innovative group was called, Sisters Working Encouraging Empowering Together (S.W.E.E.T). It was primarily formed as "a network for intentionally sharing Womanist perspectives and undergirding black women's efforts for spiritual and social liberation," according to Brown (80–81).

47. Victor Anderson, *Beyond Ontological Blackness: An Essay on African American Religious and Cultural Criticism* (New York: Continuum, 1995), 112.

48. Ibid., 11.

49. Ibid., 48.

50. Townes, *A Troubling in My Soul*, 2.

51. Anderson, *Beyond Ontological Blackness*, 112.

52. Ibid., 106.

53. Ibid., 113.

54. Ibid., 116.

### Response by Ada María Isasi-Díaz

1. Sharon Welch, *A Feminist Ethics of Risk* (Minneapolis: Fortress Press, 1990), 68.

### 9. Christian Doctrines of Humanity and the African Experience of Evil and Suffering

1. I use African and black to be inclusive of the peoples and cultures of both the African continent and the African diaspora (blacks in the Americas and the Caribbean). Throughout the remainder of the essay I deliberately use the terms African and black interchangeably to refer both to people of African descent generally and to African North Americans specifically. I also use the terms European and white interchangeably to refer to people of European descent.

2. In his evaluation of nineteenth-century African American Pan-Africanist theology Josiah U. Young critically examines a number of Christian-based anti-African ideas in the works of major black religious thinkers. See *A Pan-African Theology: Providence and the Legacies of the Ancestors* (Trenton: Africa World Press, Inc., 1992).

3. In the *Confessions* Augustine submits that "[t]he beginning of man's pride is apostasy from God; the beginning of all sin is pride." Augustine, *Confessions*, trans. Henry Chadwick (Oxford: Oxford University Press, 1991), 5, 10, 103.

4. Augustine asserts that "whatever is, is good." *Confessions* 7, 12, 148.

5. Augustine's views on the soul were mainly developed between 386 and 388 in his early writings: *Soliloquia, De Immortalitate Animae, De Quantitate Animae*. See John H. S. Burleigh, *Augustine: Earlier Writings* (Philadelphia: Westminster Press, 1952).

6. *De Libero Arbitrio*, 2, 12, 34.

7. *De Trinitate*, 12, 14, 22.

8. *De Trinitate* 7, 7. Also see R. V. G. Tasker, ed., *De Civitate Dei*, trans. John Healey (London: Dent, 1945),19, 3.

9. See Earl's discussion of what he calls the "soul-body dichotomy," Riggins Earl, *Dark Symbols, Obscure Signs: God, Self, and Community in the Slave Mind* (Maryknoll, N.Y.: Orbis Books, 1993). See especially p. 22.

10. Augustine posits that "the soul, when it is sensing in the body, does not passively undergo anything from the body, but the soul pays more attention to the passions of the body and these activities, which may be easy because of their agreement with the body, or difficult because of their disagreement, do not escape the soul," *De Musica*, 6, 5, 10; *De Quantitate Animae*, 23, 45.

11. Augustine testifies to God that "I shall look for you that my soul may live. For it is my soul that gives life to my body, and it is you who give life to my soul." *Confessions* 10, 20, 226. Also see *On Human Responsibility*, 3, 11, 12, 32–33, 35; *De Genesi Ad Litteram*, 12, 24.

12. J. G. Kristo, *Looking for God in Time and Memory: Psychology, Theology, and Spirituality in Augustine's Confessions* (Lanham, Md.: University Press of America, 1991), 71.

13. My research focuses primarily upon Protestant missionary activity (Baptist, Methodist, Anglican, Moravian, Presbyterian) in Africa, the Caribbean, and North America. Important records include: K. S. Malden, *Broken Bonds: The S.P.G. and the West Indian Slaves* (Westminster: The Society for the Propagation of the Gospel in Foreign Parts, 1933); Alfred Caldecott, *The Church in the West Indies* (London: Frank Cass & Co., 1898); Walter Hark, *The Breaking of the Dawn: Or Moravian Work in Jamaica* (London: Wm. Strain & Sons, 1904); George Blyth, *Reminiscences of Missionary Life, With Suggestions to Churches and Missionaries* (Edinburgh: William Oliphant & Sons, 1851); Mary Turner, *Slaves and Missionaries: The Disintegration of Jamaican Slave Society, 1787–1834* (Chicago: University of Illinois Press); G. H. Rose, *A Letter on the Means and Importance of Converting the Slaves in the West Indies to Christianity* (London: John Murray, 1823); Thomas Coke, *A History of the West Indies, Containing the Natural, Civil and Ecclesiastical History of each Island*, Vols.1–3

(Liverpool: Nuttall, Fisher and Dixon, 1808–1811). The Religious Tract Society, *Missionary Records: West Indies* (London: Religious Tract Society, 1834–1838); Hope Waddell, *Twenty-nine Years in the West Indies and Central Africa 1826–1858* (London: Nelson, 1863); *History of the Baptist Missionary Society from 1792–1842, vols. 1–2* (London: T. Ward, 1842); Charles Colcock Jones, *The Religious Instruction of the Negroes in the United States* (New York: Kraus Reprint Co., 1969).

14. See chapters three and four of Albert Raboteau, *Slave Religion: The "Invisible Institution" in the Antebellum South* (New York: Oxford University Press, 1976).

15. Ibid. Also see Mary Turner, *Slaves and Missionaries* and Charles Colcock Jones, *The Religious Instruction of the Negroes in the United States.*

16. In his memoirs entitled *A Voyage to the Islands*, Hans Sloane recalls that "the punishment for crimes of slaves are usually for rebellions burning them, by *nailing them down on the ground with crooked sticks on every limb*, and then applying the fire by degrees from the feet and hands, burning them gradually up to the head whereby their pains are extravagant." (Emphasis mine). See Hans Sloane, *A Voyage to the Islands: Madera, Barbados, Nieves, S. Christophers and Jamaica*, Vol. 1 (London: 1707–1725), 7.

17. Albert Raboteau provides supportive evidence in *Slave Religion*, 44–47.

18. During the 1930s, African American sociologist of religion, Benjamin Mays, argued that the Negro's God is a compensatory God who promises delayed rewards in the afterlife for prolonged unwarranted earthly suffering. Although Mays's theory of the Negro's God is not a fabricated one, his mistake was made not in introducing the theory but in narrowly applying it to black Christianity, for it can and should be most authentically identified with Euromissionary Christianity. His book *The Negro's God* aptly describes the standard white missionary's god and the Eurocentric missionary agenda. It was the white missionary who conjured up and propagated the doctrine of a compensatory god—a deity who permitted the suffering and dehumanization of enslaved Africans for the greater goal of exposing them to Christian civilization and the opportunity for redemption. It is with this god that the missionaries implored the patience and obedience of their enslaved converts. See *The Negro's God as Reflected in His Literature* (Boston: Chapman & Grimes Inc., 1938).

19. Thomas Virgil Peterson, *Ham and Japheth: The Mythic World of Whites in the Antebellum South* (Metuchen, N.J.: The Scarecrow Press, 1978), 1.

20. Ibid., 4–8.

21. George D. Kelsey, *Racism and the Christian Understanding of Man* (New York: Charles Scribner's Sons, 1965), 25–26.

22. Alexander Crummell, *The Future of Africa* (New York: Scribner, 1862).

23. Wilson J. Moses, *Alexander Crummell: A Study of Civilization and Discontent* (New York: Oxford University Press, 1989), 79–80.

24. Alexander Crummell, *The Future of Africa*, 19.

25. Ibid., 20.

26. Ibid., 18.

27. Ibid., 122.

28. James H. Cone, *A Black Theology of Liberation* (Maryknoll, N.Y.: Orbis Books, 1996). See especially pp. 110–128.

29. Jacquelyn Grant, "The Sin of Servanthood and the Deliverance of Discipleship," in Emilie M. Townes, ed., *A Troubling in My Soul: Womanist Perspectives on Evil and Suffering* (Maryknoll, N.Y.: Orbis Books, 1993), 208.

30. Ibid., 199–218.

31. James H. Cone, *A Black Theology of Liberation*, 82–109.

32. James H. Evans, *We Have Been Believers: An African American Systematic Theology* (Minneapolis: Fortress Press, 1992), 116.

33. I use the term here in a non-technical sense to refer to beliefs about the divine and commentary on religious experience.

34. Delores Williams, *Sisters in the Wilderness: The Challenge of Womanist God-Talk* (Maryknoll, N.Y.: Orbis Books, 1993), 161–67.

35. The *event* of Europe's invasion of Africa, European people's abduction of Africans, institutionalization of the modern slave trade, and modern enslavement of African people is a tangible historical occurrence. The construction of race and the racialization of Europeans as superior whites and Africans as inferior blacks created an existential *condition* of disorientation, loss of identity, double consciousness, and self-violation which are also components of Primordial Suffering.

36. I am not making an essentialist statement about human nature but a statement about the potential for all human beings or any human being to be greedy. As the impetus for violating human community, greed must be avoided and denounced at all costs; however, it is not a congenital offense.

37. One of the chief goals of the Yoruba religion which is also the most widely practiced African-derived religion in the African diaspora is to promote *iwa pele* (good character).

38. African studies scholars have noted that the recognition and honor given to ancestors as indispensable members of the community is essential for promoting abundant life. See especially Laurenti Magesa, *African Religion: The Moral Traditions of Abundant Life* (Maryknoll, N.Y.: Orbis Books, 1997), 35–94.

39. Ibid., 62–63.

40. Womanist theologian JoAnne Terrell thoroughly considers this issue in black male and Womanist theological discourse. See her text *Power in the Blood? The Cross in the African American Experience* (Maryknoll, N.Y.: Orbis Books, 1998).

### 10. In Search of a Theology of Suffering Latinamente

1. I took the term *Latinamente* from Orlando O. Espín, "Popular Religion as an Epistemology (of Suffering)," in *The Faith of the People: Theological Reflections on Popular Catholicism* (Maryknoll, N.Y.: Orbis Books, 1997), 157–69, which contains a thoughtful discussion of its meaning. In my usage, *Latinamente*, with the "*a*" emphasized, means knowing from within the distinctive experience of Latinas.

2. Dorothee Sölle, *Suffering*, 1973, trans. Everett R. Kalin (Philadelphia: Fortress Press, 1975); Simone Weil, "The Love of God and Affliction," trans. Emma Craufurd, in *Waiting for God* (New York: G. P. Putnam's Sons, 1951), 117–36. I am indebted to M. Shawn Copeland's work which significantly informed the method and spirit of this essay. See M. Shawn Copeland, "Wad-

ing Through Many Sorrows: Toward a Theology of Suffering in Womanist Perspective," in *A Troubling in My Soul: Womanist Perspectives on Evil and Suffering*, ed. Emilie M. Townes (Maryknoll, N.Y.: Orbis Books, 1993), 109–29. I would like to recognize important suggestions from Anthony Pinn, Arturo Bañuelas, Alejandro García-Rivera, Larry Gordon, Mary Lowe, Rachel Pineda, Jane Redmont, and Kirk Wegter-McNelly.

3. In this essay, I have decided to use the term "Latina" to refer to women who are of Latin American heritage. For a discussion of the range of terms in use, see Roberto S. Goizueta, *Caminemos con Jesús: Toward a Hispanic/Latino Theology of Accompaniment* (Maryknoll, N.Y.: Orbis Books, 1995), 12–14.

4. Theodicy and suffering represent two distinct but inseparable theological concerns. Theodicy focuses on how to explain belief in God in light of the existence of evil, while a theology of suffering (which is the intent of this essay) focuses on how to understand the experience of evil, namely suffering, in light of our belief in God. In recent decades much has been written in this field. Some of the more significant works include Delores S. Williams, *Sisters in the Wilderness: The Challenge of Womanist God-Talk* (Maryknoll, N.Y.: Orbis Books, 1993); Hans Urs von Balthasar, *Mysterium Paschale: The Mystery of Easter*, 1970, trans. A. Nichols (Grand Rapids, Mich.: Wm. B. Eerdmans Publishing Co., 1990); Wendy Farley, *Tragic Vision and Divine Compassion: A Contemporary Theodicy* (Louisville: Westminster John Knox, 1990); Gustavo Gutiérrez, *On Job: God-Talk and the Suffering of the Innocent*, 1985, trans. Matthew J. O'Connell (Maryknoll, N.Y.: Orbis Books, 1987); John Paul II, "Apostolic Letter on the Christian Significance of Human Suffering," in *Divine Providence and Human Suffering*, ed. James Walsh, S.J., and P. G. Walsh (Wilmington, Del.: Michael Glazier, 1985); Sölle, *Suffering*; Jürgen Moltmann, *The Crucified God: The Cross of Christ as the Foundation and Criticism of Christian Theology*, 1973, trans. R. A. Wilson and John Bowden (London: SCM Press; New York: Harper & Row, 1974); John Hick, *Evil and the God of Love* (New York: Harper & Row, 1966). U.S. Latino/a theologians have written on theodicy and suffering. See Alejandro García-Rivera, "The Whole and the Love of Difference: Latino/a Metaphysics as Cosmology," in *From the Heart of Our People: Latino/a Explorations In Catholic Systematic Theology*, ed. Orlando O. Espín and Miguel H. Díaz (Maryknoll, N.Y.: Orbis Books, 1999), 54–83; Alejandro García-Rivera, "Wisdom, Beauty, and the Cosmos in Hispanic Spirituality and Theology," in *El Cuerpo de Cristo: The Hispanic Presence in the U.S. Catholic Church*, ed. Peter Casarella and Raúl Gómez (New York: Crossroad Publishing Co., 1998), 106–33; Orlando O. Espín, "The God of the Vanquished: Foundations for a Latino/a Spirituality," in *The Faith of the People: Theological Reflections on Popular Catholicism* (Maryknoll, N.Y.: Orbis Books, 1997), 11–31; Espín, "Popular Religion as an Epistemology (of Suffering)"; Ada María Isasi-Díaz, "Elements of a Mujerista Anthropology," in *Mujerista Theology: A Theology for the Twenty-First Century* (Maryknoll, N.Y.: Orbis, 1996), 128–47; Juan G. Feliciano, "Suffering: A Hispanic Epistemology," *Journal of Hispanic/Latino Theology* 2, no. 1 (August 1994): 41–50; Roberto S. Goizueta, "The History of Suffering as *Locus Theologicus*: Implications for U.S. Hispanic Theology," *Voices from the Third World: Journal of the Ecumenical Association of Third World Theologians* 12 (December 1989): 32–47.

5. Sandra Cisneros is a novelist, poet and short story writer. Her credits

include several literary awards and honors including a MacArthur Foundation Fellowship. Cisneros has written several books including *The House on Mango Street* and *My Wicked, Wicked Ways*. Her work has been translated into five languages. Born in Chicago, Illinois, she currently lives in San Antonio, Texas.

6. Cherríe Moraga is a poet, playwright, and essayist. She co-edited the widely recognized book, *This Bridge Called My Back: Writings of Radical Women of Color*. She has written several books and plays, including *Heroes and Saints*. Her writings, in particular her plays, have won several awards. She currently resides in San Francisco, California.

7. In this essay I use phrases which imply a shared Latina experience of suffering. My decision to do so is a strategic choice made for political reasons, informed by the work of Gayatri Chakravorty Spivak and her idea of "strategic essentialism." I recognize the enormous differences which exist among Latinas (i.e., economic, racial, cultural, sexual, etc.). For well over a decade, many feminist theorists have been analyzing the problems associated with either attributing positive elements to the idea of "woman" or choosing not to, in other words, the problem of essentialism. See the articles comprising the section titled "The Question of Essentialism," in *The Second Wave: A Reader in Feminist Theory*, ed. Linda Nicholson (New York: Routledge, 1997). See also Elizabeth Spelman, *Inessential Woman: Problems of Exclusion in Feminist Thought* (Boston: Beacon Press, 1988); Norma Alarcón, "The Theoretical Subject(s) of This Bridge Called My Back and Anglo-American Feminism," in *Making Face, Making Soul/Haciendo Caras: Creative and Critical Perspectives by Feminists of Color*, ed. Gloria Anzaldua (San Francisco: Aunt Lute Books, 1990), 356–69. For an article exploring this problem in the field of feminist theology see Serene Jones, "'Women's Experience' Between a Rock and a Hard Place: Feminist, Womanist and Mujerista Theologies in North America," *Religious Studies Review* 21, no. 3 (July 1995): 171–78.

8. The legend of "La Lloróna" endures as the story of a wailing woman who weeps for her children whose lives she has taken. This legend is popular among Latinas/os in Mexico and elsewhere. For one version of "La Lloróna" see Rudolfo A. Anaya, *The Legend of La Lloróna* (Berkeley: Tonatiuh-Quinto Sol International, 1984).

9. *soap operas*

10. *You or No One*

11. *The Hollering Woman*

12. Solitude and Sorrow

13. *María of No One*

14. Grace and Happiness

15. Sandra Cisneros, "Woman Hollering Creek," 1991, in *Woman Hollering Creek and Other Stories* (New York: Vintage Books, 1992), 43–56.

16. Cisneros, "Woman Hollering Creek," 47–48.

17. Cisneros, "Woman Hollering Creek," 52.

18. Verónica A. Guerra, "The Silence of the Obejas: Evolution of Voice in Alma Villanueva's 'Mother, May I' and Sandra Cisneros' 'Woman Hollering Creek,'" in *Living Chicana Theory*, ed. Carla Trujillo (Berkeley: Third Woman Press, 1998), 323.

19. Cisneros, "Woman Hollering Creek," 52–53.

268    Notes

20. Understand?

21. Cherríe Moraga, *Loving in the War Years: Lo Que Nunca Pasó por Sus Labios* (Boston: South End Press, 1983), 141. "Te prometo. No es inglés." means "I promise. It is not English."

22. Moraga, *Loving in the War Years*, 90.

23. For an explanation of the distinction between the traditional account of the myth and Moraga's reinterpretation see Rudy Busto, "The Predicament of *Nepantla*: Chicana/o Religions in the 21st Century," *Perspectivas* (Atlanta, Ga.), no. 1 (Fall 1998): 15–18, Hispanic Theological Initiative Occasional Papers Series, 7–21. For a translation of a traditional account of this myth see "The Birth of Huitzilopochtli, Patron God of the Aztecs," in *Native Mesoamerican Spirituality*, ed. Miguel Léon-Portilla (New York: Paulist Press, 1980), 220–25.

24. Cherríe Moraga, *The Last Generation: Prose and Poetry* (Boston: South End Press, 1993), 72.

25. "According to the legend, Coatlicue, Mother of the Gods"

26. Moraga, *Last Generation*, 73. *La diosa de la luna* means *the goddess of the moon.*

27. female strength and power

28. Pragmatist philosopher Josiah Royce functions as the most prominent interlocuter guiding my interpretation of Cisneros's and Moraga's writings. I am indebted to his significant contributions.

29. Sölle, *Suffering*, 4; Josiah Royce, "The Problem of Job," in *Studies of Good and Evil: A Series of Essays Upon Problems of Philosophy and of Life* (New York: D. Appleton and Company, 1898), 15–17.

30. Josiah Royce, *The Sources of Religious Insight* (New York: Charles Scribner's Sons, 1912), 216–19, 232–39; Royce, "Problem of Job," 17–23.

31. Josiah Royce, *The Problem of Christianity*, 1918 (Chicago: University of Chicago Press, 1968), 351–55; Frank M. Oppenheim, *Royce's Mature Ethics* (Notre Dame: University of Notre Dame Press, 1993), 121. For a discussion of the importance of meaning and knowing in the effort to eliminate suffering see Espín, "Popular Religion as an Epistemology (of Suffering)," 167.

32. Guerra, "Silence of the Obejas," 348.

33. Guerra, "Silence of the Obejas," 331.

34. Frank M. Oppenheim S.J., Personal Interview by Author (Berkeley, Calif.), 27 July 1999.

35. Alejandro García-Rivera, Personal Interview by Author (Berkeley, Calif.), 15 June 2000.

36. Moraga, *Loving in the War Years*, 134–35.

37. Cisneros, "Woman Hollering Creek," 46, 51, 52.

38. See for example Sandra Cisneros, "Little Miracles, Kept Promises," in *Woman Hollering Creek and Other Stories*, 124–29; Tey Diana Rebolledo, *Women Singing in the Snow: A Cultural Analysis of Chicana Literature* (Tucson: University of Arizona Press, 1995), 49–57, 204–06. For a critical discussion of how paradigms of Chicana womanhood function, see Norma Alarcón, "Traddutora, Traditora: A Paradigmatic Figure of Chicana Feminism," in *Scattered Hegemonies: Postmodernity and Transnational Feminist Practices*, ed. Inderpal Grewal and Caren Kaplan (Minneapolis: University of Minnesota Press, 1994), 110–33. See also Jeanette Rodriguez, *Our Lady of Guadalupe: Faith and Empow-*

*erment Among Mexican-American Women* (Austin: University of Texas Press, 1994), 72–76.

39. See Goizueta, *Caminemos con Jesús*, 32–37; Rodriguez, *Our Lady of Guadalupe*, 143–58. For a related discussion focused on the experience of Latin American women see María Pilar Aquino, *Our Cry for Life: Feminist Theology from Latin America* (Maryknoll, N.Y.: Orbis Books, 1993), 159, 171–77.

40. Kenneth Surin, "Problem of Evil," in *The Blackwell Encyclopedia of Modern Christian Thought*, ed. Alister E. McGrath (Malden, Mass.: Blackwell Publishers Ltd., 1993), 198.

41. Royce, "Problem of Job," 14–16; Oppenheim, *Royce's Mature Ethics*, 72. One of the enduring questions within the field of Christology is: What is the relationship between our own suffering, the suffering of Jesus Christ on the cross and our need for redemption or salvation? See Jon Sobrino, *Jesus the Liberator: A Historical-Theological Reading of Jesus of Nazareth*, 1991, trans. Paul Burns and Francis McDonagh (Maryknoll, N.Y.: Orbis Books, 1993); Balthasar, *Mysterium Paschale*; Jacquelyn Grant, *White Women's Christ and Black Women's Jesus: Feminist Christology and Womanist Response* (Atlanta: Scholars Press, 1989); Moltmann, *Crucified God*. See also Goizueta, *Caminemos con Jesús*, 101–31, 195–96; Espín, "Popular Religion as an Epistemology (of Suffering)," 72–73.

42. Royce, *Sources of Religious Insight*, 249.

43. Ada María Isasi-Díaz, *En La Lucha: A Hispanic Women's Liberation Theology* (Minneapolis, Minn.: Fortress Press, 1993). Throughout this book Isasi-Díaz offers a thoughtful, sustained reflection on *la lucha*. See also Ada María Isasi-Díaz, *Mujerista Theology: A Theology for the Twenty-First Century* (Maryknoll, N.Y.: Orbis Books, 1996), 128–32, 174.

44. Sölle, *Suffering*, 5–6; Dorothee Sölle, "Suffering," in *A New Handbook of Christian Theology*, ed. Donald W. Musser and Joseph L. Price (Nashville, Tenn.: Abingdon Press, 1992), 464–66.

45. Royce, "Problem of Job," 24. See also Elizabeth Conde-Frazier, "Hispanic Protestant Spirituality," in *Teología en Conjunto: A Collaborative Hispanic Protestant Theology*, ed. José David Rodríguez and Loida I. Martell-Otero (Louisville, Ky.: Westminster John Knox Press, 1997), 135–36.

46. Royce, *Sources of Religious Insight*, 235. See also Oppenheim, *Royce's Mature Ethics*, 152–53; Sölle, *Suffering*, 5–7.

47. This theological term refers to the redemptive, healing character of the suffering, death, resurrection, and ascension of Jesus Christ. The term "paschal" comes from the Hebrew word *pesach*, or passover. Thus, this term symbolizes the Jewish roots of Christian belief.

48. Royce, *Problem of Christianity*, 180–82; Royce, *Sources of Religious Insight*, 236–39; Royce, "Problem of Job," 14–16.

49. Royce, *Problem of Christianity*, 186, 203–06.

50. Royce, *Sources of Religious Insight*, 252.

### Response by Dianne Stewart

1. Toni Morrison, *The Bluest Eye* (New York: Pocket Books/Simon & Schuster, 1970); Alice Walker, *The Color Purple* (New York: Pocket Books/Simon & Schuster, 1982).

2. Nancy Pineda-Madrid, "In Search of a Theology of Suffering, Latina-mente," in the present volume, 193 and 196.

3. By this I mean suffering that is generated by human design and prolonged due to powerful ideological constructs and their influence upon cultural and social institutions that shape and regulate human relationships. See Pineda-Madrid, "In Search of," 192.

4. Ibid., 197.

5. Ibid., 191. See, for example, Virginia Fabella and Mercy Oduyoye, eds., *With Passion and Compassion: Third World Women Doing Theology* (Maryknoll, N.Y.: Orbis Books, 1986); Ursula King, ed., *Feminist Theology: A Reader*; Chung Hyun Kyung, *Struggle to be the Sun Again: Toward an Asian Feminist Theology* (Maryknoll, N.Y.: Orbis Books, 1992); Elsa Tamez, "The Power of the Naked," in Elsa Tamez, ed., *Through Her Eyes: Women's Theology from Latin America* (Maryknoll, N.Y.: Orbis Books, 1989). Also see Dianne Stewart, "Christian Doctrines of Humanity and the African Experience of Evil and Suffering," in *TheTies That Bind* (New York: Continuum, 2001), 24.

6. J. G. Kristo, *Looking for God in Time and Memory: Psychology, Theology, and Spirituality in Augustine's Confessions* (Lanham, Md.: University Press of America, 1991), 71.

## 11. Bridge Building between Communities of Struggle

1. This view is shared by most nonwhite and feminist theologies and is addressed by J. Deotis Roberts in *Black Theology in Dialogue* (Philadelphia: Westminster Press, 1987), 12–13.

2. Paul Tillich, *Theology of Culture*, Robert C. Kimball, ed. (Oxford: Oxford University Press, 1959), 41.

3. Ibid., 42.

4. In the words of Orlando Costas: "It does not take much effort to show how theology—from the patristic writings to the present—has been situational through and through. Indeed it has been generally bound to the experiences and categories of western culture. . . . Biblical contextualization is rooted in the fact that the God of revelation can only be known in history. Such a revelation comes to specific peoples in concrete situations by means of particular cultural symbols and categories." *Christ Outside the Gates* (Maryknoll, N.Y.: Orbis, 1982), 5.

5. Alfred North Whitehead refers to this tendency as the fallacy of misplaced concreteness. *Science and the Modern World* (New York: Free Press, 1925, 1967), 51.

6. Roberto S. Goizueta makes this argument in *Caminemos con Jesús: Toward a Hispanic/Latino Theology of Accompaniment* (Maryknoll, N.Y.: Orbis, 1995), 164–65.

7. See for instance Roberts, *Black Theology in Dialogue*, 15–19, for an example of a dialogical methodology. Other examples can be found in Justo González, *Mañana: Christian Theology from a Hispanic Perspective* (Nashville: Abingdon Press, 1990), 28–29, and in James Evans, *We Have Been Believers: An African American Systematic Theology* (Minneapolis: Fortress Press, 1992), 30.

8. See my article, "Doing Theology as Dialogue in the Hispanic Community," *Journal of Hispanic/Latino Theology* (February 1998), where I discuss the dialogical method in further detail.

9. Ibid.

10. González, *Mañana*, 28.

11. My colleague Joerg Rieger often refers to ideologies not just as the justification of positions taken, as Schubert Ogden refers to them, but as the justification of positions of which we are not even aware. Hence, oppression may come not just from those who are intent on oppressing us, but also from those who may be unwittingly participating in oppressive structures and practices. See Joerg Rieger, in *Remember the Poor: The Challenge to Theology in the Twenty-First Century* (Harrisburg: Trinity Press International, 1998), 58.

12. Evans, *We Have Been Believers*, 27–31.

13. See my article in *Protestantes/Protestants: Hispanic Christianity within Mainline Traditions*, ed. by David Maldonado, Jr. (Nashville: Abingdon Press, 1999), 123–39, where I outline the methodology of comparison I intend to use here. This methodology seeks to trace the salient features of a theology without reducing the theology to rigid sets of categories, and in doing so, it carries the proviso that the categories are not intended to be final in form.

14. See James Evans's use of the term in *We Have Been Believers*, 23, and González's use of "innocent readings" in *Mañana*, 84–87.

15. Virgil Elizondo refers to this ability of Hispanics for being inside-outsiders and outside-insiders in *The Future is Mestizo: Life Where Cultures Meet* (New York: Crossroads, 1992), 84–85.

16. James Cone, *God of the Oppressed* (New York: Seabury Press, 1975), 33–34.

17. Evans, *We Have Been Believers*, 22; See also Orlando Espín's article "Tradition and Popular Religion: An Understanding of the Sensus Fidelium," in *Frontiers of Hispanic Theology in the United States*, ed. by Allan Figueroa-Deck (Maryknoll, N.Y.: Orbis, 1992), 62–87.

18. The roots of racism in Hispanic culture can be traced back to their respective origins in Latin America, where, as in North America, racism and classism exist in both overt and subtle forms. See Quince Duncan et al., *Cultura Negra y Teología* (San Jose, Costa Rica: Editorial DEI, 1986), 19–26.

19. Ada María Isasi-Díaz, *Mujerista Theology: A Theology for the Twenty-First Century* (Maryknoll, N.Y.: Orbis, 1996), 111–12.

20. Peter Wade, *Race and Ethnicity in Latin America* (Chicago: Pluto Press, 1997), 32.

21. See Anthony Pagden's discussion on how these categories were used to justify enslavement and the subjugation of Amerindians and Africans in *The Fall of Natural Man: The American Indian and the Origins of Comparative Ethnology* (Cambridge: Cambridge University Press, 1982), 29–30.

22. See Paul Gordon Lauren, *Power and Prejudice: The Politics and Diplomacy of Racial Discrimination* (Boulder: Westview Press, 1996), 3.

23. Ibid., 48.

24. See Kenneth R. Manning's essay, "Race, Science, and Identity," in *Lure and Loathing: Essays on Race, Identity, and the Ambivalence of Assimiliation*, Gerald Earley, ed. (New York: Penguin Press, 1993), 319. See also Paul R. Griffin, *Seeds of Racism in the Soul of America* (Cleveland: Pilgrim Press, 1999), 11–38; 124–26.

25. Wade, *Race and Ethnicity in Latin America*, 27.

26. Ibid.

27. Ibid.

28. Ibid.

29. Elizondo makes reference to similar situations in *The Future is Mestizo*, 18.

30. Gayraud S. Wilmore uses this paradigm in his article "Black Consciousness: Stumbling Block or Battering Ram?" in *Liberating the Future: God, Mammom, and Theology*, ed. by Joerg Rieger (Minneapolis: Fortress Press, 1998), 81–95.

31. Ibid., 83–86.

32. Ibid., 86–91.

33. Frantz Fanon, "The Fact of Blackness," in *Black Skin, White Masks*, trans. Charles Lam Markmann (London: MacGibbon & Kee, 1968), as excerpted and reprinted in *The Post-Colonial Studies Reader*, ed. Bill Ashcroft et al. (New York: Routledge, 1995), 323–26.

34. Ibid., 323–24.

35. Ibid., 25.

36. Ibid., 325–26.

37. Elizondo, *The Future is Mestizo*, 54.

38. Fanon, in "The Fact of Blackness," writes, "as I begin to recognize that the Negro is the symbol of sin, I catch myself hating the Negro. But then I recognize that I am a Negro." 325.

39. Elizondo, *The Future is Mestizo*, 18. James Cone refers to a similar situation in the African American reality in which blacks are defined as nonpersons. James H. Cone, *Black Theology and Black Power* (New York: Seabury Press, 1969), 11.

40. Elizondo, *The Future is Mestizo*, 18–19.

41. Evans, *We Have Been Believers*, 5.

42. In my book *Jesus Is My Uncle: Christology from a Hispanic Perspective* (Nashville: Abingdon, 1999), I make references to the image of God in humanity being in our creative ability to do God's will and love others, especially on 46.

43. See Ismael García, *Dignidad: Ethics through Hispanic Eyes* (Nashville: Abingdon, 1997), 131.

44. Pedraja, *Jesus Is My Uncle*, 55–56.

45. Roberts also affirms this citing Augustine's understanding of God's love and of the vestiges of the *imago dei* inherent in humanity in *Black Theology in Dialogue*, 71.

46. Ibid., 106. See also Elizondo, *Galilean Journey: The Mexican-American Promise* (Maryknoll, N.Y.: Orbis, 1984), 108.

47. Ada María Isasi-Díaz provides a good definition and understanding of solidarity in this respect. *Mujerista Theology*, 88–92.

48. González, *Mañana*, 73–74.

49. Elizondo refers to this ecumenism as an inclusion of diversity in his foreword in *Mañana*. Ibid., 19.

50. See, for instance, González's interpretation of the term *mañana* and the Kingdom of God as transforming the present. Ibid., 157–67.

51. James H. Cone, *A Black Theology of Liberation*, Twentieth Anniversary Edition (Maryknoll, N.Y.: Orbis, 1986), 139–42.

52. See my discussion of the Kingdom of God in chapter five of *Jesus Is My Uncle*.

## 12. African American Christian Churches

1. See Dwight Hopkins, *Introducing Black Theology of Liberation* (Maryknoll, N.Y.: Orbis Books, 1999), 31.

2. Although this statement may appear quite narrow, I acknowledge that there were other religious expressions (theistic and humanistic) that are equally authentic African American cultural expressions. See Sterling Stuckey, *Slave Culture* (New York: Oxford University Press, 1987); C. Eric Lincoln, *Black Muslims in America* (Trenton: Africa World Press, 1994); and Anthony Pinn, *Varieties of African American Religious Experience* (Minneapolis: Fortress Press, 1998).

3. In 1517, Bartolomé de Las Casas, also known as the Apostle to the Indies, after watching thousands of natives dying in corrals and burned alive, returned to Spain and pleaded with Charles V to spare the natives. Las Casas begged the king, as an act of mercy toward the natives, to import Africans to be slaves, twelve for each colonist. In 1518, Charles V of Spain granted license (Asiento) for importation of 4,000 African-born people to be enslaved each year to the Indies. The license was sold to the Portuguese. This was the beginning of the enslavement of West Africans and the Atlantic Slave Trade. See Edward Reynolds, *Stand the Storm: A History of the Atlantic Slave Trade* (London: W. H. Allen and Co., 1989), 58–62.

4. Portuguese landed in West Africa on a trading expedition. Ten Africans from the Guinea coast were shipped to Portugal as a curiosity.

### Response by Luis Pedraja

1. Paul Tillich, *Biblical Religion and the Search for Ultimate Reality* (Chicago: University of Chicago Press, 1955), 3.

2. Ada María Isasi-Díaz refers to this struggle as *"la lucha"* in which Hispanic women, and our community as a whole in many cases, find themselves immersed. *En la Lucha/In the Struggle: A Hispanic Women's Liberation Theology* (Minneapolis: Fortress Press, 1993), 43, 168–69.

3. See Orlando Espín, *The Faith of the People: Theological Reflections on Popular Catholicism* (Maryknoll, N.Y.: Orbis, 1997), 63–90.

### Concluding Observations

1. Shane White and Graham White, *Stylin': African American Expressive Culture from Its Beginnings to the Zoot Suit* (Ithaca, N.Y.: Cornell University Press, 1998), 4, 64.

2. Michele Tingling-Clemmons, "The Face of Hunger in America." In David L. L. Shields, ed., *The Color of Hunger: Race and Hunger in National and International Perspective* (Lanham, Md.: Rowman & Littlefield Publishers, Inc., 1995), 16–17.

3. Ibid., 8.

4. Emilie M. Townes, *Breaking the Fine Rain of Death: African American Health Issues and a Womanist Ethic of Care* (New York: Continuum, 1998), 29.

5. Ibid., 27.

# Selected Sources

Acosta-Belen, Edna, and Barbara R. Sjostrom. Editors. *The Hispanic Experience in the United States: Contemporary Issues and Perspectives* (New York: Praeger Publishers, 1988).

Anderson, Victor. *Beyond Ontological Blackness: An Essay in African American Religious and Cultural Criticism* (New York: Continuum, 1995).

———. Guest Editor. "African American Religious Thought and Pragmatism." *American Journal of Theology & Philosophy*, Volume 19, Number 2 (May 1998).

Angell, Stephen, and Anthony B. Pinn. Editors. *Social Protest Thought in the African Methodist Episcopal Church, 1862–1939* (Nashville: University of Tennessee Press, 1999).

Anzaldua, Gloria. Editor. *Making Face, Making Soul/Haciendo Caras: Creative and Critical Perspectives by Feminists of Color* (San Francisco: Aunt Lute Books, 1990).

Baker-Fletcher, Garth Kasimu. *Xodus: An African American Male Journey* (Minneapolis: Fortress Press, 1996).

——— and Karen Baker-Fletcher. *My Sister, My Brother: Womanist and Xodus God-Talk* (Maryknoll, N.Y.: Orbis Books, 1997).

Baker-Fletcher, Karen. *A Singing Something: Womanist Reflections on Anna Julia Cooper* (New York: Crossroad, 1994).

———. *Sisters of Dust, Sisters of Spirit: Womanist Wordings on God and Creation* (Minneapolis: Fortress Press, 1998).

Banuelas, Arturo. Editor. *Mestizo Christianity: Theology from the Latino Perspective* (Maryknoll, N.Y.: Orbis Books, 1995).

Barrios, Luis. "Santa Maria" as a Liberating Zone: A Community Church in Search of Restorative Justice." *Journal of Humanity and Society*, Volume 22, Number 1 (February 1998): 55–78.

Berryman, Phillip. *The Religious Roots of Rebellion: Christians in Central American Revolutions* (Maryknoll, N.Y.: Orbis, 1987).

Betancur, John, and Douglas Gills. Editors. *The Collaborative City: Opportunities and Struggles for Blacks and Latinos in U.S. Cities* (New York: Garland Pub., 2000).

Blassingame, John W. Editor. *Slave Testimony: Two Centuries of Letters, Speeches, Interviews, and Autobiographies* (Baton Rouge: Louisiana State University Press, 1977).

Blount, Brian K., and Leonora Tubbs Tisdale. Editors. *Making Room at the Table: An Invitation to Multicultural Worship* (Philadelphia: Westminster, 2000).

Brown Douglas, Kelly. "God Is as Christ Does: Toward a Womanist Theology," in *The Journal of Religious Thought* 46, no. 1 (Summer-Fall 1989).

———. *The Black Christ* (Maryknoll, N.Y.: Orbis Books, 1994).

———. *Sexuality and the Black Church: A Womanist Perspective* (Maryknoll, N.Y.: Orbis Books, 1999).

Busto, Rudy. "The Predicament of Nepantla: Chicana/o Religions in the 21st Century," *Perspectivas* (Atlanta, Ga.), no. 1 (Fall 1998)

Cannon, Katie G. *Black Womanist Ethics* (Atlanta, Ga.: Scholars Press, 1988).

———. *Katie's Canon: Womanism and the Soul of the Black Community* (New York: Continuum, 1995).

Carmichael, Stokley, and Charles V. Hamilton. *Black Power: The Politics of Liberation in America*. New York: Vintage Books, 1967.

Casarella, Peter, and Raúl Gómez. Editors. *El Cuerpo de Cristo: The Hispanic Presence in the U.S. Catholic Church* (New York: Crossroad Publishing Co., 1998).

Chapman, Mark L. *Christianity on Trial: African American Religious Thought Before and After Black Power* (Maryknoll, N.Y.: Orbis Press, 1996).

Cleage, Albert. *The Black Messiah* (New York: Sheed & Ward, 1968).

Collins, Patricia Hill. *Black Feminist Thought: Knowledge, Consciousness, and the Politics of Empowerment* (New York: Routledge, Chapman and Hall, 1990).

Cone, Cecil Wayne. *The Identity Crisis in Black Theology* (Nashville: African Methodist Episcopal Church, 1975).

Cone, James H. *Black Theology and Black Power*. 20th Anniversary Edition (San Francisco: Harper & Row, 1989).

———. *A Black Theology of Liberation*. 2nd ed. With a Foreword by Paulo Freire. (Maryknoll, N.Y., 1986).

———. *The Spirituals and the Blues: An Interpretation* (New York: Seabury Press, 1972; reprinted Maryknoll, N.Y.: Orbis Books, 1991).

Cone, James H. *God of the Oppressed* (New York: Seabury Press, 1975).

———. *My Soul Looks Back* (Nashville: Abingdon, 1982).

———. *For My People: Black Theology and the Black Church* (Maryknoll, N.Y.: Orbis Books, 1984).

———. *Speaking the Truth: Ecumenism, Liberation, and Black Theology* (Grand Rapids, Mich.: William B. Eerdmans Publishing, 1986).

———. *Martin & Malcolm & America: A Dream or a Nightmare* (Maryknoll, N.Y.: Orbis Books, 1991).

———. *Risks of Faith: The Emergence of a Black Theology of Liberation, 1968–1998* (Boston: Beacon Press, 1999).

Cooey, Paula M., et al. Editors. *After Patriarchy: Feminist Transformations of the World Religions* (Maryknoll, N.Y.: Orbis Books, 1991).

Costas, Orlando. *Christ outside the Gate: Mission beyond Christendom* (Maryknoll, N.Y.: Orbis Books, 1982).

———. *Liberating News: A Theology of Contextual Evangelization* (Grand Rapids, Mich.: Eerdmans Publishing Co., 1989).

Cummings, George. *A Common Journey: Black Theology and Latin American Liberation Theology* (Maryknoll, N.Y.: Orbis Books, 1993).

Deck, Allan Figueroa. *Frontiers of Hispanic Theology in the United States* (Maryknoll, N.Y.: Orbis Books, 1992).

Diaz, Miguel, and Orlando Espín. *From the Heart of Our People: Latino/a Explorations in Catholic Systematic Theology* (Maryknoll, N.Y.: Orbis Books, 1999).

Dolan, Jay, and Allan Figueroa Deck. Editors. *Hispanic Catholic Culture in the U.S.: Issues and Concerns* (Notre Dame, Ind.: University of Notre Dame Press, 1994).

Duncan, Quince, et al. Editors. *Cultura Negra y Teología* (San Jose, Costa Rica: Editorial DEI, 1986).

Earl, Riggins R., Jr. *Dark Symbols, Obscure Signs: God, Self, and Community in the Slave Mind* (Maryknoll, N.Y.: Orbis Books, 1993).

Early, Gerald. Editor. *Lure and Loathing: Essays on Race, Identity, and the Ambivalence of Assimiliation* (New York: Penguin Press, 1993).

Elizondo, Virgilio. *Christianity and Culture: An introduction to Pastoral Theology and Ministry for the Bicultural Community* (Huntington, Ind.: Our Sunday Visitor, Inc., 1975).

———. *Galilean Journey: The Mexican-American Promise* (Maryknoll, N.Y.: Orbis Books, 1983).

———. *The Future is Mestizo: Life Where Cultures Meet* (Bloomington, Ind.: Meyer Stone Books, 1988).

Erskine, Noel L. *King Among the Theologians* (Cleveland: Pilgrim Press, 1994).

Espín, Orlando. *The Faith of the People: Theological Reflections on Popular Catholicism* (Maryknoll, N.Y.: Orbis Books, 1997).

Evans, James H. Compiler. *Black Theology: A Critical Assessment and Annotated Bibliography* (Westport, Conn: Greenwood Press, 1987).

———. *We Have Been Believers: An African American Systematic Theology* (Minneapolis: Fortress Press, 1992).

———. *We Shall All Be Changed: Social Problems and Theological Renewal* (Minneapolis: Fortress Press, 1997).

Felder, Cain Hope. Editor. *Troubling the Biblical Waters: Race, Class, and Family* (Maryknoll, N.Y.: Orbis Books, 1989).

———. Editor. *Stony the Road We Trod* (Minneapolis: Fortress Press, 1991).

Feliciano, Juan G. "Suffering: A Hispanic Epistemology," *Journal of Hispanic/Latino Theology* 2, no. 1: 41–50, August 1994.

Fox, Geoffrey. *Hispanic Nation: Culture, Politics, and the Construction of Identity* (Tucson: University of Arizona Press, 1996).

Frazier, E. Franklin. *The Negro Church in America* and C. Eric Lincoln. *The Black Church Since Frazier* (New York: Schocken Books, 1963).

Garcia, Ismael. *Dignidad: Ethics through Hispanic Eyes* (Nashville: Abingdon Press, 1997).

Garcia-Rivera, Alejandro. *The Community of the Beautiful: A Theological Aesthetics* (Collegeville, Minn.: Liturgical Press, 1999).

Garcia-Rivera, Alex. *St. Martin de Porres: The "Little Stories" and the Semiotics of Culture* (Maryknoll, N.Y.: Orbis Books, 1995).

Gebara, Ivone. *Longing for Running Water* (Minneapolis: Fortress Press, 1999).

Giddings, Paula. *When and Where I Enter: The Impact of Black Women on Race and Sex in America* (New York: Bantam Books, 1984).

Goizueta, Roberto S. Editor. *We Are a People! Initiatives in Hispanic American Theology* (Minneapolis: Fortress Press, 1992).

———. *Caminemos con Jesús: Toward a Hispanic/Latino Theology of Accompaniment* (Maryknoll, N.Y.: Orbis, 1995).

González, Justo L. *Mañana: Christian Theology from a Hispanic Perspective* (Nashville: Abingdon, 1990).

———. *Voces: Voices from the Hispanic Church* (Nashville: Abingdon Press, 1992).

———. *Out of Every Tribe and Nation: Christian Theology at the Ethnic Roundtable* (Nashville: Abingdon Press, 1992).

———. *Hechos* (Miami: Caribe, 1992).

———. *Santa Biblia: The Bible through Hispanic Eyes* (Nashville: Abingdon Press, 1996).

Gordon, Lewis R. Editor. *Existence in Black: An Anthology of Black Existential Philosophy* (New York: Routledge, 1997).

Grant, Jacquelyn. *White Women's Christ and Black Women's Jesus: Feminist Christology and Womanist Response* (Atlanta, Ga.: Scholars Press, 1989).

Griffin, Paul R. *Seeds of Racism in the Soul of America* (Cleveland: Pilgrim Press, 1999).

Guerrero, Andres G. *A Chicano Theology* (Maryknoll, N.Y.: Orbis Books, 1987).

Gutiérrez, Gustavo. *The Power of the Poor in History* (Maryknoll, N.Y.: Orbis, 1984).

Harris, Forrest, et al. Editors. *What Does It Mean to Be Black and Christian?* (Nashville: Townsend Press, 1995).

Hayes, Diana L. *And Still We Rise: An Introduction to Black Liberation Theology* (New York: Paulist Press, 1996).

——— and Cyprian Davis, O.S.B. Editors. *Taking Down Our Harps: Black Catholics in the United States* (Maryknoll, N.Y.: Orbis Books, 1998).

Hennelly, Alfred. Editor. *Liberation Theologies: The Global Pursuit of Justice* (Mystic, Conn.: Twenty-Third Publications, 1995).

Hopkins, Dwight N. *Black Theology U.S.A. and South Africa: Politics, Culture, and Liberation* (Maryknoll, N.Y.: Orbis Books, 1987).

——— and George Cummings. Editors. *Cut Loose Your Stammering Tongue: Black Theology in the Slave Narratives* (Maryknoll, N.Y.: Orbis, 1991).

———. *Shoes That Fit Our Feet: Sources for a Constructive Black Theology* (Maryknoll, N.Y.: Orbis, 1993).

———. Editor. *Black Faith and Public Talk: Critical Essays on James H. Cone's Black Theology and Black Power* (Maryknoll, N.Y.: Orbis Books, 1999).

———. *Introducing Black Theology of Liberation* (Maryknoll, N.Y.: Orbis Books, 1999).

———. *Down, Up and Over: Slave Religion and Black Theology* (Minneapolis: Fortress Press, 2000).

Hord, Fred Lee, and Jonathan Scott Lee. Editors. *I Am Because We Are: Readings in Black Philosophy* (Amherst: University of Massachusetts Press, 1995).

Hull, Gloria T., Patricia Bell Scott, and Barbara Smith. Editors. *All the Women Are White, All the Blacks Are Men, But Some of Us Are Brave: Black Women's Studies* (New York: The Feminist Press, 1982).

Isasi-Díaz, Ada María, and Yolanda Tarango, *Hispanic Women: Prophetic Voice in the Church* (San Francisco: Harper & Row, 1988).

———. "Mujeristas: A Name of Our Own," *The Christian Century* (May 24–31, 1989): 560–62.

———. *En la Lucha: A Hispanic Women's Liberation Theology* (Minneapolis: Fortress Press, 1993).

——— and Fernando Segovia. Editors. *Hispanic/Latino Theology: Challenge and Promise* (Minneapolis: Fortress, 1996).

———. *Mujerista Theology: A Theology for the Twenty-First Century* (Maryknoll, N.Y.: Orbis Books, 1996).

Jimenez, Alfredo. *Handbook of Hispanic Cultures in the United States: History.* Vol. 2 (Houston: Arte Publico Press/University of Houston, 1994).

Johnson, Paul E. Editor. *African American Christianity: Essays in History* (Berkeley: University of California Press, 1994).

Jones, Major J. *Black Awareness: A Theology of Hope* (Nashville: Abingdon Press, 1971).

———. *Christian Ethics for Black Theology* (Nashville: Abingdon Press, 1974).

———. *The Color of G.O.D.: The Concept of God in Afro-American Thought* (Macon, Ga.: Mercer University Press, 1987).

Jones, Serene. " 'Women's Experience' Between a Rock and a Hard Place: Feminist, Womanist and Mujerista Theologies in North America," *Religious Studies Review* 21, no. 3 (July 1995): 171–78.

Jones, William R. *Is God a White Racist?: A Preamble to Black Theology* (Garden City, N.Y.: Anchor Press, 1973/Boston: Beacon Press, 1996).

——— and Calvin E. Bruce. Editors. *Black Theology II: Essays on the Formation and Outreach of Contemporary Black Theology* (Lewisburg, Pa.: Bucknell University Press, 1978).

Jordan, Winthrop D. *White Over Black* (New York: Norton, 1977).

King, Deborah K. "Multiple Jeopardy, Multiple Consciousness: The Context of a Black Feminist Ideology," in *Signs: Journal of Women in Culture and Society* 14 (1988): 42–72.

King, Martin Luther, Jr. *Where Do We Go from Here: Chaos or Community?* (Boston: Beacon Press, 1967).

———. *The Papers of Martin Luther King, Jr.* Vol. 1–4. Edited by Clayborne Carson (Los Angeles: University of California Press, 1992–2000).

Kirk-Duggan, Cheryl. *Exorcising Evil: A Womanist Perspective on the Spirituals* (Maryknoll, N.Y.: Orbis Books, 1997).

Kunnie, Julian. *Models of Black Theology: Issues in Class, Culture, and Gender* (Valley Forge, Pa.: Trinity Press International, 1994).

Lancaster, Roger N. *Thanks to God and the Revolution: Popular Religion and Class Consciousness in the New Nicaragua* (New York: Columbia University, 1988).

Lauren, Paul Gordon. *Power and Prejudice: The Politics and Diplomacy of Racial Discrimination* (Boulder: Westview Press, 1996).

Levine, Lawrence W. *Black Culture and Black Consciousness: Afro-American Folk Thought from Slavery to Freedom* (New York: Oxford University Press, 1977).

Lincoln, C. Eric, and Lawrence H. Mamiya. *The Black Church in the African American Experience* (Durham: Duke University Press, 1990).

Long, Charles. *Significations: Signs, Symbols, and Images in the Interpretation of Religion* (Philadelphia: Fortress Press, 1986).

Lovell, John Jr. *Black Song: The Forge and the Flame: The Story of How the Afro-American Spiritual Was Hammered Out* (New York: The MacMillan Company, 1972).

Maldonado, Jr. David. Editor. *Protestantes/Protestants: Hispanic Christianity within Mainline Traditions* (Nashville: Abingdon Press, 1999).

Martin, Clarice J. "Womanist Interpretations of the New Testament: The Quest for Holistic and Inclusive Translation and Interpretation," in *Journal of Feminist Studies in Religion* 6, no. 2 (Fall 1990).

Matovina, Timothy. "Theological Table-Talk: Hispanic Faith and Theology." *Theology Today*, Volume 54, Number 4 (January 1998): 507–11.

———. Editor. *Beyond Borders: Writings of Virgilio Elizondo and Friends* (Maryknoll, N.Y.: Orbis Books, 1999).

Matthews, Donald H. *Honoring the Ancestors: An African Cultural Interpretation of Black Religion and Literature* (New York: Oxford University Press, 1999).

Maynard-Reid, Pedrito U. *Diverse Worship: African American, Caribbean and Hispanic Perspectives* (Downers Grove, Ill.: Intervarsity Press, 2000).

Mays, Benjamin. *The Negro's God as Reflected in His Literature* (Boston: Chapman & Grimes, 1938).

Mitchell, Henry H. *Black Preaching* (Philadelphia: Lippincott, 1970).

———. *Black Belief: Folk Beliefs of Blacks in America and West Africa* (New York: Harper & Row, 1975).

——— and Nicholas C. Cooper-Lewter. *Soul Theology: The Heart of American Black Culture* (New York: Harper and Row, 1986).

Moses, Wilson Jeremiah. *Black Messiahs and Uncle Toms: Social and Literary Manipulations of a Religious Myth* (University Park: The Pennsylvania State University Press, 1982).

Nash, June. *We Eat the Mines and the Mines Eat Us: Dependency and Exploitation in Bolivian Tin Mines* (New York: Columbia University Press, 1979).

Nicholson, Linda. Editor. *The Second Wave: A Reader in Feminist Theory* (New York: Routledge, 1997).

Oboler, Suzanne. *Ethnic Labels, Latino Lives: Identity and the Politics of (Re)Presentation in the United States* (Minneapolis: University of Minnesota Press, 1995).

Pagden, Anthony. *The Fall of Natural Man: The American Indian and the Origins of Comparative Ethnology* (Cambridge: Cambridge University Press, 1982).

Pedraja, Luis. "Doing Theology as Dialogue in the Hispanic Community," *Journal of Hispanic/Latino Theology* (February 1998).

———. *Jesus Is My Uncle: Christology from a Hispanic Perspective* (Nashville: Abingdon, 1999).

Pilar Aquino, María. *Our Cry for Life: Feminist Theology from Latin America* (Maryknoll, N.Y.: Orbis Books, 1993).

Pinn, Anthony B. *Why, Lord? Suffering and Evil in Black Theology* (New York: Continuum, 1995).

———. *Varieties of African American Religious Experience* (Minneapolis: Fortress Press, 1998).

Raboteau, Albert. *Slave Religion: The "Invisible Institution" in the Antebellum South* (New York: Oxford University Press, 1976).

———. *A Fire in the Bones: Reflections on African-American Religious History* (Boston: Beacon Press, 1995).

Recinos, Harold J. *Hear the Cry! A Latino Pastor Challenges the Church* (Louisville: Westminster/John Knox, 1989).

———. *Who Comes in the Name of the Lord? Jesus at the Margins* (Nashville: Abingdon Press, 1997).

Reeves, Gene. Editor. *Process Theology and the Black Experience*. A special issue of *Process Thought*, Vol. 18, No. 4 (Winter 1989).

Reynolds, Edward. *Stand the Storm: A History of the Atlantic Slave Trade* (London: W. H. Allen and Co., 1989).

Riebe-Estrella, Gary. *"Latino Religiosity or Latino Catholicism?," Theology Today*, Vol. 54, No. 4 (January 1998).

Rieger, Joerg. Editor. *Liberating the Future: God, Mammom, and Theology* (Minneapolis: Fortress Press, 1998).

Rivera-Rodríguez, Luis R. "Reading in Spanish from the Diaspora through Hispanic Eyes," *Theology Today*, Vol. 54, No. 4 (January 1998): 480–90.

Roberts, J. Deotis. *A Black Political Theology*. Philadelphia: The Westminster Press, 1974.

———. *Liberation and Reconciliation*. Philadelphia: Westminster Press, 1971.

———. *Black Theology in Dialogue*. Philadelphia: Westminster Press, 1987.

Rodriguez, Clara. *Changing Race Latinos/as, the Census and the History of Ethnicity* (New York: New York University Press, 2000).

Rodriguez, Jeannette. *Our Lady of Guadalupe: Faith and Empowerment Among Mexican-American Women* (Austin: University of Texas Press, 1994).

Rodriguez-Holguin, Jeanette. "Sangre llama a Sangre: Cultural Memory as a Source," in *Hispanic/Latino Theology: Challenge and Promise*, ed. Ada María Isasi-Díaz and Fernando Segovia, 117–33.

Rodriguez, Jose David, and Loida I. Martell-Otero. Editors. *Teologia en Conjunto: A Collaborative Hispanic Protestant Theology* (Louisville: Westminster John Knox Press, 1997).

Rooks, Shelby. *Revolution in Zion: Reshaping African American Ministry, 1960–1974* (New York: Pilgrim Press, 1990).

Rossing, J. P. "Mestizaje and Marginality: A Hispanic American Theology." *Theology Today*, Volume 45, Number 3 (1988): 293–304.

"Roundtable Discussion: Christian Ethics and Theology in Womanist Perspectives," in *Journal of Feminist Studies in Religion* (Fall 1989).

Sanders, Cheryl J. Editor. *Living the Intersection: Womanism and Afrocentrism in Theology*. Minneapolis: Fortress Press, 1995.

———. *Empowerment Ethics for a Liberated People* (Minneapolis: Fortress Press, 1995).

Segovia, Fernando F. "Two Places and No Place on which to Stand: Mixture and Otherness in Hispanic American Theology," in *Listening: Journal of Religion and Culture* 27, no. 1 (1992): 26–40.

———. "Reading the Bible as Hispanic Americans," *The New Interpreter's Bible*, vol. 1 (Nashville: Abingdon, 1994): 167–73.

———. "In the World but Not of It: Exile as Locus for a Theology of the Diaspora," in *Hispanic/Latino Theology*, ed. Ada María Isasi-Díaz and Fernando Segovia, 195–217.

Sernett, Milton C. *Bound for the Promised Land: African American Religion and the Great Migration* (Durham: Duke University Press, 1997).

Smith, Theophus H. *Conjuring Culture: Biblical Formations of Black America* (New York: Oxford University Press, 1994).

Smith, Timothy L. "Slavery and Theology: The Emergence of Black Christian

Consciousness in Nineteenth-Century America." *Church History*, Vol. 41 (1972): 497–512.

Snyder, Eloise C. Editor. *The Study of Women: Enlarging Perspectives of Social Reality* (New York: Harper & Row, 1979).

Sobrino, Jon. *Jesus the Liberator: A Historical-Theological Reading of Jesus of Nazareth*, 1991, trans. Paul Burns and Francis McDonagh (Maryknoll, N.Y.: Orbis Books, 1993).

Sobrino, Jon, and Ignacio Martin-Baro. Editors. *The Political Dimension of Faith* (Maryknoll, N.Y.: Orbis, 1990 [orig. 1980]).

Spelman, Elizabeth. *Inessential Woman: Problems of Exclusion in Feminist Thought* (Boston: Beacon Press, 1988).

Spencer, Jon Michael. Editor. *The Theology of American Popular Music*. A special issue of *Black Sacred Music: A Journal of Theomusicology* 3/2 (Fall 1989).

———. Editor. *Sacred Music of the Secular City: From Blues to Rap*. A special issue of *Black Sacred Music: A Journal of Theomusicology* 6/1 (Spring 1992).

Stephen, Lyn, and James Dow. Editors. *Class, Politics, and Popular Religion in Mexico and Central America* (Washington, D.C.: American Anthropological Association, 1990).

Stevens-Arroyo, Anthony, and Ana María Díaz-Stevens. Editors. *An Enduring Flame: Studies on Latino Popular Religiosity* (New York: PARAL, 1994).

——— and Segundo Pantoja. Editors. *Discovering Latino Religion: A Comprehensive Social Science Bibliography* (New York: PARAL, 1995).

——— and Andres I. Perez. Editors. *Enigmatic Powers: Syncretism with African and Indigenous Peoples' Religions among Latinos* (New York: PARAL, 1995).

——— and Gilbert Cadena. Editors. *Old Masks, New Faces: Religion and Latino Identities* (New York: PARAL, 1995).

Stuckey, Sterling. *Slave Culture: Nationalist Theory and the Foundations of Black America*. New York: Oxford University Press, 1987.

Tarango, Yolanda. "National Pastoral Plan for Hispanic Ministry," *Origins* 17, no. 26 (December 1987): 10–19.

———. "The Hispanic Woman and Her Role in the Church," *New Theology Review* 3, no. 4 (November 1990): 56–61.

Terrell, JoAnne. *Power in the Blood? The Cross in the African American Experience* (Maryknoll, N.Y.: Orbis Books, 1998).

Thistlethwaite, Susan B., and Mary Potter Engel, *Lift Every Voice: Constructing Theologies from the Underside* (San Francisco: Harper & Row, 1990).

Townes, Emilie M. *Womanist Justice, Womanist Hope* (Atlanta: Scholars Press, 1993).

———. Editor. *A Troubling in My Soul: Womanist Perspectives on Evil and Suffering* (Maryknoll, N.Y.: Orbis Books, 1993).

———. *In a Blaze of Glory: Womanist Spirituality as Social Witness* (Nashville: Abingdon Press, 1995).

———. Editor. *Embracing the Spirit: Womanist Perspectives on Hope, Salvation, and Transformation* (New York: Orbis Books, 1997).

———. *Breaking the Fine Rain of Death: African American Health Issues and a Womanist Ethic of Care* (New York: Continuum, 1998).

Valentin, Benjamin. "Nuevos Odres para el Vino: A Critical Contribution to Latino/a Theological Construction," in *Journal of Hispanic/Latino Theology* 5, no. 4 (1998): 30–47.

————. "Going Public: Negotiating the Intersections of a Hispanic/Latino and U.S. Public Theology" (Ph.D. diss., Drew University, 2000).

Vasconcelos, Jose. *The Cosmic Race/La Raza Cosmica* (Baltimore: Johns Hopkins University Press, 1997).

Wade, Peter. *Race and Ethnicity in Latin America* (Chicago: Pluto Press, 1997).

Walker, Alice. *In Search of Our Mothers' Gardens* (San Diego, Calif.: Harcourt Brace Jovanovich, 1983).

Walker, Theodore. *Empower the People: Social Ethics for the African-American Church* (Maryknoll, N.Y.: Orbis Books, 1991).

Washington, Joseph. *Black Religion: The Negro and Christianity in the United States* (Boston: Beacon Press, 1964).

————. *The Politics of God* (Boston: Beacon Press, 1967).

West, Cornel. *Prophesy Deliverance! An Afro-American Revolutionary Christianity* (Philadelphia: Westminster Press, 1982).

West, Traci C. *Wounds of the Spirit: Black Women, Violence, and Resistance Ethics* (New York: New York University Press, 1999).

Williams, Delores S. "The Color of Feminism: Or Speaking the Black Woman's Tongue," in *The Journal of Religious Thought* 43, no. 1 (Spring–Summer, 1986).

————. *Sisters in the Wilderness: The Challenge of Womanist God-Talk* (Maryknoll, N.Y.: Orbis Books, 1993).

Williams, Preston. "The Black Experience and Black Religion," *Theology Today*, Vol. 26 (October 1969): 246–261.

————. "James Cone and the Problem of a Black Ethic," *Harvard Theological Review*, Vol. 65 (October 1972).

Wilmore, Gayraud S. *Black Religion and Black Radicalism: An Interpretation of the Religious History of Afro-American People.* 2nd ed. (Garden City, N.Y.: Doubleday, 1972; Maryknoll, N.Y.: Orbis Books, 1983).

———— and James H. Cone. Editors, *Black Theology: A Documentary History, 1966–1979* (Maryknoll, N.Y.: Orbis Books, 1979).

————. Editor. *African American Religious Studies: An Interdisciplinary Anthology* (Durham: Duke University Press, 1989).

———— and James H. Cone. Editors, *Black Theology: A Documentary History, Volume II, 1980–1992* (Maryknoll, N.Y.: Orbis Books, 1993).

Wimbush, Vincent E. Editor. *African Americans and the Bible: Sacred Texts and Social Textures* (New York: Continuum, 2000).

Witvliet, Theo. *The Way of the Black Messiah: The Hermeneutical Challenge of Black Theology as a Theology of Liberation.* Translated by John Bowden (Oak Park, Ill.: Meyer Stone, 1987).

X, Malcolm. *Malcolm X Speaks: Selected Speeches and Statements.* Edited by George Breitman (New York: Grove Weidenfeld, 1965).

————. *The Final Speeches* (New York: Pathfinder Books, 1992).

Young, Henry. *Hope in Process: A Theology of Social Pluralism* (Minneapolis: Fortress Press, 1990).

Young, Iris Marion. *Justice and the Politics of Difference* (Princeton: Princeton University Press, 1990).

Young, Josiah. *Black and African Theologies: Siblings or Distant Cousins?* (Maryknoll, N.Y.: Orbis Books, 1986).

————. *A Pan-African Theology: Providence and the Legacies of the Ancestors* (Trenton: Africa World Press, 1992).

# Contributors

**Victor Anderson** is an Associate Professor of Christian Ethics at Vanderbilt Divinity School. His most recent book is *Pragmatic Theology* (State University of New York Press, 1998).

**Lee H. Butler, Jr.**, is Assistant Professor of Theology and Psychology at Chicago Theological Seminary. His most recent publication is *Loving Home* (Pilgrim Press, 2000).

**Ada María Isasi-Díaz** is Professor of Theology and Ethics at Drew University. Her numerous publications include *En la Lucha/In the Struggle: A Hispanic Women's Liberation Theology* (Fortress Press, 1993).

**Justo L. González** has held numerous teaching posts and appointments including president of the *Asociación para la Educación Teológica Hispana*. His books include *Mañana: Christian Theology from a Hispanic Perspective* (Abingdon, 1990).

**Dwight N. Hopkins** is Associate Professor of Theology at the University of Chicago Divinity School. His publications on black theology include *Down, Up, and Over: Slave Religion and Black Theology* (Fortress Press, 2000).

**Luis Pedraja** is Academic Dean and Professor of Theology at Memphis Theological Seminary. He is the author of *Jesus Is My Uncle: Christology from a Hispanic Perspective* (Abingdon, 1999).

**Nancy Pineda-Madrid** is a Ph.D. candidate in theology at the Graduate Theological Union, University of California at Berkeley. Her research interests include theological themes within Hispanic women's literature.

**Anthony B. Pinn** is Associate Professor of Religious Studies at Macalester College. His publications related to African American religion include *Varieties of African American Religious Experience* (Fortress Press, 1998).

**Harold Recinos** is Professor of Theology, Culture, and Urban Ministry at Wesley Theological Seminary. Widely published, his most recent publications include *Who Comes in the Name of the Lord? Jesus at the Margins* (Abingdon, 1997).

**Chandra Taylor Smith** is Director of the Women's Studies Program and Visiting Assistant Professor of Women's Studies at North Park University, Chicago. Taylor Smith has completed a dissertation at Vanderbilt University titled "Toward a Womanist Theology of Nature: A Postmodern Challenge for the Black Theology Project."

**Dianne M. Stewart** is Assistant Professor of Religious Studies at the College of the Holy Cross, Worcester, Massachusetts. She is currently preparing a manuscript titled "The Evolution of African-Derived Religions in Jamaica: Toward a Caribbean Theology of Collective Memory" for publication.

**Benjamin Valentin** is Assistant Professor of Systematic and Constructive Theology at Andover Newton Theological School. He is the author of "Nuevos Odres para el Vino: A Critical Contribution to Latino/a Theological Construction," *Journal of Hispanic/Latino Theology* (May 1998).

## African Americans and the Bible
*Sacred Texts and Social Textures*
EDITED BY VINCENT L. WIMBUSH

"[Of] enormous contemporary relevance . . . destined to become a standard reference work in American higher education for years to come." —Cain Hope Felder

## Beyond Ontological Blackness
*An Essay in African American Religious and Cultural Criticism*
BY VICTOR ANDERSON

" . . . represents a moment of clarity and adjustment in Afro-American philosophical and religious thought, . . . Anderson has given creative testimony to the central question of the moment: What do we make of blackness?" —*Theology Today*

## Breaking the Fine Rain of Death
*African American Health Issues and a Womanist*
   *Ethic of Care*
BY EMILIE M. TOWNES

"This book fills the huge gap in resources on medicine and bioethics from a black perspective. General studies in religious ethics will be enriched by Townes' commitment to concrete realities and pointed and practical proposals." —*Religious Studies Review*

## Katie's Canon
*Womanism and the Soul of the Black Community*
BY KATIE GENEVA CANNON

"This is vintage Katie Cannon—challenging, prophetic, self-critical, and womanist to the bone." —Cornel West

## Why Lord?
*Suffering and Evil in Black Theology*
BY ANTHONY B. PINN

"Exciting, thought-provoking, encyclopedic, and theologically unsettling in its critical treatment of the problem of evil in Black theology." —*Cross Currents*